Leah Purcell is an award-winning actor, singer and writer and one of Australia's leading young talents. Born in Murgon, Queensland, she began her professional acting career in 1993 in *Bran Nue Dae*, before roles in 'Police Rescue', 'Fallen Angels' and her own one-woman play, *Box the Pony*. *Box the Pony* was the smash-hit of the 1997 Festival of the Dreaming and played to sellout seasons in Australia and London. Leah has recently starred in the feature film *Lantana* and several theatre productions.

Leah has won numerous acting awards and the play-script for *Box the Pony* won the NSW and Qld Premier's Literary Awards.

Black Chicks Talking is Leah's second book and has also been made into a documentary which she directed. The documentary premiered at the Tribeca Film Festival in New York and was also shown at the Sydney Film Festival. Several of her other books and short stories are currently in development or pre-production for television or feature film. Leah lives in Sydney with her partner Bain and daughter Amanda and is a proud Goa Gungurri Wakka Wakka woman.

Deborah Mailman, actor

Sharon Finnan, netballer

Frances Rings, dancer

Liza Fraser-Gooda, businesswoman

Cilla Malone, mother

Tammy Williams, lawyer

Kathryn Hay, Miss Australia

Rachel Perkins, filmmaker

Rosanna Angus, community police warden

leah purcell

black chicks talking

HODDER

WARNING: Care should be taken when reading or viewing this
book as it contains the names and photographs of people who have
recently passed away.

Every effort has been made to contact the copyright holders of
material reproduced in this text. In cases where these efforts have
been unsuccessful, the copyright holders are asked to contact the
publishers directly.

A Hodder Book

Published in Australia and New Zealand in 2002
by Hodder Headline Australia Pty Limited
(A member of the Hodder Headline Group)
Level 22, 201 Kent Street, Sydney NSW 2000
Website: www.hha.com.au

National Library of Australia
Cataloguing-in-Publication data

Purcell, Leah, 1970- .
  Black chicks talking.

  ISBN 0 7336 1070 6.

  1. Aborigines, Australian - Women - Interviews. 2.
  Aborigines, Australian - Women - Social life and customs.
  3. Aborigines, Australian - Government policy. 5. Aborigines,
  Australian - Government relations. 6. Aborigines,
  Australian - Adoption. I. Title.

305.89915

Cover photo by Jim Hooper
Inside cover and back cover painting by Bianca Beetson
Inside cover photography by Lisa Tomasetti
Leah Purcell portrait photograph by Scott Cameron
Portrait photography by Brenton McGeachie
Edna's Table II dinner photography by Lisa Tomasetti and Emma Brasier
Documentary stills photography by Jo-Anne Driessens
Photo of Leah Purcell and Robert Hannaford by Tim Bauer
Photo of Kathryn Hay and the Queen by Geoff Harrisson

Cover design by Ellie Exarchos
Typesetting and digital production by Bookhouse, Sydney
Printed in Australia by Griffin Press, Adelaide

To Cherene and Jenalee

Contents

Foreword

VALERIE COOMS

These remarkable women in all their emotions are a testament to the spiritual strength of Aboriginal people.

This is not a story of one particular issue—these stories stretch across a range of issues facing Aboriginal people, particularly women, in this country today. The frankness, openness and honesty of these women is remarkable, while their suffering, spirituality, strength, dignity, pride and beauty permeate their stories.

When we look closely at how these women have been brought together to share their stories with the rest of the world, one can understand that their gathering alone would have created a unique cultural and spiritual environment.

The bringing together of these women not only highlights the cross-section of Aboriginal people in Australia today, but it is also a powerful work of cultural art that depicts the immense spirituality and diversity of Aboriginal women. Not only does this give the world an insight into the lives and thoughts of Aboriginal women, but it leaves much behind for future generations to learn from, and reflect upon.

Leah's ability to step through people, women, communities and issues in this way is a further attestation to the immense spirituality and commitment of Aboriginal people. In short, *Black Chicks Talking* encompasses humour, politics, leadership, family, identity, survival, culture, land and country, together with racism and suffering, in a unique format and from a diverse group of strong, courageous Aboriginal women.

This will not only leave us all more proud and powerful as Aboriginal people, but it will intrigue and enrich the lives of many people throughout the world for generations to come.

Valerie Cooms is related to Oodgeroo Noonuccal (Kath Walker) of the Noonuccal tribe of North Stradbroke Island. She is completing a PhD in history.

Introduction

LEAH PURCELL

Bloody hell, second book!

I wasn't really excited about a second book; I was thinking of the workload and dealing with the English language. See, I'm not very good at spelling, which makes it very frustrating when you are writing and you have to stop because you can't think of how to spell a word. People say, 'Don't worry about it, you have spellcheck now', but even my computer doesn't know what I'm trying to spell in some cases. Then there was everything else I was doing or wanted to do: working on my sitcom, evolving and performing my one-woman show *Box the Pony* all over the world (well, Edinburgh at the time and then London), being a mother, feeding my three cats etc, etc. I'm getting tired just thinking about what I was doing.

I can hear it now, though, all the established authors saying, 'Be grateful, you've got a book deal!' Well, to tell you the truth, I am. I have fallen in love with writing. I have learnt so much. Discipline, discipline, discipline and dealing with the Queen's English. As you can imagine it's not a favourite with me since I come from country Queensland and we have our own language, thank you very much, eh?

So I began the journey of *Black Chicks Talking*. First there was the big meeting to establish who would be in the book. Names were thrown around, drawn from hats, pulled from magazines and from my past. But I believe that there was a higher power working with me on this project which made everything fall into place. With a little persuading, and to great relief, all the nine girls agreed to be interviewed, thank goodness.

The chicks included a couple who I knew, but a few were complete strangers. Part of the selection process was that we had to have something in common besides our Aboriginality: ie 1999 Miss Australia Kathryn Hay—1987 Miss Murgon Leah Purcell; Sharon Finnan, world champion Australian Netballer in my favourite position, GD (goal defence)—Leah Purcell, netball freak. You get it?

One of the girls feared my motives, some were intimidated and a couple intimidated me, but once we met and got into the interview something happened and a great bond formed. I for them and they for me, supporting each other in this great journey.

Now I had to actually write the book.

I thought straight interviews would be boring and wanted to come up with a way that would entice the women to look at their stories differently and find it interesting (for them) to talk about.

A colleague I spoke to about the project in the early stages thought, 'Why not ask them what sense, out of the five senses— touch, taste, sight, smell and hearing—they relate to the most, and then get them to talk about their earliest memory of that "sense".' I liked it and away I went. There ya go Scotty Rankin (co-writer with me for *Box the Pony*) there's your acknowledgement for coming up with that great idea, thanks mate.

Another tool for interviewing was to get the girls painted as they sat for their interview. Robert Hannaford 'Alf', one of Australia's pre-eminent portrait artists, got the job because he was a friend of a friend. When Alf was told the gig would be painting ten black women he jumped at the opportunity (there is only so much enjoyment you can get from painting politicians, high court judges and people like that). Fortunately, or unfortunately depending on how you look at it, some of the girls got out of that interview technique due to where they were painted, or me being busy with something else.

I was actually interviewed for another book at the time of my portrait sitting, because that was the only time I could fit it in, and man it was hard. (You couldn't use any other part of your body, other than your mouth, to tell a story. So expressing something with body language was out of the question.) But I was the leader so I had to know what I was putting the other chicks through—mother hen had to go first (whose bright idea was that?!)

After travelling around Australia and interviewing the chicks one on one, we all got together for a dinner in Sydney. It was amazing to watch the chicks interact and helped me get to know them all a little better too. The dinner conversation ranged from some big laughs to a few serious discussions. You can read all about it in the dinner chapter at the end of the book (p. 336)

The chicks' stories range from a few heart wrenching ones to a few of the women discovering their Aboriginality to being very political.

At the time of picking the women I really had no idea what their stories would be like, or how they would pan out; that's why I truly believe that there is a higher power working with me. Pity they can't help out a bit more in the spelling area, but hey, ya can't have everything. Even the other women would comment on certain things and say that this book was meant to be and that they felt so privileged to be a part of it.

We are women, hear us roar! About love, children, human-ity, mother earth, weight, time, our fellow brothers and lovers, our mothers, fathers, past hurts, future gains, positivity, life, *ly'rhn*, sisters, Michael Jackson, guardian angels, rodeo riders, dancing, netball, identity, the senses, culture, needs, wants—our pasts, present and futures all summed up in a good old yarn . . . We still have a long, long way to go but we're havin' a go! We are women!

It was a wonderful experience for me to share in the stories of these women's lives and to be able to give them to you. I guess for me that is what this book is all about: to give you an insight into the lives of these contemporary Aboriginal women who not only speak for themselves but can be related to by people of all races. My play *Box the Pony* allowed you (for those who have seen it) to see into the world of an Aboriginal woman of fair skin from the bush with a black mum and white dad. It allowed you to experience how I dealt with the circumstances that evolved out of that and it hopefully helped you reach a new under-standing. If these sort of books aren't written then there will be another generation that will grow up in ignorance of the plight of Indigenous Australians. So this book is our way of giving you a little look into some of our lives.

Australian Aborigines are not all the same, just like the rest of the world is not. We are all individuals and we all have our own stories to tell.

I hope you at least enjoy these stories and possibly get some-thing out of them. And if you don't then that's okay too, we can't please everybody now, can we?

When an understanding develops between two people, even if it started out as a fight, you have reached a point of respect and respect is what it comes down to: respecting the individual. We must acknowledge that we are different and we must accept the diversity in all our multicultural communities. The only true way we can understand our fellow human beings is by knowing their stories, and these women are giving you theirs. No one can deny them their stories because, to deny them their life stories means they do not exist. These are their lives.

May my ancestors walk with all those who read this book.

'Alcheringa Yirra Baiame!'

I want to commend any and every woman who has done anything in this country for themselves or for others. Good on you!

To all the women who participated in this book: I love you and thank you for your stories and time. Without you ladies this book would not have happened and I wouldn't have nine new sisters.

To their families, thank you. It's hard for anyone to hear a family member speak about stories from within their family circle. I believe, however, that speaking and reading these stories will allow for enlightenment, encouragement and understanding. I hope you will be proud of the love, honesty, courage and loyalty that these women showed as they told me their stories.

To my ancient ancestor who roamed this land a long, long time ago, to that woman (and man) who bore my first generation family member: I thank you. The deeper I dig back into my family's past, the deeper in culture I become, wrapped in the purity of the culture of this ancient land.

To the Australian multicultural society: this country's culture is yours too, to learn and respect. It's awesome: get into it!

To my daughter Amanda, I love and cherish you. Thanks for being patient. Are we there yet? Are we there yet? Yes, we are!

To my partner in love, life and business, Bain. To his feminnine side (which he is not afraid to reach into) I respect and love you deeply; but also to his testosterone side—without that baby,

I wouldn't be with you. Thank you so much for your support, without it I wouldn't be where I am today.

To Hodder Headline Australia, my publishers; in particular, the Sydney office and publishing director Lisa, and editors Pauline and Deonie (the white chicks behind the project)— thanks for giving me the time and space and guidance.

To my mother Florence and grandmother Daisy—the two women that gave me my determination and drive—I honour, love, respect and miss you.

To all my nieces and nephews and great-nieces and nephews: Aunty Leah loves you all and ya know where I am if ya need me.

To my dearest and oldest friend Jodie: thank you for your friendship and for helping me out in Brisbane in the very early stages on my journey of discovery. I really mean this: Thank you!

To all those family members and dear friends who have helped me out and listened to my story over and over again, thanks!

Enjoy your read.

Love,
Leah

Performance Brought Me More Than Fame

Deborah Mailman

actor

DEBORAH: EVERY PARENT ONLY wants the best for their child. Some-times you don't understand some of their ways of thinking or doing things or talking. You don't question it because they are your parents and you do as you're told, as a good kid does. But at some stage in your life, usually around about the age of twelve years old when you start really thinking about circumstances for yourself, you may question yourself on what you hear them say. But you still don't question them; or you do, but it usually ends up in an argument, not the discussion you hoped for, because it's that status thing within families: 'What would the baby know?' But once you have left that environment and are making a world for yourself you do see things a little clearer and make your own judgment on matters.

It wasn't until I got to university in Brisbane that I realised what my dad was dealing with. And it was only after I started doing historical plays, black plays about Aboriginal history, that I understood his past and how he could feel about the future. I love my dad very much, my mum too, she's my best mate, but my dad denied me my Aboriginality. Denied maybe too strong of a word, but he didn't encourage the exploration of my Aboriginality.

It took me a while to understand where Dad was coming from. When I was a young kid, I guess I didn't think about it much. He was Dad and you did as you were told. He didn't try to brainwash us, or anything to that extreme, but it was the silence on the issues that would arise in the town or on the television or in our family. It was that whole sense of shame, I guess. And the realisation for me didn't hit me until I was in my senior years at school.

It's funny, you know, that even today some of the family are still thinking that way. When I was given that whole label of being the 'first Aboriginal' to win an AFI award, one of my relatives phoned up Mum and Dad and said, 'She's got no right saying that, because she's not Aboriginal.' For some reason they don't acknowledge their Aboriginality. I look back now and see that Dad and the family wanted the best out of life and what they were seeing around them, in their time, from society in general, or what was being portrayed of black communities in the media, was not positive.

Dad would tell us that we were better than that. I think what he meant to say was that we could do something with our lives. We have opportunities out there to improve our lifestyle if we choose to take them. And choose them I did. But for a long time, when I was a teenager, Dad and I used to have huge arguments: he'd say, 'No, you are not Aboriginal.' Knowing that we were, I was really confused about being a 'Blackfella', but there were also the issues of dealing with being an overweight kid.

Leah: Every black person has dealt with that circumstance of denial to some degree, or knows of a circumstance where some of our old people thought it best not to say that you were black. Or they chose not to pass on culture because when they were removed from traditional lands to government- or missionary-run settlements, they were told our culture was wrong or that our cultural practices were witchcraft. They were harshly punished for being proud of their Aboriginality and practising their cultural ways, and so they thought that the future generations didn't need that pressure in life—it was better to deny it.

Recently, I went back to one of my elders to ask questions about my past. This lady did not want to talk to me. Not only did it hurt her to bring up all those memories, she thought it was best to let it alone. But I am grateful that her daughter is also on the path of discovery, and looking for the truth, and she urged her mother to tell me. After that old girl opened up, I cried for two hours—I could not stop. And for about a week after that I was very emotional. The pain, the hurt, the shame that I saw in that old girl's eyes, the tremble in her voice, how she hollered my mother and grandmother's names because she could see them in me—she was wailing for them. But then the triumph that they had survived and here she was still alive and in good mind to tell me my story. And it was the truth . . . I got the truth. I feel complete.

Through the pain and tears, it made me understand the old people's ways of thinking about the shame and denial. I could see why it is so difficult for them to talk about it, yet it is so important for our old people to give us those stories. Not only will it ease some of their pain, but it is important for 'us'—the next generation—to understand the hurt that they went through to get us to this day. And the young feeling for the old—we feel for our old people—and therefore let the truth and the understanding of the past be a release for young people so we can focus on being positive, not on the negative. Only then can our anger subside, and maybe then we can move on and take advantage of what the white man brought to our society and bring our mob into the future.

So Deb, do you know where your mob is from?
Yeah. Dad's mob is from Augathella, West Queensland way, from a big family. My dad was born on the bank of the Warrego River

under a tree. There's a story that I read in one of Dad's stories in the newspaper which explains where we got the name 'Mailman' from: his mother was asked who her husband was and she said, 'Charlie the mailman', so hence the name 'Mailman'. I love that story. Dad had little schooling but loved to work with the land and animals—cattle and horses. He became the master of rodeos and an excellent groundsman [he kept the grounds for the rodeo in top condition]. I'm not sure whether Dad had or received an exception card from the government of the time, but he was a man that was able to walk wherever he wanted to go. He addressed everyone the same and he was well respected in the black and white worlds of the time, and today, but especially in the world of rodeo. Even today his name is a name that is mentioned in high praise in many a rodeo circuit.

Mum never speaks about her Maori heritage. She's Maori—Ngati Porou from the East Coast of New Zealand—both sides. I remember last year I said, 'Mum, we should go home, you know, see your family.' She's going, 'Oh no, I don't want to do that.' Not interested. I kind of leave that there.

Dad and Mum met when Dad went to New Zealand for an international rodeo. Dad was representing his country because at the time he was one of the Australian champs. [He was Australian Champion Bull Rider, Bull Dogging, Saddle Bronc and he held a few titles in New Zealand.] They usually held the competition over a couple of days and there would always be some sort of function held on the nights over the tournament. I'm not sure whether they met at the first or last function, which was the ball; either way Dad asked Mum to dance and that was it—they fell for each other.

Dad left the country but he couldn't get Mum out of his system, so he spent nearly a year saving up his pay and went back looking for her. I think they may have kept in contact a couple of times through correspondence, but Dad just went back over and searched until he found her. He proposed and they

The Mailman family

married on the traditional homelands of my mother's people and then he brought her back to Australia. She took on the role of the woman behind her man and mother of his future children, which started pretty soon after they got back: literally nine months later my sister was born.

My mum is my best mate. She raised up four kids and kept her husband happy on one income.

Before I was born, Dad was offered the job of caretaker for one of the biggest rodeos in the country. At this time Mum and Dad were married and had my older sister. They were living down in Augathella, which is Dad's area . . . anyway, because he'd been really strong with the rodeo circuit, when he eventually retired from riding he was offered work up at Mt Isa as the Mt Isa Rodeo Caretaker. This was a huge offer for my father as the caretaker of the rodeo grounds was like an honour and you were well respected in the community of rodeo. It was a very big job caring for the grounds and part of the deal was free rent, electricity and everything like that, and getting to live on the premises. Mum and Dad packed up their little growing family and moved to Mt Isa, where I was born.

There are no remote communities close to Mt Isa so it has a large population of Blackfellas. I think the closest communities are like Doomagee and up the Gulf area in Normanton where a lot of the people come in from. A lot of them mob would be on the main street there, West Street, lining up for their pension at the post office and stuff like that. Mt Isa's a segregated place: you had your blacks and whites . . . and then the Mailmans roughly ten kilometres out of town.

The great thing about being outside of the town is that we had an endless sky where you could see the stars. There were no lights to kind of distract us. Now and then Dad would kind of . . . out of nowhere, he'd tell us a story about a star . . . because he hardly ever spoke about culture or in a cultural way about things . . . that was very rare. Very rarely, he'd kind of tell those stories, so when he did, we really listened. It was a teaser in a way because there was this side to Dad that he would rarely let anyone into and every now and then he would open up and talk about this great stuff, but then just as quick and easy he'd close it off. I loved those times and would let my imagination run wild filling in the story with my overactive mind. I lived in my own fantasy world.

In the rodeo grounds there was this amazing playground and when the rodeo wasn't on it was all mine. There was a ferris wheel, train, merry-go-round, a huge slippery dip, as well as these metal dinosaurs. I could climb up on them. I had the best playground in the world. So I grew up with all that . . . but no one came to play. I pretty much played by myself. Yeah, I mean I had my brothers and my sister but she was a bit too cool and a bit too old to be with her little sister, because by then she was into make-up and Michael Jackson, teenage stuff. I didn't have any friends come out, not even black friends . . . Dad wouldn't allow that. Maybe one or two girls who were part of the Gun Club, because the Gun Club was on the premises as well; I met a couple of young kids through that.

There was always plenty of action happening around our place. I remember once when one of my brothers was giving Mum cheek and he took off running toward the rodeo ground, next thing Mum's jumped into the Subaru, chucks it into fourth and chases him across the field. He stops in the middle, jumpin' around by this time, a little scared I'd imagine, and Mum gets out and throws her shoe at him and gets him right in the back. She just climbs back into the car and leaves him there, not knowing what hit him! Ya laugh now, eh?!

But I pretty much grew up by myself. I wasn't sad or anything for not having anyone to play with. I kind of managed to make my own little world.

Could that be where the acting side came into it? Your imagination, being able to run wild?
Could of. I hadn't thought about it like that.

So what was school life like?
I was shocking as a kid—really awkward, really shy. I found it really difficult to be in groups. I hated being away from my mum and dad. I always had to have one of them with me because I just hated being on my own, just really self-conscious. I was five years old, and being teased a hell of a lot because of my weight. Not just big, but overweight. I've struggled with my weight since then. Hated the seesaw, hated any of those things . . . where I had to be balanced by someone, because there was no one who was heavy enough to balance me. I didn't have the physical ability; I would find even just hanging on to the monkey bars for more

Deb at pre-school: the little cutie back left corner

than five seconds quite painful. So I stuck to things I knew that were safe, like marbles. So a lot of the time I didn't join in on any group activities.

There was a time in my early school years where I hardly went to school because of my weight. Especially one year when, for a class activity, the teacher did up a 'Weight Tree' and everyone in the class was weighed and the results put on a graph and displayed in the room. So there I was in class trying to concentrate and there on the wall in bright-coloured marker pen: my name and weight, way out and up on a branch of its own on that 'Weight Tree'. Constantly being reminded. And then there was always one or two kids in the class that would take a dig at me, so I was very depressed that year and hated going to school and hated having to deal with this. So I just stayed home with Mum.

When I was a kid, I would grab my mum . . . I was trying to hide myself. Having anyone near was a sense of security. When Mum would go shopping in Kmart I'd wait in the car. It'd be sweltering—it'd be really hot!—but I'd wait in the car because I didn't want to go into the shopping centre where there were heaps of people. When I would go in I felt that everyone was watching me . . . I hated, hated, hated being in crowds, hated social events, hated anything like that.

And here you are, winner of an AFI Award—that's really a profound journey. From an almost phobic fear of people to the most people-orientated profession, and to reach the pinnacle of that form. Then receiving an award in front of people, Australia-wide, on the strength of your talent and this ability which people love in you to be incredibly personable and open and to put yourself in a vulnerable position . . . that's a really huge achievement.

It's weird why I've actually chosen acting as my kind of thing to do. It's my job because like, I mean I love what I do, I love the idea of reading a story and being able to make it come to life, but I hate all that red carpet, full-on bullshit, I hate it. I hate it with a passion. I hate opening nights; I hate any of those awards events. I'll play the game, I can play it, I can put on the smile, but, you know, deep down I just hate it. I mean more or less it's like . . . the whole pressure of physical form—beauty and labels. It's the 'look'. You have to have 'that look'—and guess what? I don't have it. And it's hard, and I guess people say you got the talent and that's what really counts . . . but it's always there in the back of your mind.

Even as a kid I didn't have the best clothes or the latest clothes because none of them looked good on me. Even to this day I find it really difficult to go shopping for a dress or some clothes because none of them fit me, or to the point where I'm comfortable. I'm comfortable in trackies and stuff, but it's not the 'scene', is it? Beautiful woman? It doesn't fit . . . I mean, it's nice that people say that. Even when they are genuine about it, but something inside me kind of squirms a bit because, as much as I believe what they're saying, I find it very hard to believe in myself. I think that's one of the reasons why I kind of connect strongly with touch more than any of the other senses because I can feel my weight, I can feel my body, I'm very conscious of it.

I think, given a week, four days out of seven, I'll feel quite depressed. This is a physical thing, I know, but I get quite depressed about what I look like. I touch myself and I kind of hold my tummy and feel how much weight is there. But, you know, I try not to buy into it a lot of times. I know it's really stupid thinking, I can't help it though. It's something that I've struggled with since I was five years old, but sometimes I just go, 'No, this is me and I love this, be positive, I'm really happy for this.' But I'm a woman and the weight issue always sits in the back of your head.

Did you ever think there was a time when you wouldn't be alive? Like in terms of being successful now or just like in general?

I mean physically alive.
Oh, right!

That you wouldn't cope with the pressure from your situation in the early stage of your life?
No, I mean, I don't have . . . I don't think I've ever had any sense of not wanting to live or anything like that. No.

Weight is such a hard issue for anyone to deal with, but especially if you're a woman because there is more pressure from society—in ya face kind of stuff, black or white. But the hardest is in the entertainment industry. So it goes to show how strong and determined Deb is. Although it probably kills her inside, that strong mask she puts on not only helps her, but other women as well. The entertainment industry can make a size ten feel insecure. I could add my insecurities here but, really, when I look at myself I shouldn't complain—there's bigger and I would feel like a boodagha jalda or a self-centred bitch to go 'poor me'. But it is television, it adds ten kilos to you and you can't hide when you are out there.

Did high school offer you any relief?
That's when I started to feel a bit more comfortable with my ability. I eventually became really good at T-ball, softball, hockey and netball.

I liked all of them. I actually did okay at school. I wasn't a straight A student, I was pretty average really, but all the rest of the mob, they were like bloody getting Ds and Fs, they didn't give a shit about school, whereas I did. And because of that, they used to give me . . . not all the time, but they gave me a bit of a hard time. Even my best friend, who is a Murri, she'd like . . . cause she had no interest in school, she'd tease the shit out of me sometimes. But I did enjoy the social aspect of high school and all those bad '80s fashions. Remember those little plastic sun visors and the big 'Choose Life' shirts? Well, I remember a school disco and I was wearing one of those sun visors with my fringe tucked under it and swayin' there with that fella—shame, hey?! I said to Mum, years later: 'Mum why did you let me walk out the house like that!' Laugh!

How did your acting begin? Was it an escape from reality?
I ended up in drama class because I didn't want to do Business Principles and I thought it would be a bludge lesson. Anyway, kind of ended up falling in love with it because it gave me somewhere I could go and be creative and I was good at it. One of my big roles at school was Dorothy in 'Wizard of Oz'. Even that was weird because I didn't want the role of Dorothy; I wanted to be the wicked witch of the east, but my friend got her and I got Dorothy. So my friend and I complained to the teacher, saying, 'Miss, I don't think Dorothy is black?' and the teacher said to me, 'Deborah, Dorothy can be any colour she wants to be' and then she sent us up to the office.

Were you stereotype-casting yourself, Miss Mailman?
Yes! Anyway, we go to the office and the principal wouldn't swing in our favour, so I had to play Dorothy. Gunnar, we made our little yellow brick road and my mum made my Dorothy outfit by her own hands . . . I've got a photo of me in that outfit somewhere . . . anyway, I remember we did a couple of performances and this one time I was up the front of the stage and there were some kids down the front and I heard them say, 'So that's Dorothy!' I could have killed them, but it was great fun and I really enjoyed it.

I met and fell in love with Miss Deb Mailman when I went and saw her first professional gig at La Boite Theatre company in Brisbane; I think it was her first performance out of college too. It was Shakespeare's Taming of the Shrew. *I was auditioning for a Shakespearean piece with another company and I was scared shitless, so someone told me to go and check them out. There was another Murri woman in the piece as well as Deb: Miss Lesley Marller, another deadly Murri tidda. So along I went and absolutely loved the production, but loved the girls even more. Deb was great. I could see her drive, her want for perfection, not only from herself but she demanded it from the rest of the cast too. I have the same drive.*

All three of us have finally had the opportunity to work together, after being friends for six years or so, on a project of mine. If it was a game of footy we would have been the heart of the team: the play starters and finishers, supporting each other; we feed off each other. It is a powerful professional relationship, but more importantly a beautiful friendship has blossomed between us. In this industry your 'friends' can range from . . . well, those who want to use and abuse you, to those who are truly there for you. It can be a lonely world, the world of performance.

So from Dorothy to AFI award-winning female actor of the big screen, how did you feel when you won?

Disbelief was probably the first emotion. Bit confused. Utter shock and then all the positives that come with that—the joy: 'Yeah, yeah, yeah!' It was absolutely unreal. It took me a while to accept that I deserved the award. At first I thought, 'Okay, yeah, give it to the Aboriginal girl because it's the right time and this and that, but then over a month I went and saw all the performances that I was up against, Rachel's [Griffiths] and Cate's [Blanchett], I went, 'Oh wow, I'm up there, I'm up there.' It took a little while but then I thought, 'No, I deserve this.'

On the steps of the Sydney Opera House with a storm brewing in the BG (film talk: background)—couldn't ask for better setting. And this white-faced character is standing beside her director, as if waiting for instruction on the scene they are just about to run (do). This black girl fresh down from Queensland, standing there with Barry Kosky (one of Australia's prominent directors), waiting to see if she wins the 1998 AFI Award (the highest accolade in Australian cinema) . . . yeah and guess what?

Meanwhile, I was in the audience that night at the presentation. I knew Deb was performing in Sydney so I said for a joke that day, when I rung up to wish her luck for that night, 'If you win I will go up and get your trophy.' She made a little chuckle, like saying, 'Like hell ya will!' We both laughed—I was joking. Low and behold she won the bloody thing and I had the cheek to panic! For a moment I thought I might have to go up there but of course they crossed back to the live link of Deb. She did a great acceptance speech and I cried. After winning the award I raced back into the Opera House and rang home. Mum answered and when I told her that I'd won she didn't believe me at first. She asked how did I know because they were watching it on TV in Mt Isa and it hadn't come on yet (daylight saving, they were an hour behind). She got excited and happy then, but we made a pact not to tell the rest of the family until it was announced on TV. After an hour I called home again and my pa answered. He was so proud—he was more emotional

1998 AFI winner

then my mum . . . we cried. My parents don't drink but Dad always had a bottle of Bundaberg Rum in the cupboard, so this night they had a shot or two, it was a beautiful moment for my dad because that's what he wanted for us: for his children to succeed in life to their full potential. My brothers and sister were happy for me as well. Everybody was happy for me. The only slack I got was from a relative that rung Mum and Dad to say that they had no right in saying that I was the first Aboriginal to receive an AFI. I guess that family member is still in denial over their Aboriginality. But I did not let that spoil what I had just achieved and I don't think that my mum or dad let that worry them either—if anything it allowed my father to be proud of his heritage.

There was the same reaction from a family member to Kathryn Hay when she won Miss Australia, being the first Aboriginal. Just thinking about that now, that has to be really weird to have some-one say that to you. You can understand someone doing there damnedest to claim their Aboriginality, but to deny it? That's a whole different mind spin. It has to be. But it's great to see the girls stand up for what they feel is true. And what they are proud of. Kathryn has always said that she was proud of her Aboriginality, but just doesn't quite understand it yet. Fair enough.

Where is the award now?
It sits on my mantelpiece wherever my home is.

Do you think that will help you get more work?
They actually say it's a curse! It gets you an acknowledgment for your work, which is great. You are the girl of the moment, which gets you press and publicity, but I don't think you get a one-way ticket to the top. You know, I haven't seen another feature film script of late where I'm the female lead.

The world of performance is . . . crazy, to say the least. What do you think about the acting world?
It's weird, you know. I'm sure you have to sit back; I don't think there's an actor yet that I've met who hasn't done that kind of process where they've gone, 'Hang on, where am I?' I think you do, in particular when you're kind of shoved into that limelight, you must. I do it all the time, I get to a point a lot where I just go, 'Is this what I want to keep doing?' If tomorrow I wake up in the morning and go, 'No, I really don't want to do acting any-more, I want to do something else,' it doesn't make me less successful than what I am. That's what I'm trying to learn, to teach myself that I'm successful no matter what, because I'm happy really. I've got a good life, a really good life. I've got so many choices that a lot of people don't have, I can't complain!

So I just think I'm really fortunate, really lucky where I am. You know, I'm happy with that.

Your career and personal life seems to be in order but where are you at culturally? And is it an issue with you?
It's only probably been in the last ten years or so that Dad told me about his side of the family, Bidjara mob. Augathella: that's where Dad's family tribal and cultural links are. Dad and Mum moved around south Central Queensland from Augathella, Mitchell, Roma and Charleville, with work and the rodeos. I don't know exactly where they lived, if they had a place there or they lived with family. But basically Mum and Dad moved up to Mt Isa not knowing anyone really. Kind of making this new start away from family.

But yeah, I'd say growing up we were kind of told that . . . not that we were told anything else . . . kind of saying that we were better than being Aboriginal. For a little while I took that on board, as any good kid that listens and trusts her parents would.

Early high school days I never associated with any other black kids, I'd always had white friends. I never used to go to the Aboriginal support unit. I never used to go there. They had their own little common room and stuff like that where they could always mingle at lunch and stuff—I never went there. Probably only in Year Eleven or Twelve, I woke up and kind of went . . . what are my parents saying?

Nowadays, culturally I feel confident and strong in both my parents' families. I mean, I'm still learning, there's still a lot of things I don't know about Dad's family, even Mum's family, but like I'm proud of saying that I'm Aboriginal and Maori. I recognise both sides but I don't . . . I don't know a lot of things and I tell people when they want me to be a spokesperson for this and that, you know, my experience is very limited and I'm still learning. I'm not a political person and I think that there are people out there who are better speakers than I am when it comes to talking politics and it's something that I would prefer to leave to those that know. I have my opinions on issues, but they are only mine and who am I to say? I don't want to say that I am not interested, because you can't help but be . . . but I'm still learning and you don't jump in and big-note if you don't know what's going on. But where I can, I try to help out. I like the role model thing in that I am a country kid, a Murri country kid, and I have made it in the outside world. It can be achieved; it's up to the choices you make. And one of my choices is to become culturally satisfied.

Dad would use words in language, like 'yarraman' and 'ngurran' for dog and stuff like that, and he'd kind of just use them in his everyday life, like for cold he'd go, 'yakile'. So he still had that kind of language, but he always made sure that he said to us, 'You're better than this.' So I grew up for a long time thinking like this and I got called 'coconut' [a slang term Blackfellas use when they think another Blackfella is acting white or trying to be better than the others in an ignorant way] a lot at school.

So what turned you around?
Through drama, life's experience and meeting different Blackfellas in the industry and elsewhere, I'm becoming very strong with who I am. I started to educate myself in history through the plays that I started to do when I came to Brisbane, I didn't know about the referendum and stuff like that until I did those school education plays and then I could go home and have really long in-depth talks with Dad. And then he had the opportunity to see what I did on stage, and how I'm quite a positive role model, not just to Murri kids but to kids from the country. I think through that Dad went back and reclaimed a lot of that . . . his identity. He really opened up, yeah, he really did! I mean, sometimes he would still make really outrageous comments, like 'Blackfellas are all this and that'. You'd just go, 'Dad!

You can't say that!' But through our talks and my work he began to understand and he went on his own personal journey, and before he died he was so proud to call himself a strong black man, a Bidjara Murri man, and that's beautiful for him and for me to hear. And I guess by acknowledging that, there has to be a peace within him. So peaceful, in fact, that he wanted to be buried on his traditional land, and that's where we laid him to rest. I miss my dad.

From the girl who hated the seesaw, stayed in the car at Kmart, wanted to hide herself behind anyone for security, and was teased from a young age, to becoming Australia's number one Female Actor of 1998 is certainly a journey of discovery. From not understanding your background to finding an identity; from being quite happy to stay in her own little world to now having a profession where you are required to be absolutely open with complete strangers—you have certainly come a long way. You have a lot to offer, not just to complete strangers, but also to yourself, so enjoy words like touch, worth and beauty.

I'm learning to say yes. I mean, it's actually taken me a long time to go, 'Yes, I am beautiful in my way, yeah.'

Do you ever make a conscious decision about a role, throwing into the decision-making your Aboriginality and what comes with that?
Depending on what the role is, take the Kelly character of 'Secret Life of Us', okay, there was this episode and she was drinking a bit too much to drown a problem and one woman came up to me and she said, 'Don't you think you should be careful how you portray this woman because the younger Indigenous people see this.' Now that's a big ask. First, Kelly's just a character, and yes, these characters portray life, but hey, I can't change the world and really it's up to the individual to do the best that they can for themselves. And you know a lot of people my age, black or white, deal with situations like this this way. But then you do

do roles for the social impact that they have on an audience . . . it's a hard balance to hold.

It would be a total mind blowout if every time you went to take a job you had to think about the politics, the impact on society. You know, does anyone ask Kylie Minogue these sort of things?
True, hey. I wonder what she would say?

Mmmmmmm.
    Out of the five senses, you said you related to touch, but I guess it was slightly on the negative, is there a fond memory of touch?
Oh, yes. You know, with my mum and dad, my brothers and sister. Rough fun stuff and then family loving touch. And I guess in lovemaking with that special one, otherwise we wouldn't do it! Hhhheeeeyyy!!

Out of the five senses which one could you lose?
I could live without hearing. Noise actually irritates me. I like silence, quietness, and being in the city really, really irritates me. If I don't find some peace and quiet, and most of the time that's at three o'clock in the morning, I lose it. I like peace and quiet and I think that society could do with a little more of that. Tolerance, patience, bit more silence. People finding a bit more time in their day to just stop and listen. It's also because my mum is almost deaf and relies on a hearing aid, so I would want to be able to understand the way she communicates and feel what she is going through, that mother–daughter thing, I guess. But it would also be the one that I would want enhanced because I'm not a very good listener. I find I get distracted very easily from conversations. That's why a lot of things can't stick in my head, I guess for whatever reason I choose not to listen. I find it hard to read too. I find it very hard to keep knowledge up there in the old stuff between the ears. I don't like to read.

So how the hell do you make it in the acting world, may I ask? See, I never liked reading out loud because I got shamed out by a teacher in Grade One. So I hate cold reads and I always ask for my scripts early to read over them a couple of times, mainly to see if there's any big words I don't know or stuff I don't understand. So how do you deal with your problem?

I physicalise. It's easier for me to do things physically so I can remember and learn. Like taking direction: I take that direction, physicalise it and put my lines to it so I can remember them.

If there was to be a sixth sense, but I think it's already there, it's to be a bit more intuitive, listen to that little voice or that gut feeling, being observant about things. Our senses are heightened in terms of listening, also reading. As well as reading signs, it's also hearing. After saying that and saying what I said before about me not liking to read and listen, maybe I don't tap into my sixth sense as much as I should.

Is it about reading into your experience? About being in the moment too. I think because so many people nowadays are so stuck in their own kind of nine to five routines, got their paths, their daily paths—catch the train, catch the bus, I get to work by this time and I have to be here by this time etc, etc. Then something happens, you don't notice it, you don't register it, 'it' could be someone falling over, two people kissing, seeing a beautiful flower bobbing in the breeze... we miss it because we're thinking ahead. Nothing wrong with that but it's important to balance up. It's about being in the moment and that's a very hard thing to do. Look around you, what's happening? What are you hearing? What are you seeing? What are you smelling? You know, as people, we don't do that often enough because it's all about money, paying the rent, paying bills, being stressed by all that, having a million and one things to do... but do we really need to do or have all those things? When was the last time you did something purely enjoyable for yourself?

Good question. I know with my workload you do miss stuff; espe-
cially with your kids, you really notice it. So I make rules to stay
in touch with my daughter: we have quiet moments or showers
together and we talk. Sometimes I just go in and watch her sleep.
I write songs for her and some mornings I go in and wake her up
by me singing to her instead of the alarm blurting out that horrible
sound. So I try and it's physically draining, but it is so rewarding
when they think that you're cool.

Is it important to have a network of support behind you in your
career and life? What do you get from them?
It is very important to have support. I've met a lot of good people
along the way who've kind of had absolute faith in me. My mum,
my dad, an Aboriginal liaison officer in high school, my drama
teacher at high school and my partner. And, of course, all my
fellow black thespians, especially Wesley Enoch [director/writer],
they give me strength and inspiration to keep doing what I'm
doing. Meeting you, Margaret Harvey and Lesley [Marllar],
meeting all these amazing and incredible, strong artists who
know what they want.

Something else that I have tuned into, being around more
Blackfellas in the last ten years or so, is that whole non-verbal
way of communicating—save you a lot of breath and energy.
A nod, a wink, a hand gesture can say so much. Blackfella
way . . . bang! They just know what you're talking about. It's a
whole other way of communicating. Maybe there's another
sense.

I love it too and miss it when you are not around mob. Tell ya a
yarn. All us mob, we were over in Perth with Bran Nue Dae, *the first*
Aboriginal musical by Jimmy Chi, anyway we were all sitting out
on the footpath waiting for whatever and this migloo (white) woman
come over and asked if we knew where a certain shop was and we
all knew and we did that lip point (puckered lips pushed in the

direction of what you are indicating to) and this woman just looked at us. And then we all went, 'Ooohhhh' and raised our arms and pointed her in the right direction to the shop. We all burst out laughin' then.

Tell us about your belief in relationships of the heart?
Gosh, that is a hard one, Purcell. Life is about experiencing different emotions with different people. I wasn't one for thinking too ahead of myself in believing that this is it, he's the one, I'm in love. But as I experience relationships and life . . . you are still learning and growing, just trying out new things. I'm at a stage now where I'm just waiting and seeing what will happen. I don't want to put limits or expectations on things, I just want to enjoy.

But there was a time, when I was younger, you struggle with the thought that maybe you should be with a black man, because I wanted my children to have that black skin, but that doesn't matter anymore. They're going to be black no matter what because it's about knowing, knowing your culture. I'll make damn sure that they get to meet Dad's family, and Mum's family hopefully. I want to take them back to Mt Isa and show them where I grew up, so eventually they get to understand about our heritage, not have my confusion that I had when I was growing up. My kids will be gorgeous either way. And if one of my children has a weight problem, I will tell them that they are beautiful. Relay my experience and give them a pre-warning that it's not going to be easy because society can be very cruel. Remember that your family love you for who you are, live your life to its fullest, enjoy it.

Do you believe that 'things happen for a reason'?
I believe there's a reason for everything in life. As hard as it is sometimes—you go, 'Why me?'—and we may not know the answers until we are older or have an opportunity to look back on things and realise things happen for a reason. As much as we

kind of have the choices, I think there is a certain journey, a path, it's already there for us, it's just how we deal with it. If it's guardians or something like that, I feel that . . . no matter what choice I make, it's taking me somewhere. That's going to end up being a good lesson for me. The pain of life makes you who you are.

So we have to live with a certain amount of pain, but there are also opportunities to move in the other direction—to go forward—and that's a choice people have to take.

So where do you think that strength came from to do this type of career?
As I said before, I've met a lot of good people along the way who've kind of had absolute faith in me.

You must of had faith and belief in yourself?
Yes, I do. I have to, to be able to get up and do the things I do on stage and television. I'm just being modest, but yes there is a belief and faith within me and that's okay.

What is the next challenge for Deb Mailman?
I was always like really nice—really nice to people, like always wanted to be accepted, wanted to be popular or seen to be having friends. So I was accommodating to everyone like I'd . . . and I think I still do that even today where I'm trying to please everyone and make people happy. It's funny, you know, like I'm just getting to the stage where I know what works on stage. I know what my skills are as an actor in terms of . . . I got the big cheesy smile—Deb Mailman, bubbly, bubbly Deb—and quite frankly I'm sick of it! To be honest I'm really sick of that kind of . . . oh, not sick of it . . . Look, I know it works; I know that. I think the next challenge is to find something that drives . . . that pushes me away from that into another area where people can kind of see something a bit different. But people employ me

for that bubbly Deb, a certain kind of charm comes with the smile. I know sometimes I am simply employed for that reason. It's okay for a while but I get a bit bored with it. So I'm looking for a challenge in my work—I want to be pushed in my work, find that challenge again. But hey, sometimes you just got to take the work to pay the bills. Keep in touch with the industry.

You know, even with 'Secret Life of Us' my character Kelly is not that intense. It's not so difficult for me. I mean, I don't think I've ever had an experience with a character where I've found it really hard to shake something off, you know, once you get home. I mean, I'd love to have the opportunity to have something that's really intense . . . where I'm forced to actually have to shake it off. Where the transition from you to the character is so far removed that you have to go to a completely different head space. Because most of the roles that I've played are very similar to my energy anyway. Kelly's very similar in person and so is Nona from *Radiance*.

I think the hardest thing is dealing with the other part of the job, which is publicity and all that kind of public recognition. That, for me, is the hardest thing at the moment to be comfortable with. Everything else is fine. Like, I love being able to get into a rehearsal room and go through that and be on stage or in front of the camera. It's just everything else that kind of happens beyond that, that you don't have much control of. With my work I have control. I'm with people who I trust and stuff. When I'm out on the street I can't control people's reactions to me and that's kind of uncomfortable sometimes.

So what's happening now?
I am now working on the Channel Ten show 'Secret Life of Us' as the character of Kelly. It has been great to be in full-time television work. But it has its drawbacks. The recognition from the public is very weird—in how to deal with it. I know I'm just me, but to the general public I am Kelly and they think that they

Deb at Mt Isa rodeo grounds

know me. It's weird all these people that sing out to you and ask you questions about the show, like the storyline. And that's okay and I don't mind, but it's really weird to not be able to walk into a pub or a store and just be me because all these people just look at you—just really stare. I don't know what it is with this staring stuff or becoming the untouchable or just what television does to people's perspective of us actors . . . it's just all very weird.

Anyway, I'm now living in Melbourne, which I love, so the AFI has a new mantelpiece to sit on [alongside the Silver Logie Deb just won for her work on 'The Secret Life of Us']. I've got a great place that I call home, my little English cottage with daisies and lavender out the front, great big backyard to have a great game of cricket in. I have a boarder and that's great company. One of my brothers is living in Melbourne so that's great to have family close by.

The sad thing . . . my dad passed away over a year ago now. That was really hard.

But I'm happy at the moment in where I am with my life and my choices so far. Everything hasn't been smooth sailing, I have taken a few wrong turns . . . no not 'wrong', just unexpected ones in my journey, but they have sorted themselves out . . . but yeah, life is good, Purcell . . . life is good.

You know, I used to say, oh, years ago in interviews, I'm an actor first and foremost—and bugger that bullshit off. I'm an Aboriginal woman who is an actor and it's taken me a long time to kind of reverse that kind of description. It's like, No. My whole being is Aboriginal woman. That's who I am and I'm fucking proud of it.

In the Zone

Sharon Finnan

netballer

SHARON: I BEGAN PLAYING club netball when I was nine. I made my first rep side when I was twelve. I played representative level all through ages eleven, twelve, thirteen, fourteen, fifteen, under seventeens, under nineteens, up to twenty-ones and open. In the early stage of my representative career I was still playing for fun, but when I got to, like, under seventeens, that's when I felt I had some type of talent—the reality kicked in: I was selected in a representative netball team, that was really exciting for me. Getting all your uniforms and other stuff was really exciting. I played for St George for many years before transferring over to play with Randwick.

I went to a very multicultural school, St Josephs at Kogarah—it used to be the old St George Leagues Club there on the corner. I just blended in. There were Greeks, Italians, Arabs, Asians; you name it, we had it. Being Aboriginal was never an issue for me, like people wouldn't look at me and say, 'Oh, you're an Abo!' or whatever, nothing was ever spoken about my Aboriginality. I never really identified, it wasn't something that was an issue. So why bother speaking about it? I knew very little about my heritage.

See, my dad is white and he raised my brother and I. Mum, who is Aboriginal, left home when I was about twelve, I was just starting high school. She was just never there, even before she left. Not as a mother should be. There were no cuddles or kisses. No motherly things done. She was the disciplinarian. Dad would be always saying, 'Ask your mother!'

It wasn't until later in life that I now see why Mum was the way she was and I understand. I can't ask her anything about her childhood because she's very emotional. But I have spoken a little bit to my grandmother, her mother, and she has and wants to explain a few things. I only met her three years ago, she's been sick lately, so I hope to get back up there and talk to her.

Leah: Where's your mum's mob from?
She was born in a place called Ebor, which is up near Armidale in New South Wales. It's a really small town. She's Anaiwan Tribe.

My grandmother had a large family, in two lots, kind of thing. To the first husband she had six kids. My mum was in that lot. Then she left him and had another six children to her second husband. Times were tough and there were lots of pressures placed on Aboriginal families in those days. She basically had to give them up, the first six, which my mother was a part of. My grandmother just couldn't cope with all those kids, I suppose.

Mum was adopted out to a white family with one of her sisters, and I think a couple of the other ones went to other white families. But before being adopted, Mum actually went to Cootamundra Girls Home. She never talks about it, I don't really know what happened there or if anything bad happened. She never talks about the people she was adopted out with. You can only presume that it was a bad experience for her.

But talking about mums and how you think mums should be: there to sew things for you, cook and just do the 'motherly' things. By them doing that you learn from observation. But here's a story from my very early days in the representative team for netball and, because I didn't have my mother around to observe and learn from, this is what happened.

I was given a patch to sew on to this netball jacket that some-one had lent me for a 'do' that I was to attend and I'm like, 'Should I do it myself? I don't want people to know that Mum's not here at home with us. Or should I take it to somebody?' I thought, 'No, I'll do it myself.' So I've sewn this patch onto this jacket, the jacket wasn't even mine, and I've completely ruined the jacket. I don't know what I'd done but I started cutting things and every-thing. And I turned up at the netball 'do' with this jacket on, and I looked at everybody else's and I thought, 'Oh shit, mine looks different to everybody else's!' And I just felt so embarrassed.

The blazer had a New South Wales emblem on it, I think it was for the first state team that I made and I didn't have my jacket yet, so I had to borrow someone else's. And they said, 'Just put this new patch over the old New South Wales emblem and no one will ever know the difference.' But she meant to just pin it, but I've gone and cut the other patch out and sewed this one on! I was so embarrassed! I just thought, 'If I had a mum to do that for me, she would have known better.'

I never remember Mum doing the motherly things, like cud-dling me, doing my hair, putting it in pigtails and things like that. Like what mothers are supposed to do for their young daughters.

So where was she then?
Out having a good time. She got a job working nights, like shift-work and that, so she was hardly ever home, and then after shiftwork they'd all go out and have a drink and she always came home very late, if at all. She just enjoyed that sort of life and I guess it was more appealing to her than the home life.

Mum and Dad got married when Mum was sixteen and Dad was twenty-six; she moved from the country down to the city, they met and got married and had me and my brother Glen pretty quick. She didn't really have a teenage life. I think that's one of the reasons why when I was thirteen they broke up. Reason behind it, I think she just really missed out on all her teenage years, she felt pretty tied down and she just wanted to get out. But I just don't remember Mum ever being around. Even though she was there, I don't remember her being a 'mother'.

I think something happened when she was adopted out into that white family. See in those days a lot of those families, not all, had the wrong attitude toward Aboriginal people and their reasons for adopting, especially toward the child. Maybe she didn't get any type of love, so I guess Mum found that really hard to pass affection on to us. I don't ever remember her doing the little things that mothers naturally do. It was always Mum doing all the hitting or smacking and Dad was always the kind one.

I remember a lot of fights with Mum and Dad. When we were kids, me and my brother used to just run out of the house and go up to the park to get away from them; you couldn't hear the fighting when you were away. We would call the police and they'd come . . . my dad's six foot nine inches, he's a very tall man, Mum's like five foot nothing, and we'd call the police because we just couldn't cope with all the yelling. They'd come in and look to take my dad away but I'd be saying, 'No! She's the one doing the terrible things to Dad!' They'd look up at Dad and they'd look down at Mum, and they'd go, 'Yeah, right! You're kidding aren't you?' Mum would get the pots and pans out, she'd be throwing them or knives. Back then I hated her for it. I guess she just had a lot of anger inside that needed to be released somehow.

That's why I don't like to remember a lot of my childhood. I wanted my mum to be like all the other kids' mums at school, they had a mum that they'd go home to and they'd have dinner on the table and they'd sew the uniform up if something went wrong . . . just the little things like that. I never had that, it's just something I wish I'd had. I don't have any regrets about my childhood, but it wasn't always a real happy one. I'm having a better life now, as an adult, that's for sure!

Are you close with your mum now?
I am. She's studying Indigenous health and had some part-time work at Southport Hospital for a while; I'm really proud of her and how she's studied hard to get where she is now. She's really family-orientated now—she always goes to those family-type things, birthday parties and other family gatherings. But I suppose losing your family and being screwed up by other people, I guess you just want to be around family and loved ones. I guess it's the way she wants to heal her wounds, she's gathering her strength. She's very close with her mother now, and Mum and I are starting to develop our relationship again.

But she's [Sharon's grandmother] been in hospital on a dialysis machine so she's not real well. As I said before, I only met her three years ago. I don't know her very well. I don't feel that close to her. But I know she's keen to sit down and have a good yarn with me. I told her that I'm really interested to know what happened and she did actually tell me about the time she had to give the first lot of her children away.

Their father, her husband, he used to beat her and she just couldn't cope with the whole thing. He's not alive now to defend himself, but she doesn't speak very highly of him at all. The frustrating thing is that Mum never talks about anything. Like when I do try to talk about certain things, just so that I can get a clear picture and try to understand the reasons behind her actions when I was a child . . . Mum'll just cry at the drop of a hat! So I try not to ask her unless she wants to tell me.

And is that something that you hope to achieve with her, for her to talk to you about what happened?

Sharon and her nan, the first time they met

Yeah, I think so. But now I look back and I know what she must have been going through. I can understand some of the pain that she must have been feeling. I know that she is keen to make up for lost time and so am I.

I missed my mum a lot when I was growing up for sure, but Dad was just amazing; he was like the rock of the family. He was working three jobs to keep my brother and I at Catholic school, and we'd be left at home a lot on our own because he was always out working. But we had this great dog called Crumpet that would protect us every night.

What sort of jobs did your father do?
He was a computer manager, he worked for a place called Gordon & Gotch, which was a magazine distributor, he was the manager of the computer section. He worked at South Sydney Juniors at night-time doing some bar work. And then he worked

for the gas company at North Sydney. He had jobs all over the place. Trying to juggle three things at once and raise two teenage children. We never, ever went without; we had everything we needed. When we used to go to school, everyone thought we were rich because we'd take two dollars every day for lunch . . . like, back then, two dollars was a lot of money.

Dad used to say, 'Yeah, just take it off the shelf.' He'd have his little dollar notes up there. You'd come home and your dinner would be there ready, he'd cook dinner for us and then he'd take off for work.

It's funny though, I can say, 'I love you' to my mother, but I can't say it to my dad. Yet my dad's the one that's closest to me. That is so weird! Even if I do say it, it's like, 'Oh you know I love you, Dad.' It's a muck-around type thing.

But Mum on the phone, I'll go to hang up, she goes, 'Oh, I love you' and I go, 'I love you too.' But Dad, I can't do it, can't say it to his face. Don't know why.

I had the same trouble with the 'I love you' to the face with my mum, but I think that it is the unspoken words and the things that you do for one another, and the peace and easiness you feel when you share moments—that's when you really know what love is. Sometimes I think those words are thrown around too easily; you have to really know someone before you can honestly say 'I love you' and have the true feeling of sincerity in it.

Are you affectionate with your dad?
I'll give Dad a hug and a kiss. Sometimes I'll want to keep the hug going longer, but he doesn't. He's never ever said, 'I love you,' to me either, yet I'm the closest thing to him in his whole life. And it's just so weird. God, why is that?

One day I'd had a few drinks, and that's when I said, 'Oh, I love you, Dad. Like, you know, I really do love you.' I actually said it to him, and he goes, 'I know that, I love you too.' He could tell that I'd had a few drinks. I don't know what he really thought, but it's just so weird that it comes so easy to Mum, and not to Dad.

Do you believe that it's important to say 'I love you'?
I do. Because I keep thinking if I never say it to Dad, and something happens to him and I haven't said it, I'll regret it. I reckon it has to be said.

Right, what's his number? Let's ring him.
I'll tell him when I go home tonight.

It was a big decision for me to move to Queensland with my work, because I knew my Dad wasn't well. But he said, 'Look, you can't live your life around me. Like you've got a lot to do, go off and do it! Don't worry about me.' He's so good that way.

But I see him more now than I did when I was living with him. I'm down in Sydney so much, and I always need to stay somewhere, so I stay at his place. So I think it's worked out for the best.

Have you found a man as good as your father yet?
Um . . . no! No way! If I did I'd grab him, I tell you! Like my dad's just amazing! He's so smart too, he was dux of his school.

Aside from your dad, was there anyone else who encouraged you when you were at that impressionable age?
Probably my first netball coach, Mrs Lloyd. She was a sweet old lady who had so much faith in me as a junior player.

And just good old Dad! He's my superstar!

I didn't have anyone else there that was . . . I guess as a mentor or someone that was guiding me in the right direction. It was all pretty much just feeling my own way and just having Dad there as that steady influence.

With my personal relationships I'm very choosey and careful about who I'm with, because I don't want to end up the same way that Mum and Dad did. I just don't want to go through that sort of pain again.

Describe the pain.
There was a lot of frustration, confusion, anger. I was lost . . . lost in a sense of direction as a woman because I didn't have a motherly influence. The lies you keep so that everyone thinks the family was together and strong because you didn't want to be different from other families. Little did I know some of them were probably going through the same thing. The life you have to learn to deal with when you only have one parent. The responsibility that is placed on you because of that.

But it can only make you stronger, I guess. And here I am at the pinnacle of my chosen profession.

What sense out of the five would you relate to? The most?
Taste, because I love food so much, and I'll eat anything and everything. I'm an affectionate person too, so I like touch as well. I'll always cuddle someone, if I know them really well.

Your earliest memories of a good time with your family relating to taste?
I've just always got excited about food, whenever there's food around, like I always used to love going to parties and always loved Christmas time because I knew there was going to be food there. I couldn't wait for the dessert to come out. Even now if I know I'm going out for a dinner party I think, 'Oh great, there's going to be some great food there.'

What's the first Christmas you remember?
At Raymond Terrace, all my aunties, every year with Mum, Dad, my brother and me. We'd jump in the car and we'd drive up to Raymond Terrace. And we'd get in the old Ford that Dad had, it was a blue station wagon Ford. We'd drive up every Christmas

Sharon, aged 5

to have it with Mum's family. We were living at Oatley then. I used to remember . . . approaching . . . like every time . . . I'd get all excited because we were going to see my cousins and all that.

Even though every year they'd just be doing the same thing. They'd put on a big spread and everyone would just come over with the spirit of the festive season. We'd stay there for the six weeks holidays over the Christmas period. We'd always find stuff to do. We'd be going swimming in a river or in a waterhole, or go for a drive. We'd always have such a good time with them and it was good to get away from Sydney. I grew up in Oatley, but spent my first three years living at Glebe. I've only got one brother, he's a year older than me. So getting together with my girl cousins and playing was good; I always had a lot in common with them, and we'd muck around just playin' and eatin' as kids do.

Ever since I was five we've been going up there for Christmas.

My aunty used to live in this little old fibro house that was at the top of this hill, everybody used to just jam-pack into it. My aunty's slaving away in the kitchen over a hot stove, it was always hot. You'd walk in, there'd be baked things like potatoes, vegetables and roast ... it would be lamb, pork, turkey and chicken, then you'd have all their different sauces.

I've always been a meat eater. I used to love the meat. I'd have like five different ... I'd have the pork, the chicken, the turkey, everything. I'd mix it all in, never really liked my greens. I always liked my carbohydrates, so I like my pasta and my potatoes and I'd go for the pasta salad with all the creamy sauces. I just loved food. Like fattening stuff. Then I'd get stuck into the smarties, the lollies, the bullets, soft drinks and all that sort of stuff. I probably had a bit of a bad diet when I was a kid, but all this yummy food was laid out on one big long table and we'd just sit around and eat and have a good time.

I remember the night before Christmas we'd go down to the main street of Raymond Terrace; there was this big Christmas tree, it was always lit up with lights, they had Christmas carols playing. I love that whole Christmas feeling. I love Christmas. And the main reason was just the fact that we were all together. We were together with family. And then, of course, the presents, Christmas carols, the tree, the food, the decoration, still believing in Santa Claus—getting tucked into bed and waiting for Santa to come; and the next day finally arrives and the floor would be covered in presents. Everyone would just be rummaging around trying to get to their presents and would be checking out each other's gifts. I guess the reason I like that so much was because later on in my life ... when Mum left, it was never the same again. Then after that, as I got older, I still liked going up there because it was still like bringing the family together again, but never quite the same because of the strain between Mum and Dad. But I think that Christmas after she left, Dad didn't come up because it was a bit strained. But ever since then they've been best of friends, and now we still get together at Christmas and it's just like old times. It's like they never really broke up.

I'm hoping to get everyone to come up to the Gold Coast for Christmas, just for a change; the Raymond Terrace Christmas will be a hard tradition to break though. I like the idea of cooking for everyone, wouldn't be anything too flash, I'm not the greatest cook, but I would make the effort.

Do you like cooking?
I do, as long as I've got someone to cook for. I hate cooking on my own. When I came home from training I just couldn't be bothered cooking if I was there on my own. Like I'd just have a piece of toast or a bowl of cereal and go to bed.

As I sat talking to Sharon, I was envious of her beautifully toned body—her legs are awesome. Before I became a writer/ actor/ director/ mother and my time was no longer my own anymore . . . I was fit, I had muscles on muscles. I was playing netball seven nights a week and doing kickboxing as well and was always dreaming of representing my country in a sport . . . Netball!

So getting Sharon Finnan, until recently the Aboriginal goal and wing defence for the Australian Netball Team, was so cool for me personally, because of my love for netball. And Sharon actually fulfilled one of my dreams: playing for Australia. I am so proud of the sister having been up there doing her thing. So, as we finally got to the training/netball part of the interview, I got quite excited and wanted to take her on there and then. See, we also play the same positions—GD, goal defence. But she was the one

playing for Australia and I'm still dreaming about it, so she is
pretty bloody deadly.

The next question: being an elite athlete the right diet is essen-
tial. As a teenager did you suffer the pressures that are placed on
young girls about their appearances? Because when I was younger,
still in high school where looks were everything, when I trained I
would wrap myself in Glad Wrap and train every night for two
hours, doing like a thousand sit-ups. I always exercised after dinner
time and wouldn't eat until the next morning (one Weet-Bix), then
for lunch only an apple, then coming home and having dinner, then
training, and on weekends I'd drop six laxative tablets. I was also
very active at school as well so I was getting plenty of exercise.
I guess I was suffering from borderline anorexia or some sort of
eating disorder. But it really is more of a mental disorder. When I
looked in the mirror I was never skinny enough. I was not over-
weight, even in my childhood.
I've done all that! Don't worry.

I think through my whole adolescent life, I always thought
I had a weight problem. That was when you're really into boys
and everything. You were always worried about what you were
wearing and made sure you always wore what everybody else
was. I never ever felt comfortable in what I wore. I always felt
like I was overweight the whole time, it was a constant battle.
But it probably wasn't! People would look at me and say, 'There's
nothing wrong with you.' But I just thought I was.

But I overcame that problem because there I was playing for
Australia, we'd recently won all the championships, and after I
came back from competition all I did was eat and drink. And
then I thought, 'Oh, I've got to really start getting back into my
training.' It was a real conscious thing for me, like people would
perceive you to be this elite athlete and you've got to have a
certain image. It was a constant battle and stressful to try and
maintain that the whole time. Look at all the Cathy Freeman
stuff that was said about her when she took her break! But I

know how she feels, she just wants to be normal for a little while; the workload, physical and mental strain that woman puts herself through, we couldn't even fathom. A break is good because by the end of it you come back better and stronger. When you are in training you can't let yourself go, you can't enjoy yourself too much and, in the back of your mind, even when you're out there celebrating . . . and I don't drink that much anyway, but when I do, it doesn't do anything for me anyway. It would take me twice as long to get back into my fitness if I let myself go.

Even now I have to be so careful with what I eat because I have intolerances to certain foods. I just love food so much. When I was a teenager, I would gorge myself and I'd think, 'Oh shit, what have I done?' Then I'd go out and run around the block or do a hundred sit-ups! Or I'd be checking myself out in the mirror thinking, 'Oh God, look I've already put on a kilo.'

But yeah, always paranoid about my weight. Like I was never an overweight kid, but as I started getting around about the twenty-one to twenty-two-year-old mark I started to put on a little bit of weight. I was actually eight kilos heavier than I am now when I first played for Australia. I don't know how I made the team! I'm very conscious about that sort of thing, I'd go out and run around the block and do all those crazy things. Just to get rid of what I just ate, not knowing that it wasn't going to do anything at the time. But when I was playing I stuck to a hard but sensible fitness schedule and eating program. I needed to, I was an elite netballer. Now that I'm retiring maybe I can let it all go and let it all hang out, but only for a short time.

So we'll call this chapter 'Sharon Pigs Out!'
Yeah!

Eating disorders are a serious issue with our young teenagers; more so the girls, but boys are affected too and the issue needs addressing.

I think it is a mental issue. Giving our children an understanding of how the body works and what it requires to keep it functioning is so important. Just recently I was involved in a project with my daughter's school and it was great to see that, whenever the girls got an opportunity, they ate. So that was encouraging—maybe they aren't so hung-up about body image and are just having a good time being teenagers. That's how it should be: be positive about who you are as a person, eat and play sensibly and let nature develop you. And later in life when you have stopped growing then, and only then, should you worry about your image.

Here is my theory: when I was at school I starved myself and didn't feed my body properly; I reckon if I did I would have been taller and had bigger tits, true's god. And now I am having trouble maintaining a good weight and eating habits. When I see old school friends who were bigger girls—not overly, they actually looked really healthy for themselves at the time—now they look fantastic. I think when you are a teenager you should just have an active lifestyle and eat, eat healthy, so when you are ready to grow your body can. My daughter, when she was born they called her the little Michelin man [a rolly-polly advertising figure for tyres], then she went really skinny as she started to grow and I did everything to get her looking healthy, again the rolls came back. Now she is thirteen and looking good. She is tall and still growing, she's got great shoulders and the busts are filling the front, she's got a waist and a great little butt, she's my baby, she's beautiful and it's all happening naturally. So to all you young girls out there, let nature take its own course and, when that stops, then you can work at it sensibly to keep it there.

To make the Australian netball team you have to be playing at state representation level and you played for the Queensland Firebirds. There was a whole eight years where you weren't picked for the Australian team. Tell us, what were you doing?

I was working for the Commonwealth Bank, ten years with the bank.

I was just coasting along with my boyfriend of the time. Going back about four years ago now, my boyfriend at the time came up to me one day and said, 'Look, I've got these magazines from Robert Tickner's office. I want you to read them!' He goes, 'Because you're going to have to know about all this stuff [Aboriginal issues and cultural awareness] one day!' That's what he said, he did! And he just said, 'Read it.' And I'm like, 'Yeah, yeah, whatever.' And I never touched them.

Months later he'd say, 'You haven't even picked one of those books up, have you?' And I'd say, 'No, I'm not interested. I don't want to read it.' Then after a few more reminders to read the books I finally gave in and I started reading them. Two weeks later I had a job offer at the Department of Sport and Recreation as the Aboriginal Project Officer for the government. And I'm thinking, 'Oh shit! Lucky I started reading some of those books!'

They'd employed me thinking, being Aboriginal, you're going to have all this knowledge about Aboriginal issues, so I'm thinking, 'Yeah, I'll go along with it and I'll fake it till I make it!' You know? A lot of non-Indigenous people think you're natu-rally supposed to know everything about the Aboriginal culture and issues because you're Aboriginal. I started going to meetings with ATSIC and all these important people, and I'm thinking, 'Who the hell are these people? And what do they do?' I had no idea! But I'd just sit in on meetings and I'd just listen and I'd soak everything up and try and read up as much as I could. But when you think about it, if you were going for any job really, and looking for a challenge—you may want to extend your knowledge, aim high for a job that might stretch the bound-aries—you do research and study up on the issues or how to use the machinery etc. Well, that's what I did for my job with Sport and Recreation with the Indigenous Unit.

Then all of a sudden that three months probation period led to three years and I ended up getting promoted to Aboriginal Coordinator, being in charge of all the Aboriginal Sport Development Officers throughout the State, coordinating their programs, which required a lot of office hours. I didn't mind too much, it was a great experience.

That's when another opportunity opened up for me. Somebody's given me something special: my ability to play an elite sport, to be in a world championship team, to wear the green and gold. I've got to give back to the community in a more hands on way; I feel if I didn't, that it'd just be an absolute waste for me to just go and do a normal desk job. That's why I left Sport and Rec. I mean, although I was an Aboriginal Liaison Officer there and I was doing stuff for the community, I was sitting behind a desk writing reports, being a bureaucrat, and I thought, 'Stuff this!' And that's when Dave Liddiard—retired professional football player for the Eels and the Panthers, founder of NASCA [National Aboriginal Sports Corporation Australia]—came up and said: 'Come work for us and we'll get you out into the communities, out running clinics where the kids would love to just meet you.'

It was a natural transition for me. I'm actually going out into Aboriginal communities and running netball clinics for kids and identifying talent. And the talented kids that we identify—we run development camps for them. And I start off by talking to them about my story and how I got to where I am and the fact that I might not have grown up in an Aboriginal community or out in the country, I'm a city Aboriginal, but I still know about some of the problems and some of the things that you go through in your community. So to get to where you want to be in sport requires a bit more effort than if you were living in the city.

I tell them a little bit about how I grew up with a single parent and some of the things that I had to go through to achieve my goals. I say, 'I know it's not easy, there's things that we've got to deal with to get to where we want to get to.' I like them to know that I've experienced enough hard times to know what they could possibly be going through. Most certainly on different levels, but an understanding is there. I can relate to the girls and they look at me and they think, 'Wow, look where you are! Like, that's where I want to be!'

They look at me like I'm so special, but I feel weird when they say that because I don't look at myself the way they do. I think I'm just a human being that happens to be good at netball! And the series of events that led me to making the World Champion Australian Netball Team, I look back and I think, 'Yeah, it was hard work', but I don't see it as anything real special, the way they do. But the weird thing is that to some of them my name, 'Sharon Finnan', means, like wow! It's up there. But I don't see that side of it. I wish I were on the other side, I'd love just to take a step out of my shoes and see what all the fuss is. But I guess if I look back at how I used to look up at my role models, I can understand it a bit more. Role models really are important and the effect that we can have on people.

When you take on the responsibility of working with communities and then children, on the very personal level you are opening yourself up to some pretty hard emotional issues. I know that there's been a couple of girls that I've coached who have been sexually abused and that has affected their netball and their training. So I always pay a bit more attention to them and just try to be there for them as Sharon, not the World Champion Australian Netballer, but as a friend and sister. Some of them are absolute talents and it'd be a shame to lose them. Any one of them could be the next best player coming through.

I remember one kid came up to me, we were in Dubbo doing some clinics, and this kid was shaking! She's like, 'Oh my god! Sharon Finnan!' My god! She just wanted to touch me! I said,

'Dave, look at this girl! Like this is great!' And she just made my day. Absolutely made my day!

I know how you feel.
I just want to make it as easy as possible for those girls. I mean, some of them might not have a very good family life, you just don't know. Some of them may have, but the majority probably don't. I always say to them, 'Ring me, whenever you want.' I had one lady ring me up one time and she goes, 'I can't believe I've got a direct line to Sharon Finnan! Like I've got your direct line!' And I thought, 'Well, what's wrong with that? You can ring me whenever you want. I don't care.' I guess they see that as special. I guess I get a little bit embarrassed when people make such a big deal about it, because at the end of the day I'm still Sharon, just Sharon Finnan, a normal person.

That's a great thing too because we can see that.
And I say to the kids, 'Here's my number, pick up the phone and ring me whenever you want.' But they're all too shy, they never will. They get their mums to ring up if they want to ask anything. I love being able to just speak to them on their level and just let them know that I understand. To see a child's perspective of life change to a positive one and realise that there is a chance to succeed, it's just the best. It makes all the hard work worth it. I love my job, I'm getting paid, and I love it! It's not hard work, but it's a challenge and it's just something I love doing.

What advice do you give them?
'Don't be afraid to have a go at something. Like if there's something you want to do, then go for it!' Like I always say to them, 'Look, I know you're all very shy, and I was like that when I was young, but if there's something you really want to do, do everything in your power to go and do it! Believe in yourself that

you're able to do it.' Because that was one of the things that I never had, like I didn't believe that I was able to do anything. And, having missed out on the Australian team for so many years, I tell them this story: 'I had no belief. I'm thinking, no, they're not going to pick me, they haven't picked me in the last eight years! And my boyfriend then, he was really supportive, he was such an influence in my life, he just said, "How do you know you're never going to make that team again? Like just, how do you know?" And I said, "Well, I just know, because they're not going to pick me." He goes, "If you train your butt off, and you do the right thing and you get out there and show them, they'll have no reason not to pick you! Like you're going to make them look stupid, because you're just playing better than everybody else." So he was the one who motivated me to keep training and to just train as hard as I ever have in my whole life, and sure enough, like it took eight years, but I got back into the team.'

After the clinics in the communities, what happens with the ones that you have identified as talent?
I go on to selecting a State Indigenous team. I've got a squad of twenty girls, I can pick ten only for the team and sadly the others have to miss out this time round. But I always say to them, 'Listen, before I announce this team, I just want you to know, the ten that miss out, don't be disappointed because missing out on this team doesn't mean it's the end of it. It's not over. Keep trying, keep going!' Then those selected get an opportunity to be involved in extensive training programs, overseas tours and the opportunity for mainstream selectors to check out their talent.

I got invited to Uluru one year to a career's conference that they hold up there for the young girls in the area to show them the opportunities they have if they want them.

Yeah, I've been invited two years in a row but never made it because of work commitments!
So we go out to this remote community near the foot of the rock; I've never been to a community quite like that. Like, I mean, that's just out there! Amazing. And they put on a bit of a barbecue and a song and a dance for us.

Being up there opened my eyes to a lot of things. I also learnt a lot from those young girls. I just feel like I've missed out on so much as a kid: learning about the culture . . . and not having been brought up in a traditional Aboriginal family, not so much traditional but not having that input of culture in my life because my mum lost her culture by being put into a home and then adopted by a white family and she wasn't there for me. So I feel now that it's my duty to get out there and put something back into the community and at the same time find my connection to my Aboriginality through them. I'm not religious but I just feel like God or someone's given me this chosen path, I've been given a special gift and I should use it as best I can, and one of those ways is to help others.

So do you think you've learnt more about your Aboriginal culture in these later years?
Absolutely.

Going back to the senses. You said you also liked touch. Do you like being touched or do you like to be the one giving it?
Both.

So, not receiving a lot from your mum, if you were to have children, do you think you're more likely to repeat what your mother did?
No. I'd go overboard the other way!

Definitely the other way, for sure, because I know how important it is for a child to be shown that affection and nurturing. I'd certainly make sure my kids have seen that from me.

I want to ensure that my kids have my one hundred per cent attention, I think that is very important, particularly in their early years.

What do you crave?
I crave peace, happiness and acceptance.

How do you get people to like you?
I think I just be myself. That's all I do, I just be myself and I think people can see that I'm a genuine person. I find it very hard to lie. I cannot lie! I'm like . . . someone will ask me a question and it might be a personal question and it's really none of their business, yet I still tell them.

Fantastic, that's great for the book!
No, serious. I'd just rather not say anything, because then I don't have to lie. I don't like lying and I can't lie. So if somebody asks me something, I couldn't lie.

Where does that come from?
I think it's just the way I am. I've always been an open, honest, genuine person. I can pick genuine people too. I try and mix with those sorts of people. If I've been introduced to a group of people, I suss people out quite quickly and I'll speak to the people who I think are actually genuine.

How do I rate?
Well, I'm still here talking to you about myself! But I've been a fan of yours from afar. I think you are one of the most gifted, talented and genuine people I know, and I haven't known you for that long, but it didn't take much to pick you as genuine. Cause you are upfront and I know where I stand with you, which is great.

Oh, thank you!
I guess, like anyone, I crave love too. Just to have somebody there. Like I don't think I've ever been single; I've always had a boyfriend. I've always gone from one to the other, and I've always felt like I've had to have somebody there. I guess I crave that, I feel a bit weird if there's nobody there. But, as I get older, that feeling of having someone around isn't as important to me, I guess. Like I've been through a few break-ups and I know what it's like, and I've had time on my own, and this last time I've actually enjoyed it! Like I've thought, 'Well, this isn't so bad after all.'

What's your attitude toward netball?
I'm very competitive. I always have to be the best in anything I do. So either in training or competition, whether it was running or training or sprinting or whatever, I never wanted to come last . . . I don't want to be just ordinary, or average. I want to be . . . exceptional!

Everything is perfect when I'm at my fittest. When I know I've done the work. I would walk out on that court and I'd be so confident and know I looked better than anyone else out there, that in itself is an intimidation factor.

Your opponent would look at you and they'd go, 'Fucken' hell, I've got to compete against that!' But that's the impression I wanted everyone to have of me. I'd worked hard and I felt good, I knew I looked good and I was out there playing. And when the four quarters were over, I knew I could go another four! I was that fit, I was smashing everybody. And it was just a great feeling. And yeah, I was 'in the zone' then. I remember 1995 was my best year. I remember it as if it were yesterday. Everything was just falling into place and I'm . . . I'm pulling intercepts out of the air that I never, ever thought I'd get to. You know, freaking shit like that was happening. At the end of that game I just felt so great and to top it all off it was our final, it was a National League Final. I was in the zone then!

How do you describe that sensation of being 'in the zone', when your whole body is in the moment? It's a level of human experience that not a lot of people experience. Do you think that it could almost be spiritual?

I suppose. It's funny though, you have this thought process before you hit the court and certain things go through your mind, something might trigger the right thoughts that you need to hit your full potential that game, I guess that's the first stage to get into the zone. The mind really is amazing, a lot of things are achieved by mind over matter. My boyfriend at the time was so supportive with the things he said to me. He'd send me a fax before every game, and he'd say, 'Now, you are the Queen of the Court! You've done the hard work, you've done the training, your people are out there watching you. Like the kids are out there watching you!' He only had to say something like that and that's enough for me; it just triggers something inside and I'm off, I'm away, I'm out there! I'm going to have the best game!

I felt pretty spiritual up there singing the national anthem, getting my Gold Medal in New Zealand! I'll tell you! It was a feeling I've never ever experienced before. Total elation and I was screaming the national anthem at the top of my voice! I was that excited. I just wanted everybody to hear me. And I was at the front too, I didn't care who I was blocking out behind. I thought, 'Stuff these bitches!' They were on the court, I didn't get on the court; I'm going to stand in the front, I'm going to get my head on the screen!

Did you cry? They [the television station broadcasting the Netball World Cup] didn't broadcast the presentation.
That's a shame they didn't show that!

No, jerks never do! They'd do it for any other sport except for netball!

World Champion netball team (Sharon's in the middle, thumbs up!)

I cry every time I get up there and sing the national anthem. Whether it's out there just before a game or whatever, because I just think of the hard work that's gone into being prepared for the game and playing for your country, knowing there is a nation relying on you to win . . . yeah, I always cry, always.

Especially when it's sport! You must have felt very happy and proud when you were representing your country—it is a huge honour. It also helps when you live in a country that is sport-mad. I love playing in a team sport or anything really to do with a team effort. I would love to represent Australia one day. I guess I have represented Australia when I took Box the Pony *to London, but I didn't get the tracksuit, and that's what it really comes down to in the end—the tracksuit, the tracky dacks! With the name of your country on it, you just stand twenty feet high.*
True!

. . . to put on the green and gold. I've done it in my dreams!
Yeah, man, I tell you what! Another honourable moment was when the whole Australian Netball Team received an OAM in 1991 because we were the World Champions and it was the first World Championship Australia hosted and we were the champs, so we got the recognition for furthering the sport in this country. I didn't really understand what the OAM was all about when I received my letter telling me this was going to happen; I got Dad to explain it and then realised what a great honour it was and I got really excited about it.

Are you spiritual?
No, not really. I mean I grew up and was educated at Catholic schools all my life and Dad was a pretty full-on Catholic going to church. It's where Mum and Dad met actually, at church.

Everything I was ever taught at school, I didn't know whether I believed it . . . It was just something that I thought I had to believe, just because I was going to the school. So I still don't have any real strong views on religion or anything like that. My ex-boyfriend was the one that's actually been telling me that I should believe more in . . . in the Dreamtime and all those sort of things, and that's when I started reading up a little bit about it and wanting to know more about it. And I still want to know more because I don't know enough, but I mean I'm not spiritual in any way, and I'm not religious, but I believe that there's a better place that we're all going to go to.

So you'd say you were a competent kid? Comfortable within yourself?
Yeah, yeah I was. I was always like the clown of the party, or I was always the leader in a group, I was always appointed captain. I was Sports Captain at high school. I was a counsellor, like a prefect; I always had trust put in me for things. I guess that gave me that confidence, because I knew people trusted me. So

I was quite a confident kid, but shy. Confident but shy. I don't know if you can be that, but I was.

It's almost like two separate people in a way?
Yeah, it's almost like I'm still trying to create the perfect world or scenario for me; I never had it as a kid. I'm shy of situations because I was young and had to deal with an adult world before my time, because I didn't have my mum to rely on and was unsure of what to actually do in certain situations. Although Dad was my knight in shining armour, there's stuff a mother and daughter have to go through. Then I was overly confident, because to get what you want, you have to be out there. I found that confidence through the strength of getting what I wanted and knowing that I was good at what I was striding for. I just wanted to make sure everything was in place, and everything was perfect, I guess. Or the way I would have liked it when I was a kid.

Are you escaping from the past?
I don't think so. But I'm having a much better life now.

Are there other dreams you had as a kid, or was it always netball?
I used to be a good singer when I was at school. I always remember in kindergarten they used to have the music come on the radio and you had your little singing books. I reckon I was the best singer in the class, went in all the talent quests. I remember singing Abba songs and I was always one of the best singers. And I always thought I was going to be a singer because I had this great voice! But I probably should have trained myself when I was younger, to keep the voice going.

So when did *you* know you were good?

I still don't! I don't know. I've never trained though. I tried a couple of times but I felt that the teachers were trying to change my style.

I work on the theory that emotion makes a song, and your body language in expressing it. I guess a voice that can hold a note helps too. And I'm lucky I inherited my mum's talent for singing. She loved to sing.
You're just a natural.

... I guess ... yeah ... when did I find the faith in myself? It came after I wrote 'Run Daisy Run' I think, my grandmother's song about her story of being stolen. That was my third song that I wrote in '92. That song made me cry!

When I sung that to my family for the first time I was petrified. All my sisters could sing, they have these operatic soprano voices, and I always thought of myself as a foghorn in the background. So when I got the courage to sing in front of them, you know, I could have sung in front of whoever, the elite singers of the world, and it wouldn't have mattered what they would have said, but I had to impress the family, and I did. When I looked up and saw the family crying on hearing 'Run Daisy Run' for the first time I said, 'Oh, was it that bad?' And they said, 'No, dummy, listen to what you've captured in that song and how you sung it.' So I think it was their acceptance or acknowledgment that I could hold a note, I thought, Oh, okay. Maybe I do know, sort of know, what I am doing in the singing department.
So you never really trained?

No, in nothing. Just straight from the bush out from under my little gum leaf and here I am.
Really? How brave is that? That's amazing.

Thank you.
So, Leah, when did you first pick up a netball?

Hang on, I thought I was interviewing you?

Well, I want to know about you! I've heard of you and all the work you do, not only professionally but for community as well, and I've always praised you from afar.

I played all sports at school, but netball was . . . I loved it because it was a team sport. I did athletics and all those sort of things, and I just didn't like being out there on my own. I liked having my friends around me, so I chose netball. I suppose it was what I was really good at out of everything. I was nine years old.

I used to play basketball, I was in Grade Five when I first started basketball. By Grade Seven I wasn't satisfied with basketball; the girls that I was playing with were so good it was hard to crack the team for a full game. So one day we were playing a game of basketball and I was off, I started to watch the netball game that was being played about a hundred metres from where we were and I thought to myself, 'Now, that's art. That sport has discipline.' They looked really good playing, it was like it was neat and tidy. There was a certain style about it; whereas in basketball it's a bit all in, if you know what I mean. There is discipline and style to basketball but netball has . . . space and placement, I just think it's a great sport and I happened to be better at netball than basketball. I played goal defence, GD, from the word go, but I have also enjoyed playing centre because I was usually the fittest on the teams I played for. I also loved playing shooter or goal attack but that's for indoor netball. But my favourite position is GD. I never contact—I am a clean, hard, fast player. I have a great lean and a great defence zone play, I never contact or play dirty.
Neither do I! Actually you have similar views as I do as a defender. I always say, 'I'm one of the cleanest defenders in the league' . . .

. . . I don't smash people.

Nup, no need to if you know what you're doing.
. . . I always try and pull out of things . . .

Exactly.

. . . I'm not rough . . .

You know, you could be as dirty as the next person, but it is the art . . .

Yep.

. . . *to defend and even when I rebound, I don't touch nobody!*

Same here.

. . . *And the umpire will pull me up and you accept it; you have to. But usually the player that I am supposed to contact turns around and says, 'But you didn't touch me' . . .*

I think we may have got a bit sidetracked here, back to the subject of this book.

Yeah! We're off track!

We'll have to have a game somewhere?

Yeah, definitely.

Hey, you had an opportunity to play with the first Indigenous netball player, Marcia Ella, sister to the famous football Ella brothers. What was that like, did she give you any advice?

Marcia was very shy but she was very glad to be playing with another Koori. She didn't verbally give me any advice but she did take me under her wing and stirred me here and there, but she was close to retiring so I think we only had one or two games together. But that will be one of those memories you treasure forever, because she was my idol, I really looked up to her.

So are you really pissed about not having a run in that world championship game, to be able to say that you physically helped with that win?

Yeah! Big time!

I'd just won a world championship, but I still didn't feel like I'd achieved my goal yet because I hadn't been on the court. I wanted to ... my goal ... the whole purpose of training so hard, everything was about playing in that final against New Zealand, and it just didn't happen. I feel like I've done everything I possibly can, but I still haven't achieved that goal.

I spoke to a few coaches and I spoke to a few friends about retiring and they said, 'Look, once you retire that's it! You can't go back.' Well, you can, but you ... I hate people that do that, say they're going to retire and they go back. So I decided I'd play as long as I could, and just try and plan my work a little bit better so it fitted in better with my training, so that I wouldn't be so hectic and I don't just react to people ringing up saying, 'Oh, can you come here for NAIDOC? Can you do this, do that?' And that's what I was doing before, I was just trying to please everybody ... I can't say no, that's my problem. I always have to say 'Yeah, I'll do whatever I can.' I put myself out if I have to. I'll give my mum my last cent even though I need it. Things like that, you know. But I came to the realisation that sometimes you just have to say, 'No!' I needed to just be a little more careful with my time and look after myself for a change.

That's one of the reasons why I wanted to keep playing— because the kids would still recognise me. Now that I'm not playing, I still want to be in the public eye, kids forget very easily. You know what I mean? And I still want to be up there so I can motivate and encourage.

Why do you need to be in the public eye?
I get a lot of satisfaction out of it. Not for myself, but for the kids, they need that constant 'in your face' role model to keep them motivated. I get a good feeling from it. I know how much the kids love it, I guess we're providing something for them—that dreams and goals can be met with a little hard work and some encouragement and a little helping hand. Give them something

exciting in their lives. Give them a purpose and when they see me on TV playing it makes them proud and gives them strength.

I mean this program we run, it's not just a quick fix, we talk to them about employment opportunities and different directions that they can take in the sporting industries, and we try to work in with a lot of the Sport and Recreation offices in leadership skills in the community. Running coaching courses and things like that. So we're trying to do something positive for the community.

When you go out to some of these remote areas and you see how disadvantaged the communities are . . . you appreciate your life a lot more and really want to make a difference. I'm not going to be able to change the whole community's attitude, but at least we're making a difference with some of the young people's lives and exposing them to what opportunities are available to them outside of their community.

We held this camp, one of many, but this one in particular stands out, this teacher rang me up and said, 'Look, these kids are great, can I bring them to the camp?' I said, 'Yeah, bring them in.' And she said, 'What do they need?' And I said, 'Oh, you know, as long as they've got some shoes and a pair of shorts.' She said, 'I don't even think they've got shoes,' and I said, 'Well, I'll try and get some if I can.' Like I'll try and get them a pair, and then she said, 'We might be able to scrounge a pair up from their aunties or something like that?' But see, the thing is, if a kid like that went to a white club, turned up with no shoes, the coach would go, 'What the fuck are you doing here?' Maybe not that harsh, but the same intent; that's the whole reason why NASCA exists! Because we want these kids to feel comfortable; if they turn up barefoot I don't care, they can play with no shoes on. I don't give a shit! I want the kids to feel comfortable in this environment, I don't want them to feel like they have to pretend if they don't have the right gear or equipment, I just want them to soar to great heights with their natural sporting abilities, and to give them hope.

And these kids that get selected will represent their state through NASCA's 'State of Origin' series: they have an opportunity to also be selected to represent an Australian Indigenous Team and travel overseas, which also helps to broaden their social skills and learn about other cultures. What we aim to achieve with NASCA is great for their whole personal development. So hopefully we can keep up the great financial support that we have already, it is always the hardest, but this program does work and you've got genuine people working in this organisation who really care for these kids.

What does NASCA need, like in terms of financial support? How's it going?
It's going okay. Dave is just amazing in getting funding, but we are always needing more. Westpac have thrown money towards the golf program. The New South Wales Department of Sport and Recreation provide a lot of funding for general admin costs and things like that, that's just for three years. Alan Jones [radio personality], he's on our Board of Patrons, he's been very supportive. When Dave took the first Aboriginal team overseas, we didn't have a sponsor, and Alan Jones announced it on his radio program and within four hours we had enough money to take these kids overseas! Bob Hawke is another big name, he helps out when he can.

We've had a lot of support, a lot of corporate support. We don't rely on the government much at all! It's all mainly corporate, except for the Sport and Recreation money that comes in. We just want it to get bigger, and it's going to get bigger, better and stronger. But I really need a major sponsor for my netball program, hopefully soon.

How many kids are you currently mentoring?
Hundreds! We keep records of all the kids, we keep track of them so none of them slip through the program. If they do, they

sharon finnan   65

can come back any time and try again; we'll give them another opportunity. But we are always looking for financial support, we're always looking for that little bit extra.

What are your concerns for the future? It's a very big question.
It is.

Your work with NASCA is right on the edge of one of the biggest issues for Australian society.
I'm concerned with what our kids are getting into and I'm talking about the negative stuff: drugs, alcohol, violence, etc. I see that it's just a vicious cycle and, until it's broken, nothing's ever going to change for the better. I believe that some of the programs that we're doing out there in the communities are creating an awareness of some of those issues and problems, and by using sport as a tool to break some of those cycles and attitudes, I feel, and know and believe, that what we're doing is beneficial.

If you suddenly had a huge amount of money to do what you like with, what sorts of things would you suggest?
Health problems—they need to be looked at. We need some more sporting facilities in remote communities, we need proper housing out there for our people. Find out what the community wants first by asking them and then go about fixing it. I would give the money to an appropriate organisation that would do the right thing with it.

Like in some of the remote communities we've visited I didn't even see a shower or toilet. Why not put in just basic facilities in all those sorts of areas? Just things like that, just things that are going to make people feel a little bit more comfortable and if they don't want the whole works, well fine. Let's just make it the way they feel happy with. At least make it liveable for them so they can feel comfortable. If I was in politics, they're some of the issues I'd be looking at dealing with.

But go and ask the people, that's the key issue, and giving money to people who will do the right thing and put the money to the proper use.

Ask them! That's what I found, working in government, that they don't consult enough . . . you really need to go out and consult with the community before you run in there and start doing things. And that's one big thing that NASCA didn't want to do, was to just start running around the communities without adhering to protocols.

We work through the local people and say, 'Well look, we can provide this and we can offer this. Is this something that you'd like us to do?'

We went on the footy show and we promoted the programs. The next thing we know, we've had two cars donated to us through Aussie Home Loans! I drive one of them and Dave has the other; it's all painted up in really deadly Aboriginal art which was designed by our chairman John Moriarty's company, Balarinji. That's the same company that painted the Qantas planes. It's got my netball program on it and all that sort of stuff, so I'm promoting Aussie Home Loans while we're promoting our program. Driving around the Gold Coast, there's no black faces on the Gold Coast, so I'm driving around in this car, at first I felt a little bit paranoid because it just drew so much attention. First time I was like, 'Oh shit! I can't hide!' It's just a bright car. But now I feel great driving around in it, very proud!

I would have so many ideas if I had an endless amount of money and I had control of it. Jackie Kelly, the former Federal Sports Minister, I was on a panel with her and we were down in Canberra at a Sport and Rec conference. The audience were asking us questions and someone asked me, 'What will you do when you retire?' And I said, 'Oh, maybe go into politics, Aboriginal politics.' And as soon as that conference ended, she came straight up to me and said, 'Which party do you support?' And I said, 'I don't really know!' She goes, 'Well, here's my number, give me a call at some stage.'

So I said, 'Look, I don't think I'm really ready for it yet.' But it is something in the future that I would really think about. That's maybe a future goal for myself.

So what are your future plans now that you're retiring from the game? [Sharon has just decided to retire.]
I will be the assistant coach for the Firebirds [the Queensland team in the Commonwealth Bank Trophy Competition] and will be tested for my Level Two Coaching Certificate—it's important that I get that, it helps out with getting jobs; especially if I choose to go overseas, which may be on the cards because my current boyfriend, he's a TI [Torres Strait Islander] boy, is a very talented cricketer and there may be an opportunity with him to go over. But I made the decision to throw myself into my work with NASCA and I've told the coach all that and they are pretty cool with that. So I can spend like once a week training and be there for home games, so I'll still be in the scene. But work and living a normal life are my priorities this year. I've bought a place on the Gold Coast and just want to make a home for myself. And I would like to start a family soon, at the end of the year realistically.

What brought on the decision to call it a day?
The heart wasn't in it anymore. Like turning up to games going, okay, let's get this over with. Looking around at training going, what am I doing here? The up and coming players are just so much younger these days. There was no enjoyment or satisfaction or attitude anymore, so when that happens you know it's time to go.

Was it a hard decision?

Yes and no. No because my heart, mind and body were telling me quite clearly it was time to go. But it was emotional when I was playing my last game because the realisation came when I was on the court, 'This is it, this is the last game I will be playing.' So that bit was hard because it became final. I do not regret my decision, I'm really happy at the moment. I've got good memories and I just want the simple life now.

Did you keep your Australian Netball uniform?

Yeah. What we did, actually, after the final, we all signed each other's and the bib that we were wearing. I've got that hanging up in my wardrobe, but I'm going to use that for something special. If NASCA can use it to raise funds in any way, I'll get it framed and auction it off.

Wow! That's a big give!

That is! Like that's something I probably should keep for myself really. But I've got photos all over my lounge room wall. Every time I walk into my house, I see them! And relive the moments. I get uplifted just looking at them. I've just put them all over the wall to remind me of what I've done and to motivate me to keep going.

I've had the picture of my success in my head for a long time, it's like you've grown into that, and that's a nice story, the positive thing from that is beyond the sporting results, it is this 'giving' to individual young people. It's a passion for me now.

It's actually quite a really cool and big thing that you're doing, at a grass roots level.

Well, I just hope that I can have some influence on the political people who are making the decisions out there as well. I think I'm in a position to be able to influence people that way. Not

Sharon with the world championship trophy

necessarily wanting to be directly involved in politics, but in a
sense that I at least have a say and try and change a few things.

*It's about change and that's what every great person in history has
done.*
I said to someone, 'If I die tomorrow, for whatever reason, I'd be
happy. I'd be a happy person. Because I am proud of my efforts
in helping people, my people or those who are less fortunate.'

*You have a special gift from the ancestors, you were sent for a
reason. Not everyone can give so much of their time to the young
people of this country. We don't want you to die tomorrow.*
  *May the ancestor guide and bless you. So you can continue to
work for our people.*

Voice on the Wind

Frances Rings

dancer

FRANCES: WHEN I CAME TO Sydney I was still very, very shy. I enrolled to go to NAISDA [National Aboriginal Islander Skills Development Association]. Once I was there, to my surprise, I felt that I didn't fit in anywhere. If you had a traditional look about you and were from one of those remote communities you got special attention. I was just a fair-skin, country girl and I felt that I was being overlooked; I was always overlooked. That made me work harder. I just quietly went about my own business, doing things my way. I think back and, out of all the other graduates in my year, like I'm the one that has continued on fully with dance. Everyone branches off to different things, I guess, but I stuck with my dream to dance. The hard work and determination has paid off: by becoming a principal dancer for Bangarra Dance Company and having the opportunity to dance and study overseas and now choreograph.

Leah: Yes, we are now hearing the story of the beautiful Frances Rings, our South Australian girl. On interviewing Frannie I really had no idea what her story would be about because I was literally a fan. I had seen Frances dance and was blown away. One of my childhood dreams was to become a dancer, but I realised later in my life, if you don't start at the right age then it's too hard on the body, and you can appreciate the lengths that these dancers go through to do all those steps and moves. It's a beautiful art form, one of my favourites to watch.

I have been dancing since I was five. I was always bossy too. I liked bossing people around, especially my sisters and brothers. I remember me and Gina, my little sister, we were so close we were almost like twins. I remember we would dress up and play these games or we'd have these roles we'd play out. I would always be the queen or head princess, Gina would be my maid and my stepsister Deirdre would be my husband, I was probably the dominating wife as well. But we would muck around like that and have fun. But the reality of it . . . it took away the ugly side—no money, getting teased at school and having alcoholic relatives coming around humbugging. So going out the back and playing Monkey Magic or designating ourselves to these roles to play out, it took all that other stuff, the reality of our situation, away. You see that with a lot of black kids. It's make-believe.

Tell us about your family make-up?
My mum is a Kokotha woman from South Australia who was actually married when she met my father. They fell in love and had me and Gina, but Mum went back to her husband. Mum has got, like, five other kids to him, so she went back there, to Ceduna. Dad took Gina and I with him to Port Augusta. I was a toddler and Gina was a baby. That's where he met and married my stepmum, a Nyoongar woman from Western Australia. She was to have three children to my father, my younger brothers.

Our stepmum already had a daughter so she became my stepsister, my big sister Deirdre. I remember when Gina and I were to first meet our stepsister. She had all these toys, deadly dresses and stuff, because me and Gina we never had anything like that. We'd want to wear her clothes, we'd nick her toys, all the natural things little sisters get up to.

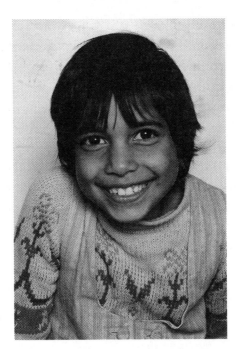
Young, smiling Frances

It kind of gets a bit bizarre here in my life at this point. I became quite distraught through this time in my life because my little sister Gina, who was like my shadow—she was always there, we travelled everywhere together, inseparable—Gina was fostered out. She was six years old. Money was extremely short. Dad not only had a wife to support but her child, as well as my brothers, who were all babies in steps to one another, and she wasn't going to give up any of her children, I guess. So Dad took it upon himself to give up one of his, and Gina being the youngest, he thought that would be for the best. So the next minute she was gone.

I went through this whole missing her kind of stage. I went through this transition of trying to replace her and to do that I would go off into my own little world . . . but it was really hard because she was just always there, my shadow.

We moved over to Kalgoorlie. Gina stayed in Port Augusta with her foster family. Dad was working on the railway and he was always being transferred, because of his transfers we lost track of Gina.

I always used to wish it were me. I thought she was getting a better deal or something. I was eight going on nine, my brothers were all toddlers. Dad and my stepmum separated, so I became a mini-mum. There were times when I would have to stay home from school to look after them with my stepsister because Dad was away working a lot . . . but I didn't mind that, that part was great really. So there were my little brothers, my older sister, and I was like the middle child, that middle child syndrome. It was like everything else was going on around me. I was being overlooked. I thought, 'Oh geez, it'd be good, I wish it was me that was fostered.' I said that once and I got a hiding. Dad clipped me over the ears.

My sister and I haven't had any big conversations about that situation, about what happened to us, to her. We want to, but it's still too painful for us.

At this stage of the story I was floored. This was an amazing story and it was just the beginning, could there be any more surprises? I felt so privileged that Frances trusted me with this story. I was using so much energy to stay in control as the interviewer and not break with the emotion that I was feeling and I think Frances knew this because she continued on with her story. There was like this other connection between us and it was that sista strength happening under the table, this energy going back and forth, she knew I was there for her.

When did you meet up again with your sister?
It was dance that brought us back together. I was eight, she was six when she left and we met up again when I was eighteen. It was so amazing. I was studying dance at NAISDA, here in

Sydney. She was in Year Twelve and she was applying to go and study dance at the Centre of Performing Arts in Adelaide. She was like full-on into the Rock Eisteddfod, just really full-on into dance in the way most of the white girls go through. It was wild, bizarre really, because I always thought like, I wonder what she is doing, what she looked like. I wondered if we looked the same. I'd always wondered about her. We were so close and then one day she was gone for twelve years of our lives; nothing. It was like there was a limb missing from me. So when we got back in touch with each other, she was dancing and it was just like, *Wow!*

The very first time we met, I went to her. She was still living in South Australia in Adelaide. I was auditioning with a friend in Sydney and she was talking about her boyfriend, who was a Nunga from Adelaide. So, out of curiosity and a stab in the dark, I asked her to ask him if he knew of my sister. I couldn't believe what I heard the next day: my sister was going out with his brother! You could have knocked me over with a feather. So, before I knew it, I was on a plane going to meet my baby sister for the first time in . . . too long. And then, before I knew it, we were both auditioning for a position with Bangarra.

You know, I had all these big dreams of us dancing together and, like, in the same company and working together and all of that. When Gina eventually joined Bangarra, when that became a reality, it was like dancing with this person who looked like me, had my mannerisms, and it was my blood, but we were complete strangers. That was really, really, really hard for us.

When you're dancing in a dance company it is very competitive at the best of times, not nasty or anything like that, just pure professional competition for the lead roles. I became one of Bangarra's lead female dancers. And then my guilt trip would start and that uneasiness between us would rise. 'Why you and not me? Why was I fostered out? Why wasn't it me that got that role?' There was that restlessness. Those questions weren't asked

Frances and Gina

out loud, this was all in the silent screaming that we were doing in our own headspace, but we could feel it. We are blood, sisters; we were once one. She was my shadow and I guess she was feeling that again, but it wasn't in a good sense anymore and nobody was giving us answers either.

I remember going up to Queensland and just, like, losing it with my father. Just like, 'I didn't create this mess but we're the ones that have to deal with it. Nobody is helping us, there's nobody that is giving us the answers. And here we are two... two sisters that don't know how to be sisters. We're strangers!' I mean, I just lost it; I saw red. I'm a pretty placid person really, but this day... I don't know. My anger, confusion, came from deep down in the pit of my stomach. I was throwing things around. I kind of 'went' for him. It had been rumbling deep down inside, building over the years. All I wanted was for Dad to say sorry. And he did. I just stopped, like everything went from me. Dad just broke down, he was really upset and he said, 'I'm so sorry, I'm so sorry for that.' And once I saw that, I saw him as my equal, I suppose; I didn't see him as my father, the man that gave away my sister, he became my friend. But my sister and I have still got to talk about this and become friends, I guess, too.

It was like she came into the dance world and made friends with everyone else in the dance company except for me and she was going out with them, hangin' out and things like that. But I wanted everything all at once—we're sisters, we should be best friends, we should be this and that. All these high expectations of what it should be like, but it didn't turn out that way.

I can't complain because I'm lucky that I have her in my life again.

What was next to happen after you and Gina found one another? I guess it was the start of the healing process for yourselves.
The next step was to find our mother.

So I started to ring South Australia, trying to find out if they knew the whereabouts of my mum; I had her name and through the black grapevine had an idea of where she had worked. Just asking other Blackfellas from Adelaide. This one fella said, 'Oh yeah, she passed away a couple of years ago.' I rang my best friend and just broke down and cried to her. Then a few weeks later I found out it wasn't her. It was like a rollercoaster ride: no, she's dead; no, she's not. I got the number for the community at Koonibba, which was her home, so I rang. I ended up speaking to my half-sister there. The next thing I know, I'm on a plane. I asked Gina if she wanted to come but she said, 'No, you go first!' So I ended up going alone; a big step.

I was in Adelaide waiting for a connecting flight to Ceduna and I was talking to these Nungas and I'm going, all happy way, 'Oh, I'm going to Koonibba to see my mob out there. It'll be my first time, I haven't seen them since I was a baby.' They're like, 'Oh, they're wild out there! They're West Coast blacks, they're wild, they'll stab ya in the back, sister or no sister!' I'm like, 'No!!' Shock, horror! I don't need to hear this, I'm already freaking out. I'm meeting all this family I never met before.

What was that like?
As the plane was landing, I looked out and there were all these black faces—crying, waving—when I got off the plane they started toward me . . . coming to hug me. They knew me. It was fantastic. Family. But who are these strangers?

They were just waiting for me to come back. It was like I was never gone. That's what I found the most interesting that, yeah, they knew I would come back . . . I talked to my old aunties, 'Oh yeah, we remember you and your sister when you were babies. You two would run up and down the street here. But we knew you'd come back. Your father took you away.' They weren't bitter or anything like that. 'We knew you'd come back.' I thought that was really, really lovely. This is my roots, my people, my blood. I wouldn't have rested until I did return, whether it happened when it did or years later. I had to return.

The bizarre thing was when I looked out I knew straightaway who my mother was. I recognised her, but I couldn't remember her. I recognised her eyes. That was the strongest thing I remembered of her. When we touched I remembered that, I remembered her touch, it was familiar. She was there . . . here I am . . . we're back!

When we sat talking I was looking at her feet, her hands, her eyes. It'll be that, that's what I'll remember, forever.

I was nineteen when I met my mum. She's beautiful. An amazing woman, I can't even begin to imagine her pain of losing her two baby girls. But she's . . . I guess like . . . it's hard talking about this.

Are you okay?
Yer, I'll be fine . . . just give us a sec.

I was grateful Frannie asked for a break, I had a huge lump in my throat so I was happy to pause.
She . . . my mother wouldn't let go of me. She'd come in and check on me in the middle of the night—I think she thought she was dreaming—to make sure I was still there. I'd wake up in the morning and she'd be there sitting on the edge of my bed waiting for me to wake up. It was beautiful.

There would be moments and she would be doing her daily duties and I would catch myself staring at her or I would look back at her or sneak a peek and think to myself, 'Wow, you gave birth to me. I've got a mum and she loves me.' That's a weird concept for me; she was never in my life.

I lasted two days—it was too overwhelming. Two days! But it was a great two days. Family coming in from the community, carloads. Like in town I'd be walking down the street with Mum and she'd be dragging me into every shop saying, 'This is my daughter!' Introducing me to everyone—whitefellas, Blackfellas—everywhere; she was so proud that I'd come back. I'd have these people coming up to me, crying and grabbing me . . . it was such an overload . . . a big shock. I had to get away. Process what I had just experienced. But I was coming back, and each time I will be able to stay that little bit longer.

I go back every year, but it's harder for Gina. I can understand that. For her it was about building up trust again with her family. Gina was fostered to a Nunga family so she did have that connection to mob, but not her blood, not her family. But they all adore Gina at home there, it's hard not to. I remember once when we went home together and the biggest carload of boys came looking for Gina! 'You gonna get this [holding up a fist] if you touch my sister!' Anyone touches her they deal with me.

I'm just very protective of her—always have been, always will be, she's my baby sister.

How was your family on your mother's side handling it?
Family wars kind of started then, nothing too dramatic, but just the fact that I had another five siblings and they all want us to be with them and then you had Mum. It got very hard and very tiring trying to please everyone.

I remember this one time when I was still a kid and we were still living in Kalgoorlie. I was outside playing and this bus pulled up. It was like, 'Oh, who's that on the bus?' There were all these black faces and Dad came out and told me to go inside, 'You don't look out the window!' I went inside, I never did look out the window. I was curious, but very scared. I didn't understand what was going on.

It was my mother who was on the bus. I was nine. She came on the bus. Some of my mum's family had seen me out shopping with Dad and word got back to Mum, so she jumped on the Community Bus to see if she could see me. Dad went out and he was wild. He didn't want her to have anything to do with me. I heard someone inside say that that was my mother out there. And when we had that big blue, in Queensland in later years, I let that out too. 'Why? Why didn't you let me see my mum?' She tried to find Gina, but I think after a while she thought it best to leave it. I don't think she ever stopped thinking or talking about us. I think it was hard. I haven't really spoken to her about this, she's very quiet and she's very shy. She's tiny, a tiny little thing. Her beautiful dark skin, her eyes, her hands and feet—it's probably the strongest feature with us, the three of us.

The first time that Gina and I went home together we were at Mum's house, which backs right up onto the bush. It was late one night, it was really freaky, wind was blowing strong. I went and opened the window and that's when I heard it. I heard the voices on the wind. They were high-pitched voices. All I wanted to do was go to my mother and lay next to her. I wasn't afraid of the voices at the time; I just wanted my mother. She was sleeping on the verandah. I went to her and slept there next to her. I felt so safe.

I think the spirits were telling me it was okay, I needed to do that. Mum needed me to do that. Once I laid down beside her I could feel them around us, the old spirits, and then they went. I'm not sure whether it was a dream or it was for real, but it was nice. Her touch, her smell, yeah . . . yeah, that was good. Then in the morning when we awoke we'd slept right next to each other all night and that felt great. We were another step to becoming closer, to being in touch with my natural mother. But it's something I will mourn for the rest of my life. That time is lost forever, it's missing, it's . . . it's gone. Nothing can ever bring back those missing years between my mother, my sister; between us, us three.

My eyes had tears in them, I couldn't hide it anymore, but I did not let them fall. I became the interviewer again and thought it best to move on. So, how did the wider community take to you? You being an outsider, what did you see?
It was hard to believe some of the ignorance of the local white people there. I could call it a lot of things, but when it comes down to it, it really is ignorance. Like, after living in the city it's like, 'You don't have to deal with this!' But I'm not a local so it's easier said than done. You know outside the bank they have grown cactuses there so after they [the Blackfellas] got their pensions, they couldn't sit there. We went into this shop, and because we weren't buying anything, they kicked us out. Another time, I jumped in this cab with some of my family, we were going over to the other side of town to see a cousin. So we get in this cab and I'm like, 'Hey, that meter's not on, what's going on?' 'It's a set fee.' I was like, 'I don't think so! You've got a meter,

use it.' He did. He picked me up again, he recognised me and put the meter straight on.

There are prejudiced people out there in this big free country of ours, it might not be plainly in your face, and sometimes it depends on the colouring of that face as to how much they show you, but it is there. It's about attitude—what they have been taught and the ignorance and fear of something unknown. That must change.

But my family is proud of me and I think the white locals are too, they see me on 'ICAM' [Indigenous Current Affairs Magazine for SBS]. But I love that country out that way! It's great. Every time I go back there, it's just like I think, 'Oh gee, I'd love to like hold up here for a couple of months and just hang out.' In each of the women there I see something that is reflective of myself. I know that I will eventually go back there and just . . . hang out.

Has your dad seen you dance?
I can't handle my family coming to see me dance. I can't handle them talking about me, like . . . praise. We were dancing in Lismore. Dad came down from Coolum with his wife. It was quite bizarre because Gina was performing as well! It was the first time that they had seen each other since she'd been fostered out.

Oh wow.
I was really kind of tense about that too, but I'm sure it was eating away at Gina more, she didn't say much; and for Dad as well, I guess. What a situation! How do you deal with that? A bit like the twilight zone. He was so proud.

My mum came to see me in Adelaide. I got her on a bus up from Ceduna. She sat in on a class and then came and saw the performance that night. The company just loved her and she was treated like a queen; she loved it. Gina wasn't dancing then but

I think Mum had seen us on TV dancing together. It's really bizarre, I guess she's seen me more on TV than in person. It must still spin her out. I can't imagine, if I didn't know where she was and hadn't found her and she was watching me on TV, would she know it was me? I think that she would have but she wouldn't have asked. It's like she was kind of somehow there all along, you know? She was never too far away, that's how I feel with her.

Dealing with all your family issues from such a young age, did you ever have suicidal thoughts?
When I was a kid, like I remember thinking: I just want to die. It was just like once or twice when I was really depressed . . . and missing Gina. Thinking that no one understood or that no one was there for me. Then I felt I had a responsibility to my brothers and they needed me so I channelled my energy into them. They replaced Gina, I guess. I needed to be needed. That kind of survival mode, where it kicks in and you'll be fine.

Automatic pilot.
Yeah. I was reading about these kids whose parents had died, these three young boys. Their parents were junkies and they both died within three months of each other. And these three little boys lived in this house . . . it was really sad . . . the oldest boy was looking after them and when he wasn't around they would freak out. I could relate to that story so much—that connection between siblings. How does a child know how to do those things? That's what a parent is supposed to do. I remember being an adult before my time; sometimes you have to if you want to survive. We draw our strengths from somewhere, maybe it's the ancestor?

And that gut instinct. Which is the way the spiritual ancestors speak to you. I rely heavily on my gut instincts, do you?

I follow it firmly. It's something that will never let you down. It's the one thing you can trust. I've always fallen back on it.

Which one of the five senses would you relate to?
Touch would be the most obvious one. As a dancer you have to know your body and when you're dancing with someone else touch is important for communication.

What's an early memory for you, relating to the senses, that was heightened by touch.
When the rain hits your face as the first drops fall ... big and fat. That smell of when the rain hits the dry dusty dirt, I like that and that's a fond memory from Kalgoorlie.

Being a performer, you do rely on the physical form, the physical sense of things. Watching, listening, not so much smelling, only when your dance partner forgets to put on under-arm! But we all come to know the smell of each other; you get very close, personal and very sweaty.

Touch, from a light, sensual touch to grabbing—hold me I'm falling. To being pulled, thrown around, to being dramatically placed gently on the floor. Then you feel the hardness and the cold or the sweat that lays there from someone else. Or you are in 'the moment' and you feel nothing but sheer performance ... whatever it is when you are there and nothing else matters.

But another early childhood memory would be us kids all sleeping in the one bed, head to toe, now that's touch. All sleeping in formation to fit comfortably in the bed. That was so nice, I always liked that—family fitting into the bed like fingers into a glove, perfect. Warm and safe.

What frees you?
When I'm performing I feel the most free. When I get there, to that moment; it doesn't always happen but when it does it's really good. You get lost in it. Time doesn't have any meaning, where

Frances in one of her many performances

you are, the theatre, the space, the movement . . . you're lost in it. It's like an out of body experience.

It happened in Washington, in Fairfax, Virginia. We were performing at the George Mason University Theatre. It wasn't a huge audience. But in this one particular part of the performance when the water is poured over us and then I'm like . . . gone! We could be anywhere in the world performing, but this one section of the dance piece brings me back to our country, it brings me home. 'It's going to rain.' Them dry country towns, you know it's coming. Us kids would run outside and like have a big party. We'd strip off and muck around. I get lost in that. That's what I love about performing with Bangarra. It's young, exciting and fulfilling to dance the dances of our country, to have a deeply rooted connection to this country's ancient culture.

Do you think we have a better understanding with that unknown sixth sense?
Yeah, definitely.

What is it for you?
It's a knowing. It's something that . . . something old . . . it's hard to describe . . . it's almost a sense of place and a sense of coming home. Like eventually you do come home and I found that through everything that's happened to me. It comes around and, with time, it does eventuate, although sometimes you can't change what's happened to you, to me—all those years taken away. A sense of knowing, that sense of belonging. The more I go home and the more time I spend with my sister the stronger it becomes.

Where does this sense sit in your body?
I feel it in the tiny hairs all over my body. It's also like when you get this warmness down the back of your neck. But I'm thinking when I was in New York and, like, I really missed home. Yeah, I really missed home and family. I was completely alone. I had to rely on myself. I really found out who I was. I found my strength and my weaknesses, but I found that wherever I walked, whatever track I took, that I always had something to come back to, and that was what I had. Nobody else could take that away from me. I am that. I have my country and I have my family there. That was somewhere, wherever I was in the world, I knew I could go back there and they'd look after me. That's something I never had before . . . where it's like a real concrete foundation.

My dad's offered me that, like he's been there all my life, he's my hero. There's no other man I look up to more than my father but . . . God, it must be a black thing . . . that whole kind of spiritual, cultural womanhood—that feeling of completion and wholeness—and that came from my mother and her people. My sister, my dancing. The more that I wanted to perform and express myself, throw myself totally into it, you know, learning all those traditional dances, hanging out with all that mob from the remote traditional communities. It becomes clearer to me what I was missing out on and what I didn't have. I thought: I've really got to find what's mine. Look at the hairs on my arm—they're up . . . that's it, that's what I'm talking about.

Well, the hairs on my arm are up too. I know exactly what Frances is talking about. It's a thirst that is never quenched. You become delirious with confusion; frustrated when you have to justify your actions to non-believers. All we really want is to know that we belong and have a purpose. We want our culture.

When we had a woman's business day down in Sydney out at La Perouse, the women from the Mutitjulu community came down to take us through the day. I was in awe, I was silenced. I became patient. They spoke language but I could understand. I was envious of this little twelve-year-old New Zealand girl, not sure whether she was Pakia or Maori, but she spoke and understood the language. My body ached—I wanted to cry, I wanted to be held by these women. I helped one of the ladies down the stairs, the one that didn't speak English at all, but she looked at me, right into my eyes. She spoke to the other woman and the other woman asked me where my mob was from. I told her and the lady that looked right into my eyes said that she knew me—maybe she meant my spirit, maybe she could see my ancestors. Maybe she could see my black soul.

These old girls were so funny and talking dirty! Comical . . . true! I had the best day. They told us our Dreaming track—it was beautiful to know and I can share that with my daughter. I took her up there to the mountains where the story ended, I can't go into detail because it is not appropriate, but God we felt so whole, so complete, so empowered, so mighty. I would just love to give this feeling to all those women of other cultures who may not have a connection to this great land or have not got that fulfilment of their own. If it was a gift I could give, I would, but I believe it is part of our individual life's journey to find that connection, then you appreciate it. And Frannie and I have found it and we are blessed by our ancient spiritual ancestors because of our hard work and determination to get there. 'Ngai alcheringa yirra Baiame.'

It would be great if everyone in our society had that feeling of belonging or that knowing. We would be more respectful of each other. There would be a feeling of reverence. Respect for life, that is overlooked and taken for granted: we wake up every morning, brush our teeth, have breakfast, go about our daily business, but do we really look around? I thank God that my mum was still alive, that I have found my sister, that I have made peace with my dad, that my career is going well. I am so thankful for these things, I wonder how many people out there have actually sat down and had a look at their lives and went, 'Shit, I'm lucky to be here, or God, I'm really grateful for all the things I've got.' All those things we take for granted. We need to acknowledge and respect them, instead of going, 'Oh yeah, okay.' Take the time before it's too late.

If you had to give up a sense which one would it be?
I think I would give up sight. I think it would make me a better dancer. That'd be good.

Why?
Because your other senses would be heightened, then you would gain more for your dancing, your sense of space. We take our sight for granted; you look for your next spot on the floor. Without sight, to get to that spot would require timing, positioning and formation, it would be quite exciting to try, especially with other dancers being onstage.

I remember once when I was fifteen, I was auditioning for a performing arts school—majority white students, white principal blah,

blah, blah. I had learnt a song but I had to make up a dance on the spot. The headmistress just turned on this music and said, 'Dance.' So I closed my eyes and I danced . . . I was off. I mainly closed my eyes because I was myall, shame, I didn't want to look at her. She actually turned the music off, but I continued to dance and then I eventually realised the music was off and stopped, feeling more shamed because I carried on. And then she said, 'Oh, you're great, but you'll have to learn to dance with your eyes open.' She didn't understand my shame. And saying that made me even more shamed.

I was accepted but when the headmistress said, 'Leah, would you like to stay and be a part of our school', I turned to my dear old mother and said, 'Are you going to stay?' She quietly said, 'No, I'm going home, back to Murgon.' I turned to the principal and said, 'Nah, I'm goin' home with my mum.' And that was that. I believe that that was the right decision then, for me. And four years after that day my dear old mum passed away. I knew I had to go home with her that day because I knew she wasn't going to be around for much longer and I needed all the time I could get.

Besides being a great dancer what else are you good at?
I'm a listener. I feel most helpful when I can help someone. I don't feel comfortable talking about myself, but I've done all right tonight, I guess. It's not that I don't like having conversations, but I'm more of a listener. And where I can, I like to help out with some advice or just be there to help or have that shoulder for them to lean on.

If I had to give advice to a fifteen or seventeen year old who had my upbringing and came from the same situation, I would tell them not to take things too personally because I take things too personally. I'm too emotional, too sensitive. I'd tell her to be more assertive—don't take things to heart all the time. And just keep going and trust that things will work out cause they eventually will.

You said before that when you first came to Sydney and to the dance school you felt that you didn't fit in. Did you experience that anytime before then?

The colour boundaries didn't come into my life until I started school, or when you took notice of them because then they were right in your face. The mentality was the same at school: I was a half-breed and wasn't supposed to get too far, or they were downright racist.

I was ten and this girl was sitting next to me just fully abusing me. All the anger from the abuse was building up inside me, because before I just turned the other cheek. 'Keep going, keep going,' I was thinking to myself. I walked over to the teacher's desk to sharpen up my pencil, real sharp too. I returned to my seat, not saying anything, and she started up again, so I grabbed her hand, held it down and I stabbed her. I was like, 'You're going to pay!' I was a child, like I knew nothing. I wanted to kill her; I could have if I put the pencil anywhere else. I just had that much anger and confusion and frustration in me . . . I was a child of ten, aren't things supposed to be a bed of roses at that age?

I guess you can see why the people that have put up with that sort of treatment all their lives go out and do some of the crime that is happening out there, or turn to drugs and alcohol. But why did that little girl say and do those things to me? . . . she's only doing what she's been taught. Thank God we are working for our younger generation to have a clearer and wider understanding of the black issues and politics in this country. But it's the generation before them and before that generation again—they are the ones, like grandparents or parents who can still influence their children into thinking negative—they need to be educated as well. Maybe we need more stories like *Box the Pony* that will reach those people. That's deadly too, sis, thanks for that.

Going back to that 'half-caste' thing where you walk the fine line. Well, I didn't really become aware of my lightness until I started dance school here in Sydney where the stereotypical traditional-looking student was put up on a pedestal. It was like they were saying that for you to know culture and be spiritual, to know your Aboriginality, you had to come from the remote communities. To a certain degree that is true, but you have to give us a chance; we don't have it at our fingertips; we had to search long and hard. I'm not a traditional woman and I'm not a modern dancer, but I am a contemporary black woman and dancer. I think I'm lucky I can have the elements of both.

But, you know, my dad was great with his advice on those times when I would go home and ask him why.

Dad being German, he knew what I was going through, him being a migrant in Australia. 'You stand up for yourself. You can do whatever you want.' He made us work hard at school, always enforcing how important it was to go all the way through to finish high school. That's what I really wanted to do, until we moved to Queensland when I was fifteen and I had to go to Bundamba High School in . . . Ipswich! Year Eleven. I cried every night for the first three months. It was hell. The black kids wouldn't have a bar of me, because they were like, 'Who are you, little uptown thing getting around?' The white kids wouldn't have a bar of me either. I hated it! Hated it! Eventually I made friends with some of them, the ones that took pity on me. But of all places—Ipswich! God, that was such a full-on place then. I don't know what it's like now. I have no desire to go back.

But I was saved, I was sent to boarding school. Dad had enough of the crying and could see my pain. So I finished my senior year at boarding school in Warwick. I loved it. I became quite academic, studying. I was enjoying learning, it became fun and was seen as a positive. It was made our responsibility.

I possibly could have played you in softball; our school went over that way to play in tournaments. I always thought that the Darling

Downs was made especially for softball because it was so flat and wide. I used to think that, gunnar gunnar, hey?
No, I didn't play representative school softball, I was into tennis at the time.

Very spiritual place with all the stories of the min min lights. Did you ever experience anything like that out that way?
There was always a 'presence' out there; you could feel that something was there. I'm a real chicken when it comes to that sort of thing—get too frightened too quick. If there were min mins around I would have closed my eyes and missed them.

When did you make the final decision that brought you to Sydney to dance?
I knew I wanted to dance the moment I saw a pamphlet at boarding school of this girl jumping up in the air, she was Aboriginal too. I thought, 'Yep, that's it.' I haven't looked back. I saw Bangarra first perform, it was the Praying Mantis Dreaming, and I thought, 'Yep, that's for me. This is something that's going to suit me. They're dancing my language.' I just thought that was the coolest thing I'd ever seen.

When I first came to Sydney, I was only on Abstudy, so I couldn't get home much. Being away and all that, you miss it. So I guess there were a few of us that felt that way, so we started our own little family group. We linked up in this house in Redfern. We were a group that was there for each other, we were, like, even if it's raining we are still going to walk to Glebe and go to school. We were the driving force behind each other, when we got slack there was always someone there to give a little push.

I'm a contemporary dancer, but it's also different again because I know that in that dance world there's something that sets me apart. It's interesting because recently I was choreographing and working with the traditional women from South Aussie. Not just telling them what I wanted or how I wanted them to dance—it was a crossover of knowledge. The old women were teaching me the dances of my people and, in working with the women, we are all learning tradition. And then, in the same situation, I was building on to the dance by adding contemporary moves or adding my style to a completely new dance.

I went and saw this production and it was excellent. I told Frannie that she had patience, and working with mob teaches you that. Us urban mob are caught up in the rat-race of city living, but that's how you got to live if you choose the city. The stories the women from South Australia shared were beautiful because I had just learnt a couple of similar dances from the Mutitjulu women from the centre. Frances has her own style which is very refreshing. I hope, and I'm sure, we will see more of it in the future. Frances' touches added that contemporary feel for us urban Blackfellas, because that's our corroboree, that's our reflection of living, our stories, our journeys. It was a beautiful piece of work. As I sat and watched I just wished I could have joined the ladies on the floor, not necessarily as a dancer—although I wouldn't have said no—but I felt I needed to be down on the floor with them to really appreciate the power of the dancers and stories.

One of my aims as a choreographer is to bring our unique styles, Aboriginal styles, out. We have a particular way of holding ourselves, we have a particular way of using our hands, our mannerisms, how we talk to each other, how we laugh and throw our heads back—it's all so full of these gestures, it's brilliant and that's what I want to work with. I'm comfortable with this now. I feel I can achieve this . . . I have a better sense of who I am, where I'm from, what I have to offer.

And girlfriend you have a lot to offer, not only from your brain and spirit, but that well-toned dancer's bod-tay. Tell us about the FHM shoot.

FHM magazine? I really enjoyed working on that, it was good fun. They were great. No, they were really kind. I felt comfortable. It's very hard doing that kind of thing [an underwear photo shoot] because you don't quite know what to expect, but I was extremely happy with the shots. I think they were done with taste. My husband loves them.

But I did get a bit of slack from a few people in the community, the black community. Some people liked it and some didn't—not so much the end product, but more the fact that I was in underwear looking sexy. Maybe their view is still that kind of missionary thinking where it's like: cover up. I get a bit fiery about that sort of thinking, putting their standards onto other people. If someone goes to me, 'No, you can't.' I'll go, 'Yes I can.' We are beautiful women, if it's done with taste and respect then there's nothing wrong with showing our beauty. I think my shots show that, as well as style.

I told Frannie that not long before her shots came out in FHM *(which my partner liked too and when I told a nephew I knew her I quickly became the legend aunt), I saw the first black centrefold in a* People *magazine. She was wrapped in the Aboriginal flag, she looked gorgeous and her shots were done with style as well, but the best thing was that she looked very comfortable with what she was doing. Some people are fine with nudity and others aren't, and that's fine, but they can't expect others to take on their modesty. Everyone has a right to do what they're comfortable with—it's their body, after all.*

And, you know, how long am I going to have a body like this for? Gravity's going to take control one day. I'm just enjoying myself.

How did the shoot come about?
I got the gig when their editor saw me on 'ICAM' and he thought, 'Wow! That's a good idea to have an Aboriginal woman in the

mag.' He rang SBS Publicity and the publicity lady for 'ICAM' was really pushing me to do it. My initial feeling was 'no', but then I thought: no, hang on, this could be fun and a challenge for me. I've danced around stage, in less, in front of live audiences so, hey, why not? My husband being so supportive helped me to go ahead with it. The following month we [Bangarra mob] went and had a look to see if there were any responses to my photo spread—there was! This one fella wrote me a poem like, 'I'll be your slave, come and live with me', and all this other wild stuff, and I think that was hard for my husband. He's worried I'm now susceptible to crazy kinds of people. Touch wood, it's been pretty good so far, like I haven't received any kind of unwanted attention. Like, if you're in a restaurant, you have to be careful of what you are saying, or you'll be out having a big bitch about something, swearing away, and like sometimes my friends have got to pull me up, they'll go, 'They recognise you, so can you stop swearing?' And what about when ya start talkin' dirty?! But, you know, I preferred to be in the background.

Where did you get the confidence you have now?
It wasn't until I came to Sydney. I had done public speaking at high school, that's probably where I got my confidence from. I always feel more comfortable speaking in front of strangers than to people I actually know. I also think that with the write-up in the *FHM* mag it showed people I'm not just an airhead dancer. And, of course, with time and dealing with stuff in your own everyday life you learn and get confidence.

How are you handling the pressure of fame?
It's weird being in the spotlight. I get home and check my e-mails and answering machine and there are all these messages from old, so-called friends and teachers, like from pre-school and stuff like that: 'I just wanted to say hi and congratulations on your

success.' It's strange because when I needed that encouragement, they didn't give a shit.

I can see where Frannie is coming from, but I told her I looked at it as a way of them saying, 'Maybe I should have said something and I'm sorry I didn't.'

I was thinking to myself a few days ago about when the right time to give encouragement is, because timing is so important. You could get the wrong encouragement at the wrong time and you could end up on a different journey—not on the right path that is out there waiting for you.

I think when I was trying to have discussions in my earlier days, as a young mum, I would say stuff to family and it was like they were ignoring me, and you're thinking, 'Come on people, a little bit of encouragement would be good around about now. Help me on my way here.' But I look back now and think, I'm glad they didn't say anything because look where I am today. I always say the ancestors work in mysterious ways. So you can't be too hard on those so-called old friends. They are acknowledging your efforts now. Let them give us the pat on the back we so rightly deserve. As hard workers, us performers sometimes forget to do that, forget that it's okay to accept that acknowledgment too. It's nice to be acknowledged, even when it's a bit late.

You're at a real powerful stage in your life, of having moved to the top of your chosen art. You're part of a future generation that will be driving this country, in a way. To get to that point you have to be driven, you have to be a little selfish, but once you reach the top, there is a responsibility. Selfishness and responsibility often don't go well together and that's where a lot of people fall down. But, you know, the thing with us mob is that that selfishness is not a conscious thought. I like to call it determination and drive. And it's our mob that keeps us real, keeps us grounded. Yes, there is personal gain but we take a nation with us as we do it.

How do you see yourself in this situation?
Everyone else's situation or need is greater than mine. It's important to go back to the communities, because the advice we get
from our own mob is valued and probably the best you'll ever
get. It's important for them to have their say and they'll tell you
too if you're right or wrong, which is good. But you can't please
everyone, which is one of my problems because you always
try to . . .

Yeah, me too.
I'm really generous, I'd rather give.

It's important to experience life, whether it is right or wrong
for your career or for yourself personally. But it's something that
I definitely had to go through or had to do. You have to really
find that foundation first, then you will find your own.

*Well, talking of experiencing life, Frances recently came back from
overseas, New York to be exact. How was that experience when it
was only a couple of weeks after the terrorist attacks on the Twin
Towers in New York?*
Once we learnt that the hotel we were supposed to stay in had
been demolished because of the damage caused by the terrorist
attacks on the Twin Towers, fear crept in, but Stephen Page, our
director, was really great. We had a big get together to discuss
the issues of going over there and what our purpose was, the
pros and cons of going, and then Stephen allowed us to air our
concerns and then we had time to see whether each individual
still wanted to go, and it was up to us. But the whole company
decided that we would go ahead and that there was the beginning of something special . . . the company had become one. The
trip really was amazing—it was an awakening for the company.

We arrived in the evening in Princeton, New Jersey and we
relaxed that night as much as we could. But the next morning
after breakfast, we were all put on a bus and we went straight to

Manhattan, Union Square. We felt, as strangers to this land, that we had to pay our respects to this country's people and acknowledge the great loss that they were feeling and dealing with. So we thought that we should go and have a small ceremony for healing and guidance and a blessing for the tour that we were about to commence. So our song man, traditional man, Djakapurra, started to sing. And sing and sing—he did not stop until he felt that it was right to leave. This was not a performance and it was not arranged by anyone but us, but we invited the other Australian contingent that were over there to contribute or be a part of this ceremony if they wanted to and a few of them came down, from the Cloudstreet theatre production from Company B Belvoir. It was beautiful and touching and sincere.

Of course, Americans started to come around and watch and asked what we were doing and when we explained what was going on they were really touched and moved by our offering of healing. On our way home we stopped at a fruit shop and a lady there asked why we had our *gupan,* white ochre, on and we told her we had just done a healing ceremony at Union Square and she said, 'Thank you, my brother's somewhere in the rubble down there', and she was emotionally moved. And that united the company again. It really was one big family. Bangarra's had that feeling before, but not as intense as this. I think the company can only gain from this, it will be a great next few years to come.

The tour itself was huge and tiring. We travelled across the country by bus and it really was beautiful to experience, even though there was this presence of fear and sadness in the air, but it also made the country show more compassion for its fellow man and that was an eye-opener for me because that was a big change to the last time I was over there. But the tour was intensely physical—like twelve hours in the bus, two hours proper sleep in a bed and then it's bump in time, then to perform that night and then pack it away and back on the bus. That continued for eight weeks. We got great reviews and the new work piece for Bangarra, which was 'Corroboree', was just received so well. And amazingly no injuries, no attitudes and no complaints. That trip was truly a highlight of the year, besides me marrying my wonderful husband Scott in our beachside ceremony! That was truly beautiful too, to share our ceremony with close family and friends.

So what does the future hold for you?
I have not retired from dance, but I am having a break and won't be in everything Bangarra does. But I am truly excited that I will be choreographing alongside Stephen Page in our next production, with the working title 'Walkabout'. My piece is called 'Rations' and that is about thirty-five minutes long. And I'm also helping out with the rehearsal directing. I think I'm really ready for this, like the trip to America has given me personal growth as an elder of this group. Like, as an example: when there was the outbreak of anthrax over there, all the younger members were so scared—we all were—but we had to help them through it. There's this maturity I have found now which wasn't there before.

I've enjoyed my experience with 'ICAM' as a television presenter, but I have moved on from there. I have been spending good quality time with family in Ceduna, South Australia and I visited with the old people of Port Augusta—just sat down and had a good old yarn, I hadn't been back there since I was little. And precious time with my sister Gina on our personal journeys, it's all been just great. She's been doing so well with her ventures too, I'm so proud of her. I feel so good about these next couple of years with career and family and, ya never know, maybe my own little family too. The bushfires [in Sydney in 2002] have been terribly close but we are fine because of the position we are in, but it's sad looking at all the little animals . . . laugh, although

Gina, Mum, Frances and Dad at Frances' wedding

you shouldn't, but I was thinking to myself if those little animals took shelter in Blackfella's backyards, *gunarn*, Blackfella be eating him, eh?

Frannie! But true too!
Yes, I'm looking forward to a fulfilled life of love, happiness and good fortune with me and my husband. I wish that for all.

Millennium Woman

Liza Fraser-Gooda

LEAH: LIZA CAME TO US *at the very last moment, so late that she missed the first course to the dinner we had planned for the final chapter to bring all the black chicks together. She ran up the stairs and threw herself at us; I sat back and watched as her energy filled the room and she picked up the conversation and ran with it beautifully.*

Liza is the entrepreneur of the black chicks. She started her own business, wanting to promote the black beauty of this country. She started a small publishing and promotions business to help her baby sister out, but others heard and it grew.

Liza has an amazing confidence about her. She holds herself well. She is proud. She is the positive image that we as a people want to push to the world; she is the twenty-first century portrait of our Indigenous women of the future. That's the impression I got.

Liza comes from a family who were one of the lucky ones not to be affected by the biggest issue involving the Indigenous people of Australia: the 'Stolen Generation'. Even though neither side of her family were 'stolen', her paternal grandparents were removed from their tribal area and taken to the mission called Woorabinda, 170 kilometres southwest of Rockhampton. There, her grandparents instilled in their children the message that to get along in this white man's world you had to beat him at his own game and that meant becoming educated . . . white man's way, but keeping strong to what you remembered from the old people too.

Liza: My grandparents were very strict on education, my father and my uncles and aunties had private Catholic education and it was always instilled in us to do well at school, academically being the priority. I went through to Grade Twelve and obtained a certificate IV in tourism, but I'm always doing courses like 'train the trainer' and stuff like that. I just want to learn. I want to educate myself . . . I want to grow.

How did your grandparents know that education was the key?
You know, them old people, they could see the opportunities the white man was giving to our people through education and technology. You either embrace it or get left behind. Because our family had been taken from their traditional grounds and lifestyle, they could see that that was gone, so time to move forward and embrace this new lifestyle. And, of course, by keeping your identity through family, customs, stories and identifying with your roots, you stay black. Being black is about pride in who you are.

Liza's grandparents left the settlement of Woorabinda and moved to Rockhampton, where they were one of the first Aboriginal families to get one of the departmental houses for Aboriginal families. Does this story sound familiar? It is a similar story to that of my own family.

Liza's mother and father married and lived in a nice little house, had three beautiful daughters but then later divorced—sounds like the average family life. Liza excelled in sports and her academic studies at school. She received various awards for her efforts, which made her very popular in her school environment and in the township of Rockhampton in Queensland (sorry, another Queenslander!).

So Liza grew up in a loving family environment, was spoilt with plenty of love and a few material things. Her and her siblings were, and still are, very close and have all been successful.

This story sounds like that of an average white middle class family! Well, I'll be blow'd, you mean to tell me we can have a normal black family that fits into society and lives a fulfilling life? Can't be, hey, something must be wrong somewhere, surely. No! Black families can be just as normal as anyone else, actually there're quite a few. The media don't show us them; but I will. There are families out there who are living quite happily in both worlds of black and white, but there is always the preferred world, and that is black—it allows us to be us, no gamin.

I am happy and content with life. I had a very good and strong family upbringing. We are a very close-knit family and we love each other very deeply.

Who's your mob?
I take my mother's side and that's Bidjara, so I'm a strong Bidjara woman. My mother's family originated from Augathella (southwest Queensland). With her mum, Georgina Fraser, nee Lawton, and her siblings they grew up on the banks of the Warrego River, living at the Yumba. My uncles would go out hunting for kangaroo and bush tucker to feed the family whilst my grandfather, Benjamin Fraser, would be away as a stockman on properties around the southwest country of Queensland. My dad's dad, Frank Gooda, taught himself to read and write and could recite the poems of Henry Lawson and sing the songs of Hank Williams Snr. He taught my dad to play the guitar when he was twelve. My dad's mum is Gangulu. She was born in Rockhampton, and then they were moved to Wooribinda. They travelled around Central Queensland before settling back in Rockhampton. My nana's family were all taken from their tribal area to Wooribinda . . . see, I don't know a lot of that stuff so part of my journey is to find out all about Nana's childhood and life

so I know who I am, to be complete, and then you can move forward.

I think that's where our problem lies. Because so many of our people were removed from their tribal grounds we are all a little confused, because in our culture knowing where you are from is so important. Any Blackfella knows, when you meet some other Aboriginal person you ask where they're from and if you can't say where you are from you feel a little inadequate.
But I don't think I've ever met a Blackfella that can't say where some part of their family is from.

True.

Did your family fit into white society okay?
Yes. My family is well respected in the white community because they all hold good professional jobs. Dad is the manager for Aboriginal Housing, Uncle Michael is the State Manager for ATSIC in Western Australia, Uncle Dean is the Senior Resources Officer at the Department of Aboriginal & TSI Policy, Uncle Malcom runs the CDEP at Woorabinda, Aunty Judy is a hospitality teacher at TAFE. Nana used to sit on a lot of Indigenous committees and organisations' boards. My family is actively involved with the community.

What about in the Aboriginal community up that way?
Yes, my family are well respected.

My grandparents left the mission because I think they just wanted the best for their family. My nana was a woman of pride and refused to be told any different. My nana and her ten children moved to Rockhampton: 110 West Street was the first government-issued house to the Blackfellas. A welfare worker was assigned to the house and she tried to come around and check on Nana and her kids, but Nana stopped that woman at the gate and wouldn't let her up the stairs. Nana told her, 'I know how to look after my kids, you not going to come in here and tell me how to look after my child.' So the social worker left with her tail between her legs.

So we are very fortunate on both sides that we were not affected by the Stolen Generations, but not all situations could have been dealt like that, the way my grandmother did.

The foundation of your family is strong and I know that that's what makes you a strong woman—family is so important. You are very lucky to have that.
Yes, you realise that as time goes by and as you look around at those who are less fortunate, your family is very important. So, yes, I am one of the lucky ones to have that open, honest support from my family.

Did your parents talk much about culture stuff to you?
We talk our lingo. There are lots of words we know. When I was a child my stepfather would go out hunting and then cook the food underground, *kuppmurri* style. My favourite is porcupine. We actually ate a lot of traditional foods growing up.

I recently took a trip to my mother's home land of Augathella. There I participated in a very spiritual and personal journey of visiting sacred and traditional sites with my elder, Uncle Rusty Fraser. He told me Dreamtime stories, taught me more language, showed me where my ancestors are buried. That was just so soul-fulfilling. Because we now live in this westernised world; growing up, culture wasn't a real focus, it was still present but it played a minor part in everyday life. Going out and getting an education and worrying about paying rent took priority, and this was enforced by my grandparents and parents, they knew to achieve in this world these things were important for survival. But every black person knows that that connection to land and culture are important and you need to connect, so that's why I went into Aboriginal tourism: to learn about my culture. But now I realise you learn the best from listening to your elders telling you stories. All my elders, except Uncle Rusty, are gone now and they have taken with them all their knowledge and wisdom, that's what hurts the most. I wish I could have spent more time with them.

Describe your father for me.
Well, Dad's fifty-one years old. His name is Angus Gooda. He's a strong black and handsome Murri man. He works for Aboriginal Housing in Rockhampton. He writes his own music, he plays the guitar, and when I was growing up I thought that my dad was the best guitar player in the world. As I grew up and heard about Tommy Emmanuel and other guitarists, I got very disappointed that there were other guitarists out there. I just loved being around my dad, and my stepdad, Reg Little, as well—he loves his country and western too, but my stepdad also sings and plays the guitar. Sometimes my two dads would have a jam. Country and western is in my soul.

At present my dad is a bachelor and I think he likes it that way. He can catch them women, true. I've asked him on many occasions, 'How do you get all these women, Dad?' God, he's goin' to kill me for this! And he says, 'I'm a musician, they love that guitar.' He's got a complex about growing old. Like I can go out nightclubbing and there's my father dancing up. He says to me, 'It's not how old you are, it's how you feel.' But it just doesn't stop there. I asked my dad what's his secret for looking so good. He reckons, 'It's the facial exercises and the "Oil of Ulan", bub.' Isn't that just beautiful? Dad likes his vitamins too; he's got a whole cupboard full of them.

Dad was always the one that was pushing the education side of things, always buying us stuff to do with education—computers and encyclopedias—stuff to learn from. I remember Dad made me do guitar lessons and he made my sister do the

Liza and her dad

piano, but she was the one that wanted to do guitar. See I wasn't interested in the guitar, I was interested in little athletics and running around. But Dad also encouraged that because he loved his sport as well. He was the oldest player to play A grade football for the 'All Blacks' in Rocky. He looks bloody good for fifty-one. He is conscious about his looks and how he presents himself.

It certainly is great to know that a black man of that age loves himself enough to look after himself. Too many of our men are not looking after themselves; too many of our men are dying far too young. Within one year, five male friends of mine died of a heart attack or heart-related diseases, all under the age of forty. The statistics are terrible. So it is great to have a Murri man talk about his beauty secrets. I think we need him to hold a few urban men's business meetings.

I love my dad and stepdad. I adore them both for the opportunities they have given me.

Was your dad around much when you were a small child?
He was always a hard worker, worked in the mines. He was always there but it was always Mum there for the security and emotional love; Dad too, but Dad spoilt us with material things, but he also loves us. My stepfather was always there for me. Because of my family's values I am who I am today.

My eldest sister, Stacey, is my role model. She leads us all astray; she's the practical joker. I trust no one but my sister, I can tell her my inner thoughts. She's there for support, to give me encouragement. I just love her!

My baby sister, Jessica, is very straightforward, very beautiful, talented, and is going to be a recognised person in our community. She's still going through school at the moment but she's the baby and she's got us all wrapped around her little finger. I have four younger half brothers: Peter, Desmond, Cameron and Marcus. My brothers are very special to me. Also my stepfather's children—Lisa, Caleb, Joel, Luke and Spencer—all play an important role in my life.

It's so beautiful to hear that, because some sibling relationships can be so difficult and strained.
See, with my sisters and I, I'm the middle child and they say that I've got a 'middle child syndrome'.

And what's your definition of that?
Because they gang up on me . . . but when me and my sisters get together it is fun and we love being around each other.

What would a night out with you, your mum and your two sisters be like. I reckon it would be pretty wild.

Liza and her sisters

No, no, it wouldn't be a wild one. We'd have a bowl of porridge first, to start the night off.

Porridge?

See, we love porridge; we would eat it for breakfast, dinner and tea. So a bowl of porridge before going to bingo. We love to sit down to a game of bingo. My mother's a bingo player, that's her enjoyment; she'll do anything for a bingo price. It's Mum's favourite pastime, just a time for all of us to get together and have a laugh and be silly, and then come home and sit around listening to country and western, singing and dancing.

My mother is very beautiful and loving. My mum's a gypsy, her and my stepdad just go from one town to the other. Back and forwards from family. Well, she's got no kids around her so why not? She just loves to travel. Mum's in her late forties. She had all us kids when she was quite young. Growing up, all my aunties would say that we were spoilt. And that's because of Mum.

Spoilt with love or material things, or both?
With a bit of everything. Very loving. But because of the love and closeness we were good kids. I thank her for her smile, her gentle nature and her friendship.

She can't cook and all us three girls can't cook either, so we blame that on Mum. But she's an obsessive-compulsive cleaner: she'd get up, one o'clock in the morning, and wouldn't stop until everything was spotless. When we were little we would come home from school and you wouldn't know your room because Mum would have been in there changing everything around. So it was, like, every two weeks the whole house would be rearranged.

They used to say that my mum was the best lookin' *gumbi* walkin' the Warrego River. The Warrego River is in our tribal area and *gumbi* is the word for woman in our language, so she was the prettiest woman around. She is very beautiful. She loves to dance, sing and just have a good time in life.

What is an early memory of you when you were a child?
We were living in Ipswich and I got given this big doll in a pram for my birthday, it had a bright red and green jumpsuit and I used to think it was my baby and no one was allowed to touch it. I was five. I treated this doll as if it was my own, as if it was gold. I just played the girlie games with it . . . I can't remember what I called it.

I'm very competitive. At school in Tennant Creek, I would always win the hundred metres sprint, high jump and long jump, and I would always be competing against my cousin. But there was this one event I couldn't win and that was the seventy metre walk, my cousin would always win this event. So this one time there was about ten metres to go and I started running! I

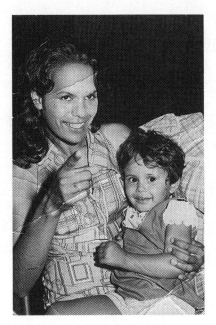
Liza and her mum

got disqualified, so I can never stake my claim at winning everything, but I came pretty close.

Where did that drive to win come from?
I think because I'm an Aries—we are born leaders, we like a challenge, we want to strive and always get the best. I'm just competitive. I hate losing; I always wanted to get that best result, ever since Grade One. I've still got all my certificates and trophies. All through high school I was competitive, I was named in the Australian under fifteens netball honorary side.

Netball again. We really need to get a netball game under way: a netball game against someone, anyone—we'll take them on.
Not only in sport, but academics as well; right down to a game of cards today, I'm competitive. To be successful in today's world you need that attribute.

Tell me a happy thought of you in school.
Happy thought?

Like a yarn or something funny that happened, or you getting up to mischief.
Oh, I was a good girl, me. I really loved school. I loved going to school. So I guess my happy thought is having the opportunity to be able to get up and go to school. I loved the aspect of learning, gaining knowledge. I was popular at school because of my sport. I was house captain . . . I was, and still am, an achiever; I just wanted to be good. And to have no barriers in thinking that I couldn't be good, because that's who I am. It comes back to my family, just their love, support and guidance.

What did you do when you finished school?
I worked at the Dreamtime Cultural Centre, Capricorn Tourism and Development Organisation, Indigenous Promotions, Byvan Management and Tjapukai Aboriginal Culture Park. I worked in various positions from food and beverage, tour guide, conference coordinating, administration, sales and marketing. This gave me ten years experience in the tourism industry. I was always eager to learn, thus developing my skills and knowledge to establish a small business with my business partner, Dina Paulson.

I was also the editor of *Tell-a-Murri*, a magazine that featured stories on the black community from Central Queensland. We would print five thousand copies and distribute them to all Aboriginal and Islander organisations. I would always be organising concerts and fashion parades for our youth. I would go to schools and present motivational talks to all the school kids, give them encouragement to follow their dreams and goals. I take pride in my involvement in my community that is also soul-fulfilling: it keeps you grounded. Mob does that to you and it's great. But I said to myself one day: I want something more; I was craving something deeper. I had this niggling feeling deep inside. I was needing something for me personally . . . it's hard to describe.

So I headed off to Kowanyama [an Aboriginal community in Cape York, Queensland] for three months, living and working there with the community. The only person I knew was my stepsister, Lisa Little, and her other half, he was the manager of the local pub there and he gave me a job in the canteen. It was just another world.

Do you drink?
No, I'm not a big drinker, only occasionally at social events, and I do not smoke.

Alcohol is a big problem in our communities, what did you see when you worked in the canteen up in Kowanyama?
It broke my heart. A lot of times I cried. The population is about twelve hundred—and a big per cent of my people would be alcoholics. In the canteen alone, they would make a substantial amount of money a week selling alcohol. It's sad. There is a big problem, but because the communities are so isolated, there is nothing else for our people to do. And then you've got younger people hanging around the fence waiting . . . waiting for their time . . . it's a cycle . . . that can't be broken, but needs to be.

The canteen was a place where it all happened, not only just the drinking but cultural activities as well. I loved working there because I was learning from my people, under all the wrong circumstances. There was something else happening at the canteen; they would bring in traditional foods and they would speak in language and they practised their traditional dances. It was like a nightclub but with traditional stuff.

I got adopted into a tribe, the Kokomanjunen tribe, known for the coloured sands of the area. I was working behind the bar with four other sister girls and all the mob would come in and get their charge. I connected with them by just talking to them, there was a connection already there just by being black, but just yarnin' with them was what got the ball rolling, and asking questions. They nicknamed me, yellow girl and corroboree girl.

Yellow girl because of skin colour, you being lighter than them, but why corroboree girl?
They had no jukebox for music, so no good. They nicknamed one old fella jukebox because he would sing and the rest would come in and do corroboree, sing in lingo and everyone do shake-a-leg instead of disco dancing. No good, all them old women be goin' for it doin' shake-a-leg, no good, all them old women came and dragged me from behind that counter and I was there doin' corroboree with them. So that's how I got the nickname.

My subconscious decision to go to Kowanyama came from a relationship break-up and a little help from a white woman. I was in a seven and a half year relationship; we were going through a rough time. I was on a bus going to see him and I was sitting next to this migloo woman, me and her clicked, she was very spiritual, and she said to me, 'Liza, you are heading in the wrong direction, you should be heading up north, I can see you amongst all these Aboriginal people.' She was looking me right into my eyes, reading my spirit. She told me she could see me wearing a white shell necklace and she said, 'When you get this necklace, you hold onto it because it is where you will get your strength. And if you ever need guidance this is where you will get it from.' I went along with it. Around about four months after that, I moved up to Kowanyama. I got adopted into the tribe, not at all thinking about what that white woman said to me on the bus. I made a special friendship with a girl called Rowena, who is a beautiful, strong Kokomanjunen with the pure blood of her ancestors running through her being. She has these big brown eyes. Rowena and I connected spiritually, we are Moon Dreaming sisters. We worked in the pub and became real close.

She would tell me stories about her childhood growing up in Kowanyama. She would share with me her cultural ways and language. One day she walked into the pub and gave me a white shell necklace, this necklace I'm wearing now, and I just started crying. That was what that migloo woman was talking to me on the bus about. The necklace is made out of shark bone. Her family adopted me into their family and tribe. They gave me dilly bags, boomerangs, spears and necklaces made from snake bone, shark bone, seeds and shells. Her mum would bring me bush tucker into the canteen all the time. They are my adopted family and I miss them greatly.

When you get your portrait done you'll have to wear that necklace, it's beautiful.
From that day on everything clicked and now I ... I cut it in half and made a choker and I've always got the other half in my bag or around my neck, so if I get nervous or afraid or need guidance I have it with me to hold.

Does it work?
Oh yes! It's just very special.

Did this experience make you aware of your sixth sense?
My sixth sense is my inner strength and spirituality, my culture. Every Aboriginal person, or every person for that matter, has that; it comes down to whether they want to acknowledge it and find it. And by me going up north to be with them traditional mob, it made me open my eyes to all things and that was special.

I get a very positive vibe from you. Every girl in the book has a different energy, different vibe, I get the impression that you're quite happy at where you are at, at the moment. You are working hard on your own projects, but I feel you have a great force behind you, apart from your family. Where do you think this other force comes from?

I believe in the power of our culture, our ancient spiritual ancestors and family.

I strongly believe in my sixth sense. My inner self, my inner spirituality. My inner spirituality would be like a sixth sense, like that gut feeling.

Is spirituality and culture important to you?
It's my identity. If I don't have that, I'm no one.

In the foreword of the calendar you put together with your business partner and company Jinnali there's a poem you wrote. It's pretty special. Was that spiritually found or enhanced, can you tell me about that?
It was three o'clock in the morning, I think it was one of my ancestors trying to speak through me and it just came to me. It was like it came from nowhere. It was really weird, I like to write poetry but I'm not a poet, but every now and then I get this urge to write. It comes from a thought, I think it's just me trying to express myself, verbally releasing myself. This is the poem:

Searching for our Ancestral Spirits

Times are changing we must adapt to survive,
no longer hunters and gatherers in the old ways,

Nowadays, we must build economic development and
self-determination the new ways,
We can't live in the past, the pain hurts too much. Help me!

Free me from this sorrow and anger that has been passed
on to me
from generation to generation. Release me!

Let me fly away from this entrapment into a new beginning,
a new century. The twenty-first century.

I want to feel my ancestors' spirits beckoning me to spread
my wings
Fly, Liza, Fly.

No longer shall we live in fear, for we must unite to destroy
that plight.
For that time has come, for us to stand tall and hold our
heads high.

No longer inequality but we are equal, for we are the true
traditional owners of this land.

*Do you think it's a great way to get things off your chest or out of
your system? And should we all do a little more of that?*
Definitely. I think through words and writing you can solve your
own inner thoughts or comment on things that you wish to
express, even if it's just for your eyes only. I've got a gratitude
book and it holds all my personal thoughts and comments from
others that have inspired me. Even little sayings that I might
have heard from somewhere else that have made an impact on
me at that time. Then when I'm feeling down or upset I go and
have a read through my gratitude book. And remember why I
am here.

Is it a nice book or just an old scrapbook?
I paid about thirty bucks for this hardcover book, it has this
beautiful picture on it of an angel with a harp and in gold print
it says, 'Musical Thoughts'. So it feels special and because I paid
a lot for it I look after it. Every page has a special note or
affirmation.

*Why did you do that, were you just browsing in a bookstore and
saw it, or did you make a conscious decision to get a book for that
purpose?*
I was watching the Oprah Winfrey show.

*Now there's another strong black woman, whether you like her or
not. She has overcome huge hurdles as a young black girl to become*

one of the most powerful and influential people in the world. Credit where credit is due.

And she was talking about a gratitude book and how you should write about your personal thoughts and the things that you appreciate in everyday life that make a change in who you are, write them down, so I just started doing it.

Do you think we've been influenced by the African-Americans? Do you think there is something that we could learn from them?

Yes, I think there is. Look at what they have achieved in their society, they're educated, professional and they're strong and they are a community that brings everybody up and supports each other, and that's what we lack. But they also have their downsides, but doesn't everybody?

I would love to, and will, send a copy of Black Chicks Talking *to Oprah. She's come from hard times, she's been down and out and she has worked hard to get to where she is. And she deserves all the accolades she's got and gets. 'You Go Girl!' She is reconciliation. She brings all aspects of life to her show and magazine. And maybe the sister will bring all us black chicks from down under on the show!*

Where do you get your inspiration?

In my bedroom on the back of my door are all the successful Indigenous people like yourself, Cathy Freeman, Deborah Mailman, Anthony Mundine—all little mementoes of people who I've met on my journey—and at night I lay back and think to myself, 'If they can do it, so can I!' That inspiration comes from seeing other successful Indigenous people out there. It's really up to you to become the person you dream of being. You are your biggest obstacle to success and happiness, once you understand what you want in life there is no limit to what you can achieve. Drive, dedication and desire are my elements to being a successful businesswoman.

So it really is important to make a big deal of those that have made something of themselves, whether in entertainment, sport or academics.

Very much so. Because if it weren't for you guys, as my role models or what we call high achievers, I wouldn't be as determined to be successful like you all.

Being called a role model is a huge title to carry around on anyone's shoulders because nobody is perfect. But I believe there are chosen ones who the ancestors have decided will have the drive, the determination and the shoulders to carry the weight. I believe that all of the women in this book are among the chosen ones. Everything they do, they do with passion. And that's what I think the key to success is: passion and determination. Unfortunately I could not write about all the fabulous women (and men) out there in the communities that do work tirelessly for community, but I acknowledge all your work and efforts, THANK YOU!

Are you a happy person, are you happy at the moment?
Very much so.

And should we all be happy?
Personally I wish everybody could be happy: to have the best in life, to achieve what they want. My happiness comes from learning more about my culture and my family, if I'm happy with my family, that's all that counts.

Today, as I was waiting for my lift to pick me up for the interview, I was sitting on the steps of the Sydney Town Hall and I was looking around and I looked up and there was the Aboriginal flag, flying high on the middle pole, and I just got so proud, so happy, it actually brought tears to my eye.

What do we need to change so we can become a complete and whole nation? Do we need to change the flag?

I personally like the 'look' of the Australian flag; I think it looks the best out of all the flags in the world. But it doesn't represent us as a nation, like the Union Jack could be removed and replaced with the Aboriginal flag. That would be deadly.

For me, for this nation to become one, Australia Day needs to be changed to a day in our NAIDOC [National Aboriginal & Islander Day of Celebration] week. Because at present all Aboriginal people look at Australia Day as 'Invasion Day'. I think that would be a good start.

But that's what they call it in Queensland. In New South Wales it's called Survival. Should we call that day Survival Australia-wide for the Blackfellas, because as they say in the song from Mixed Relations: 'we have survived the white man's way.' So we make a positive out of the negative and have a positive outlook on that day. We celebrate our survival.

My concern with an Australia Day being chosen out of NAIDOC week would be that wider Australia might think it's another one to the Blackfellas if we have it in the week of our celebration for our culture and people. I think it should be on a day that Australia, black and white, came together for the very first time and that was when the Aboriginal people were finally considered citizens of this nation because, without the vote of the white people at that time, who knows when they would have considered us citizens of our own birthplace. That could have been considered the start of reconciliation in 1967. But it's a hard one because then people might think that that day was a day to mourn. Fancy having a day to remind us that before that we were considered sub-human and not citizens of a country where most Aboriginal families can trace their link back to, at the least, a date before or pretty close to when white man arrived. I know I can. It's a hard one. Let's just draw it out of a hat maybe?

I think there should be more Aboriginal people in parliament or on boards speaking on our behalf. So far there's only ever been two black representatives in parliament, Sir Neville Bonner and Aden Ridgeway, so there should be more representation of our people. Some of our leaders need to come down, come back to reality; be a bit more involved, listen to the communities, listen to us, us young ones, because we've got a lot of ideas, we want to take part, give us an opportunity, just open that door for us, let us come in and sit down to listen and learn.

I guess most of the girls in this book, except for Cilla and Rosanna, have not grown up on communities. Has that shaped us into who we are today?
Yes, it has. But we should not be ashamed of that and should not be judged that we are less of an Aboriginal person. And the mob in communities should not think that they are the real Blackfellas because they went through a hard time on struggle street. There's this image out there where . . . even whitefellas think like this, that if you don't come from struggle street or didn't grow up on a community, then you aren't black . . . that is so unfair because what makes me Aboriginal is the blood that runs through my veins, the Dreamtime stories and language passed on to me by my elders. My Aboriginality is set firm and holds strong in my soul and it is solid . . . it is me.

I agree!
It's all about choices and if you choose to stay on the communities then that's fine, but make that work for you. Everyone is different and is allowed to live their life as they see fit.
Our old people went through all the pain. They did that so we, as the next generation, can achieve. And that's what I believe I have done. My great-grandmother wore the scar of her master's boot on the side of her ribcage and my great-grandfather rebelled against the slavery. My grandmother was stolen from her homelands and my grandfather worked hard all his life and was a highly respected man in both black and white communities. My mother went through

the generation where you kept quiet about your Aboriginality, but she was a proud black woman and held her head up high. She dealt with a lot of personal things too. The eras they all lived through were the hardest in which to gain respect and an opportunity, so it would be big shame for me to do nothing and big shame job if I did not progress with the opportunities I have been given. In anything that anyone does you've got to prove that you can do what is required and sometimes the hardest person to convince is yourself. Believe in yourself, and then others can believe in you. If you get knocked over, just get up and dust off the dirt and go again.

There is a new generation out there grabbing the opportunities and they are triumphing.

I think as long as our people are happy and if they are content, if they are growing not only in community but individually as well. It all comes back to the Aboriginal Council, back to our leaders; we need strong leaders. If we don't have a good leader, then who are we to follow? That also applies to the wider Australian communities as well.

Do you think, being in the twenty-first century, that the non-Indigenous people of this country should embrace the Aboriginal culture as theirs as well?

Yes, definitely. We are the true Indigenous people of this land, we are all Australians and the Aboriginal culture is a part of this great country's history. If they are true Australians then they should take it on as their own. Learn it, appreciate it, respect it and recognise us. If a white person comes up to me and wants to know about my culture, I will sit down and tell them all that I can.

There was a young fella that I met the other night and we got talking about Aboriginal issues and I brought tears to the brother's eyes; I was just telling him the stories, the truth that he didn't know. He called me this morning and thanked me for my time and I said that if I could help him in any way with his thesis at university then I would. Whatever I can do, I will do. We should just be one big happy family and respect each other. We live in the country with the best opportunities in the world.

Reconciliation. We have been dealing with it for the past ten years and healing. We need to move forward, I just want to get it over with, it's in the past, it's dragging us down; we've got to go forward, we've got to start building, starting our own small businesses creating employment and educating our kids, change their way of thinking. We need positive role models to get down and into the communities and show their faces, no more stereotypical Aboriginal person, let's bring the real person out within us all. Sharing our culture and making these white people and the wider community see our intelligence.

We've got to unite together. We've got to bring our culture and spirituality back and practise our ceremonies; we need this for the basis for everything. We need a language of some sort, like an area, and accept that so our young people have something to grasp. Some sort of traditional law or traditional guidelines. Our elders are to choose whether they—offenders— are to then go further into the white man's law system.

Where do we find our true elders in this day and age? You know, some people out there get to forty and think they are an elder.
Yes, very true. The community should choose and then those people must uphold their end and not abuse their situation and if they do, they should also be dealt with.

We should have a nationwide kind of board with members, but then each region has a smaller board and they deal with their community problems. Bring back traditional punishment using spears etc.

Indigenous tourism, a lot more focus on that. I mean, help to set up more small businesses so that the black man can capitalise on his culture and country. We are also educating and earning a living in something we are proud of and know, so we don't have the pressure of working in the white man's world. We can have an opportunity to develop . . . us, ourselves.

The reconciliation process must start within us as individuals. Build our foundation as a black race in this country.

All working together, we can get there, we've just got to start at the beginning and all work slowly together. The broad, community-based support for this is there. Let's work on it.

How do we build the self-esteem and determination to succeed in our young people?
We are aiming to do that with our business by promoting positive role models for our youth to follow in our footsteps, but also allowing them to create their own path. Positive, successful Aboriginal role models should be going into our communities and making their presence felt. Talking to our youth, encouraging them to excel in education, employment and career development.

Eventually, Jinnali Productions will be conducting personal development workshops focusing on issues that affect our youth on a day-to-day basis. Such as deportment and grooming, fashion, goal setting, motivation, drug and alcohol awareness, general life skills, diet, fitness, cultural issues and many more empowering courses. It will allow our young people to take control of their lives and to become confident, strong people. But I guess it will also be up to the young people as to whether they come to us and use these programs to empower themselves and to capitalise on that.

But I've had a very blessed and sheltered upbringing that has given me the motivation to go and talk to the younger kids— give them some direction and encouragement. We need to do that for them because there is not enough discipline or support or direction from their parents.

Is there a difference between black and white?
Yes, there definitely is.

Yet I look at you and see that you have made the crossover; you can intertwine the two worlds.

Me, I'm black, but I'm cool about, and comfortable, sitting in the white man's world. But it was only through my business that I have started opening up my mind to the white man's world; I can play the game. But I am most comfortable with my black mob.

Were there times in your life when the black community turned on you or your family for their good fortune, like that good old word we all hate to hear: coconut?

Yer, sad to say, all the time.

How did you deal with that?

Me, growing up and being very popular with my sport, there was a lot of attention given to me. It hit me when I went to Year Eight, to a private Catholic school, and I could hear what was being said from the state high school mob, that I was a coconut and all that sort of stuff. But I didn't want that; I'm an Aboriginal first and foremost, but I just want the best out of life or what I could get at the time. I didn't want to be barefoot and pregnant and on the pension, I wanted to achieve something in life. So in Year Nine I left the Catholic school and went to the state high so I could fit in, because I didn't want to be an outcast from my own mob.

So what happened when you got to the state high?

Because I came down to their level . . .

But why should we? We are all different. We all have different goals in life and some of us are given a little more determination than others and we capitalise on that. What's wrong with that? The different races in this multicultural society in Australia are all different in their goals and they are allowed to achieve, so why do Blackfellas always have to bring each other down? We should be encouraging each other because our race has been kept down for so long. Don't you think that they should celebrate in the glory? But instead we are cut down for 'big noting'. We can all achieve, the individual has to make that choice.

Are we capable of making that choice? Of course we are. But do we want to? Of course we do!

This wise woman told me a story once and it went like this: 'There is a white man with his bucket of crabs and a black man with his bucket of crabs. The white man is having a hard time keeping his crabs in the bucket but when he looked over to the black man's bucket all the crabs are staying in. The white man asked how he was keeping his crabs in the bucket and the black man said, 'Well, every time one looks like making it to the top, the others keep pulling him back down again.' And that story relates to us Blackfellas. Is it jealousy?

Maybe it is, but the opportunity to succeed is there for everyone. It's up to the individual to grab it.

Most things people do in their line of work really put them out there on a very lonely limb. It is very frightening stuff. Support is so important. Of course, you can't please everyone, but it hurts and it's hard when there is friction. But you can only do so much and if they can't see the good, then maybe it's their problem. People only see and hear what they want to.

If we were succeeding for our own gain then we wouldn't care what the community or people thought. But we are not.

I know I work for my ancestors and they are pleased with what I'm doing, otherwise I would not be having the success that I have been given. I feel very privileged—it's an honour to have their blessing.

I am a chosen one, I am stronger, and that's why we are where we are, we are working for the ancestors. When I'm feeling down

I feel the spirits talking, saying, 'Get up, Liza, you can do this—you are a leader. Be strong and dedicated, don't worry about what they're saying, just focus until you achieve that dream.'

All the women in this book have been brought to me by the ancestors.

What now for Miss Liza?
I'm twenty-six years old and at present I am setting up a business with another Murri woman, Dina Paulson. It's about enhancing the lifestyle and education of Indigenous women; to allow them to increase their self-esteem, confidence and personal grooming. Promoting the diversity of the modern Indigenous woman—not only are we beautiful, but also intelligent. Dina and I produced Australia's first Indigenous women's calendar. We are examples that dreams do come true, all you have to do is believe in yourself.

Congratulations on that project—I have seen one and it is great. Can you tell us how that all came about? And why?
I started submission writing in 1999, my sister was sixteen at the time and wanted to get into modelling. She was in Melbourne and signed up to an agency, but she didn't get that extra support at the agency and left. I was always given an opportunity and I wanted that for my sister too, and I have always wanted to do workshops for young women for self-enhancement. When we were growing up we had an aunty who was a beautician and she would always be on our back saying things like, 'Liza, are you cleansing? Are you eating properly? Look at your skin.' So, as I was growing up, I saw my other community sisters not looking after themselves and I wanted to give something back to the community, so I thought of the calendar. So I started submission writing and it just all came together. Like you said before, it's like the ancestors are working through us,

Liza with business partner Dina Paulson (far right) and two of the models from the calendar

that spirit pushing me. At the same time I was working at Tjapukai...

What's Tjapukai?
The Aboriginal cultural park up in Cairns. So my forté is Aboriginal tourism, I've been working in that industry for ten years.

I needed a change. I needed help with this idea I had. So I asked my ancestors for some guidance. And I ran into Dina, literally. Our paths crossed that very night. I just knew this was meant to be, I just couldn't give up. Unknown to me, Dina was trying to do the same thing down on the Gold Coast. She was working on her idea about a calendar and she was going through a difficult time in her life and for some reason she was saying to herself that she needed to get to Cairns. She didn't know why, because she had never been there before, but something was pushing her to get to Cairns. Dina mentioned her plans to a mutual friend and she told Dina about me.

That night I was out at a model's party and Dina was leaving the next day, and one of her cousins said, 'Let's go out down the esplanade, have a coffee.' In the meantime, we were in the upstairs of this coffee shop having dinner. When we came downstairs I was leading the way and Dina was coming into the coffee shop and our paths crossed and then the mutual friend said, 'Hang on, Liza, this is the woman that wants to meet you!'

As soon as I looked in her eyes, I knew we were meant to work with each other. The next day we had a photo shoot and Dina came along to see how I worked, and then after the shoot she said that she needed to get back to the Gold Coast to collect her stuff and within a week she was back up in Cairns. Then, after another week of working on the project in Cairns, Dina felt that things weren't happening for us up there in Cairns—we didn't have the resources to get to where we needed to be, we had to go to Brisbane. I had just got a promotion at Tjapukai to marketing and that's where I wanted to head, but she said, 'We got to go!' So next day I resigned, packed my whole life up, packed up the car that we christened 'Ballbags', the Laser, and cruised down to Brisbane, not knowing what was going to be in front of us.

We worked as a team to work toward our dream, to get it happening. We lived anywhere and everywhere, we were on the dole—had no money, no home, just trying so hard to get our dream up. Lived in up to seven different places, people feeding us, feeling sorry for us, and in the meantime trying to get this calendar produced. Seven days a week, twenty-four hours a day we worked and dreamt the calendar. Sometimes we would take turns in feeling down about the project, but the other would be there to keep us going.

We had no money and because most of the girls lived interstate they had to go into their Indigenous organisations to get their airfares sponsored. We got sponsorship from Stephan's hair and make-up, a website from Taylor's consultancy on the Gold Coast, we had Mununjali give us money for film, Black Diamonds program give us sponsorship for development and other expenses. NAILSS [National Aboriginal and Islander Legal Services Secretariat] let us use their office space and equipment for the whole four months that it took to produce the calendars. Three photographers that gave their time to us for nothing; one Indigenous sister, Barbara Paulson, in her first year of photography, she did most of the shots. And we got a hold of Australian model management photographer Lee Judd, we flew him up from Sydney, and Michael Pole. They all believed in what we were trying to achieve. And it all came together. And here we are now down in Sydney with the first of our calendars out there.

Tell us about Ballbags.
Well Ballbags is what I call Dina's car. See, my first car was a Datsun 120 and I called that car Ballbags because he took me everywhere. And this little car now has taken Dina and I everywhere; it has got us to our destination safe and sound every time. This poor little car hasn't had a tune-up or anything and he just gets us to where we need to be. So I said to Dina, 'We need to give him a nickname' and I came up with Ballbags Number Two. Ballbags has played a big part in our journey—from Cairns to Brisbane, Brisbane to Sydney and all around Sydney. We've only been here a few times before, but Dina will know her way around—I call her the black tracker, she just knows where to go. The black tracker and Ballbags makes for a good combination.

Well, the calendar has gone through the roof with international sales and they had to run another print to fill the orders. Most of the feedback was positive, there were a few complaints about the fair-skinned girls, but Liza and Dina put them straight; so they have been educating as they go along and that's excellent because it's not just about the beauty of these women, there is also history and culture wrapped in there as well.

I rang Liza to enquire about the Aboriginal strippers 'Hot Chocolate', as you do, and she told me that she and some of the girls had gone to Germany to work and things were going really well. They are in pre-production for the next calendar, which will be shot in and around Rainbow Beach and Augathella, and they are all excited about that, as help has come a little easier this time round, but only just. They are still working hard to achieve their goals for the company.

What does Liza want to be in the future?
I want to be a strong, successful, determined, career-minded woman. A role model for my community—someone that they can look up to. A leader. Build my business and create employment for my people, and continue to promote and bring awareness of my culture nationally and internationally. I am a grass roots woman!

You go girl and go hard!

A Mother's Love

Cilla Malone

mother

CILLA: I TOUCH. I JUST like to feel. I close my eyes and when I think back my earliest memory of a pleasurable touch would mainly be from my children. My life before that, there was not—if any—any touch that I would remember as pleasurable.

My first-born—I couldn't stop touching him when he was born. I was fifteen when I fell pregnant, sixteen when I had him and I just couldn't believe I did that and I just . . . I couldn't stop holding him. I would just touch him—with all my children really—but my first-born was special, that moment of bonding. I would trace over his face with my fingertip; I couldn't believe my eyes, I did that! On my own; I didn't have the father there—it was one of those one-night stands that went wrong, you know. Maybe I . . . at the age of getting pregnant I should have kept my legs closed! But it was something that happened. I didn't get much guidance from my mother, and everybody else was doing it. My sister Edna was always there for me, she was like a mother figure, but now there's a little tension and I'm on my own.

My first-born is a teenager now. He loves golf and has a par eleven. I'm very distant from him now though. I gave him to one of my other sisters when he was two. She took him because I was too young and wasn't coping very well. We just like grew apart, as you would, I guess. She married and they moved away from the mission, which I was glad for—I didn't want him growing up on the mission. I see him now and then, but it's not like it used to be; not as close. In those first two years that were ours, we cuddled a lot. Still am, with me and my daughters, cuddle all the time and hug all the time. Yeah.

Leah: This is Cilla: the mum of the project. She is thirty-four years old and has six children, fathered by five different men. She gave two of them, the two boys, to her sister who couldn't have children, and she has the four girls. She shares custody for the fourth girl with the father. He has a very active role in his daughter's upbringing.

Cilla lives in Cherbourg, an Aboriginal settlement in southeast Queensland. It was founded in approximately 1901 for the so-called 'wayward' blacks or people who were forcibly removed from their tribal lands or those that came of their own free will because of the promise of work and better living, which all turned out to be lies. Government assistance did not start until 1905. My grandmother, Daisy Chambers, (nee) Walker, arrived in 1910 after she was stolen from her homeland of Mitchell, west Queensland. My great-grandparents on my grandfather's side were also stolen from their homelands and dispersed throughout the east coast of Australia until they finally settled in Cherbourg because other family members were already there.

Cherbourg (Barambah Mission back then) was formed because another mission near Woodford, an hour and a bit west of Brisbane, was full and they needed somewhere to place the next lot of blacks coming in. A local well-to-do white lady offered some of her land. Since it was only of fifth grade farming standard, she gave it to the blacks. This story was told to me by a great aunt.

My mum was born at Cherbourg, she lived in Broadway Street. The third or fourth house in the street. The tree is still there that my grandfather planted, it's a real landmark for me when I go home. Sometimes I wish that tree could talk. What amazing stories it would have of those times past, gone to grave with my elders. My mum left the mission with her family when she was fifteen years old. Cilla's parents were born at Cherbourg too. Her mother was raised by her grandmother. Cilla's mum's mob came from Eidsvold, about two hours drive west of Cherbourg.

At the time, the mission was run by a superintendent and missionaries. It started out with about three hundred people from thirteen different tribes who all spoke different languages. They were told not to practise their customs or law and not to speak their language because the authorities thought it was evil or that they were planning something when they spoke in language.

As soon as the families arrived (in the hope of a better life) their children were sent to the dormitory and the parents were sent to the camp area and from there, there was little, if any, contact. When there were known clans coming in to the mission they would try and stay together and form tribal groups and consequently there were areas in the camp known as top camp, middle camp, bottom camp and Chinatown.

It almost seemed as if, at random, some of the families coming into the mission would be able to keep their children and others would be removed from their families, because there were children up in the camp. I guess if you were fair-skinned, or known to have mixed blood, then you were removed automatically with no explanation. This was the case with one of my aunties, not by blood but by clan. (She has her own book about those days and it is excellent: Is that you Ruthie by Ruth Hegarty.) Dark-skinned Murri children were placed in the dormitory as well.

You often hear the stories of the unbreakable bonds that were formed in the dormitory because the dormitory kids became family for each other.

The rules were strict in the dormitory; even though the families were just up the road the children were kept away. My great-grandparents worked in the dormitory as the black house parents who looked after the kids until the age of fourteen, when they were sent out to work as servants/domestics/jackaroos.

The camp mob lived in gunyas with a dirt floor that often shone, as my mother used to say. (It shone because the old women would sweep them until they were almost like cement.) Later the men cut down timber from the local bush for the families to build their own homes.

The people in the camp were allowed to live off the land, but that didn't last long as they were restricted to a certain area. This meant the wildlife was affected because there were too many people living off the one area. The usual practice was the walkabout system—eat and then move on to another area and let the first place rejuvenate—but they couldn't do that within the camp confines. So they ended up living off the government rations of flour, sugar and tea.

Life was not good. All the promises were now clearly lies and, over a few generations, the people became angry. Attitudes changed and the most prominent feeling in camp was a hatred for the white man authority figure. This wasn't true of everyone though, a lot of the old people did not show or hold their anger against the authority figure—they just let it go. They were really very placid people.

There were good times too, when the people were left to themselves. My old people said that they made good times in their private family lives by telling all the old stories and songs. Sometimes language was whispered around the fire late at night and my old people said that this was special time. My mum would say it was special because it was just their time. On New Year's Eve they would have a big corroboree with a big bonfire and all the different tribes would come and share their stories and dances. My father, who's white and lived in Murgon, told me about this, he said the townsfolk would come out and watch. He said it was brilliant. But that was short-lived.

In the 1930s Barambah Mission was given to the people and the name was changed to Cherbourg, but the last superintendents did not leave until about 1975. There were some good white people who *held the authority positions because I remember my mum and grandfather and my great-aunts and uncle praising the good ones. But overall there was such a great loss of culture and law and a disintegration of the whole family structure, which I think is why we have the problems that we have today in some of the Aboriginal communities. I'm not saying that communities are bad places, not at all, I've got family, best mates there, and it's the place where I can relax and feel at home, but because of the small population (Cherbourg has about two thousand people living there today) the trouble is easily seen. People would say that I have no right to comment because I have never physically lived on the community—fair enough. That's why I have invited Cilla to talk about her life on the community, because she has lived there all her life.*

I was six months old . . . yeah, six months when I was placed in the dormitory on the settlement at home there, Cherbourg; five of us, the younger ones. We stayed there for about five...five years, I think? I'm not sure, it seemed like forever, five or six years, yeah. Mum and Dad had split up and she took off and left us with Dad, and Dad was a working man and he just . . . he couldn't look after us.

I don't remember much about the dormitory, not much at all, just how big everything was. We ate in a big dark kitchen. It was dark; it was awful. I didn't like it because when we were punished we were made to sit in there and eat soup with cold fat all over the top. I hate kitchens. Dark kitchens, anyway. Wooden floors, cold wooden floors. All I remember was all these big pictures of Snow White and the seven dwarfs, all over the place. Big, framed pictures. All over the place, all of the dwarfs— they were everywhere. Where we all slept was like one big room with like twenty beds, and the cots were out on the verandah for the babies. Boys and girls, but when the boys got old enough they were made to go over to the boys' dormitory and there was this old woman there that used to take me into her bed, because

I was the only baby there. It was probably . . . where the touching comes into it, I suppose, because she always . . . she reckons she always took me into her bed. She was one of the workers, she was the only one that showed me any affection—besides my family that was in there with me. Rachael Lacey was her name, she died now . . . oh, a long time ago, twenty years ago. My first daughter is named after her, *Lacey*. I would always be there to see that old girl every time she came back to the community. She was a mother figure when I needed to bond with someone in the early part of my life.

It was strict in there . . . yeah, very strict, but the five of us stuck together. We did everything all together.

Then one day out of the blue, they were saying, 'Your mother's here, she's taking you for a holiday.' We just couldn't get out of there quick enough! Yeah, Mum came and told us she was taking us for holidays. Apparently she'd heard that the dormitory was getting closed down, they were going to foster all the kids out. So she came and told them she was taking us for holidays and never took us back.

I remember that day. I just couldn't wait to see Mum. I didn't even know what she looked like. They used to tell us that she had long hair and she was fair, and when we used to walk from the dormitory to the store, every time we'd see someone with long hair, we'd run over calling her Mum. They'd look at us real weird way, but yeah, I just remember I couldn't wait to see her and what she looked like. I just focused on her.

When she did arrive we all raced to her—the five of us groping at her—we nearly tackled her. But there wasn't a lot of fuss, she just grabbed my hand and we left with our little bags.

We all walked with her to my grandfather's place, up the top end of the camp. Where we'd never been before, all that time we were in the dormitory we weren't allowed near what they called the camp, the rest of the community. The dormitory's away from the camp. We went up to the top end now, this fella's suppose to be my mum's father. She never knew her real father; she still doesn't. But this fella we stayed with now was suppose to be her father. Just stayed with him for a while. Just went boarding, like moving from relative to relative till we found . . . till Mum got us our own house then I think, there would have been eight of us little fellas; nine, with Mum. She came back from working in Sydney.

Me and my mum aren't very close. We don't get on. But she's got thirteen children; I don't have much to do with her at all. I just always felt like she hated me for some reason. Maybe those first couple of years out of the dormitory were all right with her, but from teenager, or early teenager, I remember I started feeling like my mother hated me. I was always trying to do things to make her happy, to please her. Stuff like cleaning up when she'd come home late from cards or something. You know, because of the house, all done up, and just hoping she'd walk in and say, 'Oh gee, that's nice!' You know, I was forever trying to get compliments off her . . . and I never, ever did, no matter what I did. I did the washing, I'd do a lot of little things just to try and please her, but nothing seemed to work. Even up to today, she just . . . I don't know. I wish I knew why. But a lot of people say that we're just so much alike, I'm so much like her. Maybe that's why we don't get on? Looks, ways and everything, I've been told.

At one stage there I thought: no, she doesn't hate me, she doesn't; it's just me feeling sorry for myself. And one of my brothers were sitting there drinking one day and then he said, 'Hey, Cilla, Mum does treat you different. She does treat you like shit.' And that was the first time that anyone else acknowledged it. Mmmm. Just when I was ready to accept that she did care. You know, just not the way I wanted her to. But yer, that really broke my heart that, to hear that come from him. Yeah, but my family are my children now.

Cilla and her girls and 'prettyone-anyone' the cat (on Cilla's shoulder)

So, now you have your own children, how are you toward them?
I'm so affectionate with my children. I fill them with all the love
I can. I always said I would because we never got hugs and kisses
from Mum. And people, even at Cherbourg today, they spin out
on me kissing my kids before they go to school and that. I always
said I would show my children love because I never, ever felt it
from my real mother. I said I'd never do that to my children and
I never did. We hug and everything, all the time. Kiss. I love
them. I tell them all the time and they tell me.

I met Cilla through her younger sister; we went to high school
together. I had known of Cilla and thought she was just beautiful—
long blonde golden curls, a deep olive complexion and a smile that
would warm a stone heart because her smile was, and still is, sin-
cere. But the official introduction was at her twenty-first birthday,
which was doubling for her engagement. I would think, 'Wow',
I used to . . . I really used to . . . I don't know why now—she's a big
bitch! Nar, only gamin. There was something about her; I was drawn

to her. Maybe subconsciously there was a connection or something telling me we would become very dear and true friends.

With her pregnancy with Lacey, gee she was big. I had just found out that I was pregnant and Cilla's sister, who I went to school with, was showing with her pregnancy. Cilla was sitting on the lounge, biggest guts, and I was standing up looking at Cilla's belly thinking, 'Shit! I don't want to get that big! I could never get that big . . . could I?'

Got any labour stories for us, since you've had six children!
I didn't want to know any of my children before they were born, eh. I didn't want to know, cause I had a few scans. They'd ask, 'Do you want to know what it is or not?' and I'd say, 'No!' cause it pays off at the end of the labour to have a surprise, I reckon. I wouldn't want to know. It's hard work! That's the gift at the end of it. My longest labour was the last one, she was like five hours. My shortest was with my first-born: he was only three hours, and he was big!

When I was in labour with Lacey I was craving for white grapes. I made them [friends] drive me all over Toowoomba, where I was living at the time with Lacey's dad, looking for the white grapes, while I had the labour pains.

I said, 'I'm not going to the hospital until I get some grapes!'

So we're cruisin' and she [Cilla's friend] hits one of those speed bumps, she didn't slow down and it ruptured the membrane, the afterbirth. That's when they rushed me straight up . . . ruptured my afterbirth, not the waters.

But I got my grapes and I ate them all the way up to the hospital and in the labour ward.

I spun out because it was a big hospital compared to Cherbourg, they had like women lined up on trolleys waiting to go in and they were wheeling other women out the other side. Lining up and they even tell you to fill out a form! Standing there in labour! They're just as calm as! Whereas in Cherbourg, you just get all that attention. They would fuss over you because they hardly ever had births there back then. The hospital was suppose to stop. You were supposed to go to Kingaroy to have your babies. Cherbourg didn't have the right staff to be able to deliver, and equipment in case of an emergency. But I used to just stay home until my labour pains were like two minutes apart and they couldn't do a thing. I wanted my children to be born at Cherbourg. I always said that; I don't know why. Cause it's my home, it's where I was born.

What's the most important ingredient for motherhood?
Motherhood? A mother's love. Honesty too, you know. Just being true to how you feel toward them, and trying to get the same back. I tell them everything, my children; hopefully they'll tell me everything. But yeah, like even when I have a really bad day, like I gave up drinking for three years—if there's a down side to me it's the grog—and then when I started again, I told them, you know. I sit down and tell them. I don't just say I'm drinking again, I tell them why, I try to tell them why.

I guess when I think back to my excuses it's a kind of depression. You get caught up with all the crap that happens on the community—someone's always gossiping or trying to cause you trouble or getting into ya business. And for years the way to deal with it is drinking . . . that's all we know. We don't have any counsellors. Well now we are suppose to have, but Blackfella shame to go talk to whitefellas. And then you don't wanna talk to Blackfellas cause they might gossip, you know, so you go drown ya sorrow. And that does affect your kids, even if sometimes you try to justify to yourself that it doesn't, but deep down you know . . . but you become so hopeless . . . you are digging your own grave and it becomes hard to pull yourself out. But you'd think you'd learn by other people, hey? My children may be young but they can understand or sometimes they see my troubles and they hang on with me until I try and get over it.

But yeah, just telling them everything and just being honest about everything. About how I feel, just a lot of little things, you know?

Yeah, love! Showing them love is more important to me than anything. Love. To honestly love your children and to show it to them openly, and encourage them to do it. As important as education is, love comes before education with me, for my children. My eldest girl, she's a very emotional young girl. She's very affectionate and really appreciative of anything I do for her, of . . . of me.

Do you think they will always understand your reason for drinking? And how many times do you think a child has to take the back seat to your drinking?
No, I'm sure my children have their private talks to either friends or each other, or other people that they trust . . . and they may have asked, why does Mum do that? And I don't expect them to always understand. And as they get older they see things their own way and will deal with it differently I'm sure—they're strong girls. And a child should never have to take the back seat to drinking. That's not right, not right at all. And I have asked my kids to do that, but at those times I was drinking I couldn't even see clearly what I was doing . . . I'm just glad they stayed around.

Do you think about what you put them through?
At my lowest I thought that they would be better off without me; I really did come to that decision. I was just tired, just so tired of everything. Just tired; I'd had enough. That's when I was thinking about ending my life. I think that time was the lowest I've ever got. Through my whole life. But it was my children that brought me back and Boomi [Ngtali's dad]—I wanted another go at our relationship. But for me to do something about me I had to make that choice between a fucked life or a decent one.

What was one of the hardest times, with your children?

Losing them. Losing them to other people. Like my eldest, because I was so young and everything, it wasn't very hard because he was going to my sister, but then I had another boy and my sister ask for him as well so that my eldest could have a brother, he was lonely so I let her take him too. I still miss him, I'm still close to him. He rings me a lot . . . Daniel, yeah— Dan Dan, my little man.

Then losing the girls, Lacey and Lowana, to their father. It was a custody case and he took me to court and he got them off me for three years, and I got them back last year. I did throw the towel in really because it just spun me out. I've never been in trouble with the law, not that I was in trouble, but just dealing with all that. I just said to my solicitor, 'Just let him take them until I get on my feet.' Because the father of the girls even said, once I get off the *yarndi* and grog and sort myself out, he'd give them back to me, and I honestly believed that. But that wasn't his intention at all. I didn't get to say goodbye to them because I gave them to him for the school holidays and he kept them from there. I didn't see the girls again until I got court orders which allowed me to ring them. I was still smokin' and drinkin', but I would be straight when I would visit the girls and he would let me see them.

Then I started to sort myself out and cut right back to just about nothing and that's when he wouldn't let me see them. It pushed me back over the edge with his lies and bullshit about me, that just topped it off. He thought that I'd straightened myself up to get the girls off him but that wasn't it. I'd met some-one and we were just fighting too much when we were drinkin' and smokin', so we stopped all that to better our relationship and it worked, things started to fit in place and work for me instead of against me. But all this time I had my youngest daughter, at the time, with me, Kaylynn, bless her; I dragged her around with me. I guess she was my pillar of strength there for a while. I had her to hang on to, a lot to ask from a four year old.

Do you think you had a right to ask that from her?
No. But I wasn't going to lose her, although I was probably doin' all the things that would actually lead to that . . . she's Mummy's girl, anyway . . . she stuck to me like glue.

So what happened with the court case?
I wasn't going for custody for the oldest two girls, I was only going to get my access back. The whole court case was a big spin-out really. They found out a lot of stuff that turned against him [the father] and then one day we were going to court in Brisbane, and my solicitor rings me up early and he says, 'I'm coming to court with you, something's happening today.' I said, 'Why? What?' And the next minute this woman from Family Referrals was just talking really chirpy on the phone—they must have known. But I wasn't going for custody, I was going for my visiting rights.

We went down and it was in this one courtroom, the judge didn't know what to do, what to rule. So they put us up a floor, to a higher court. That's when in all their big words, like they didn't say it straight out, I didn't understand them, my solicitor had to . . . my barrister had to explain it to me: I will get my kids back! That's what they were saying! I just hugged, jumped all over him and everything when that judge ruled in my favour. I think everyone saw through . . . through the girls' father . . . everyone. He lost that on his own. I was honest, 'Yes, I drink, yes I smoke *yarndi.*' I was just so honest, you know. It was a big spin-out, I was only going for visiting rights.

What was it finally like to get them back?
It was lovely, because I got them back the same day they left, because of school . . . the courts would not let them go from one parent to the other during school. They wait for the school

holidays, and that's when I gave them to him, I got them back on that day. Same day, three years later! We drove over to get them. We drove to Toowoomba to pick them up and he had all their stuff out on the lawn, in garbage bags and shit, but I didn't give a fuck, I don't care about that, I just ran and grabbed them. I just . . . I'll never forget that day.

His visiting rights were granted but he never, ever did follow through. Not with even one of them; well, that's his choice!

Yeah, and the girls were waiting on the lawn too when I got there. It was twenty-five years ago . . . sort of like a repeat of what happened to me, eh? . . . I was waiting for my mum, looking through a dormitory window, and I ran to her, and now they were looking out for me and they ran to me.

In my introduction to you I mentioned that you have six children to five different fathers. The reason I mention that was that there is a conception that some women out there in low income circumstances just have children for the money, as in pension from the government. What do you think about that? Could people look at your circumstance like that?
Well they could, but they would be wrong, very wrong. Do I think about it? Not much, like, with my eldest, I was just a teenager exploring at the time. I wasn't given the advice of contraception—you're young. With my second that was my first serious live-in relationship, but the father took off before I even told him I was pregnant. Then my two eldest girls, that relationship with their father got me engaged so you think, 'Ok this one might be for real', but you know shit happens in life and there's things that are just beyond your control. But I have never, ever regretted having any of my children, I love them all equally.

What were you like at school?
I was always the teacher's pet. Spelling, I loved spelling and writing. I loved writing, yeah. Hated maths, but yeah . . . just spelling

Cilla looking gorgeous, aged 16

and sewing. I'm mad for crosswords now, I love a good, hard crossword.

Yeah, Cilla is pretty bloody good at them. She's got a brain, it just depends on whether she wants to use it. I'm always having a go at her for not trying that little bit harder to get a job or to do something that will stimulate her brain. But, hey, you could talk till ya black and blue in the face, it's up to the individual. But, ya know, as long as ya have a go. And when it's ya friend you can just keep giving subtle nudges.

My favourite teacher was Mrs Muckett. She was from Scotland; she took me for Grade Three, Four and Five. On weekends she would take us to the beach and everything, me and Bruce, a mate. She'd take us to play squash.

Cilla actually lived with me for a while. We were going wild. Kingaroy every second Friday night, pay week, RSL disco, netball. It was a real girl's home—Cilla with her two and I had my daughter. They were real fun, happy times because we were there for one another—no one else mattered. We had each other to confide in, we could babysit for each other and Cilla was a good cook. And that little yellow Datsun. The cartoon car, as the Cherbourg kids called it.

Tell ya a yarn now. I think Cilla was pregnant with Kaylynn and was living back at Cherbourg. I would go out and visit. Well, on this day I was about to leave and she walked me out to the car and, bugger me dead, I had a flat tyre. Well, I was on uneven ground but I thought I would still give it a go at changing it there and then. So I jack it up, Cilla found a brick to put under the opposite front wheel (it was the back passenger side wheel that was flat), we were following the steps. I go to take the tyre off and as I pulled on the tyre, the car being a two-door Datsun Sunny Deluxe 1000 1971, I actually pulled the little car off the jack! Lucky Cilla was there— she caught it and held it up! I had the cheek to say, 'Hang on and I'll get the other wheel and put it on!' We just cracked up laughing. We had to stop for a while after the spare was on—I was too weak with laughter to do any more. Where was a camera when you needed one?

Back to the school question—I'm going all over the place here with my memories. How was high school?
Yer, I was doing okay. I still loved English and the sewing lessons but high school in Murgon was such a socialising event. But I only got to Grade Ten and pulled out when I got pregnant. It was no big deal to drop out because of that—everybody was doing it . . . it was acceptable behaviour. Maybe not the best from other societies' view, but Blackfellas accepted it. Maybe if we didn't accept it so easily some of us might have had a chance of doing something with our lives, instead of becoming mothers,

but then that's what some of us wanted. But you always think back and wonder what if. But this is it, so deal with it. And some can't, you know, and that's why some of them kids are running wild. Make ya sorry though . . . for both.

I often wonder: Why am I still alive? I attempted suicide once. Tablets. That was when I was pregnant and I was scared of Mum finding out and I would rather die than tell her! Pregnant with my oldest. But, when I fell, I hit the floor really hard and woke everybody up! My asthma tablets. I thought Mum would only think low of me again. I wanted to please her, not disappoint. I went down to the hospital. Mum didn't come with me. Made the police take me. She just cursed me. And even used it against me when I came back—I better do this, better not do that. Hide your tablets and that sort of shit.

Have you ever worked?
I've held down quite a few jobs. Even in those times, like the late '70s and '80s when the government still wasn't paying Blackfellas the right wage. We've all been waiting for our back pay or a payout. The lucky number seven—there was a seven thousand dollar payout for unreceived wages to all those that held a job between certain years. There's an inquiry into it. I'm not sure if it's all over Australia but the Cherbourg mob have come forward now because of your Aunty Lesley, Tammy's mother, she started that off. You had to have all your papers and proof, or at least dates, so they could check with the employers.

We (my partner and I) started doing part-time weekend relieving work there, in the children's shelter [near the old dormitory site]. Here's another cycle, only this time *I'm* the manager, carer and stand-in mother. We got on really good with the ones that were doing full-time work there, but they wanted to leave. Some of the criteria was that you had to be in a stable relationship, no drinking and drugs. That's hard to find in Cherbourg, but at this stage my relationship was going well—we had both been clean for some time. So the next thing you know we are the replacement carers and I was back in the dormitory-style system again, not exactly the same but close. I didn't like that about my situation cause, like I said, I felt like I was doing to the kids what was done to us when I was in the dormitory with my brothers and sisters. So I went out of my way to not be like that. Like I'd buy pretty plates and cups and toys for them and stuff like that. I did whatever I could to make it not feel like a dormitory. Take them out on weekends, every weekend, take them fishing, swimming, we'd just get out of there.

The kids that were in the shelter were neglected or mothers stressed out, or just nowhere else to live. It's a small community but I still didn't know their parents personally and sometimes we were left in the dark as to what the situation was with that particular child or children.

We fought for a lot of changes there in the shelter when we had it, for new furniture, beds, carpets, renovations but not just material things, for counselling too. I started that off, they weren't doing anything like that. There were children in there that were abused and stuff, that weren't getting any counselling. There was a ten-year-old boy who had the mind of a three to four year old and no one had done anything to help him. He was there two years before we came along and I really fought to get him counselling. It was very frustrating; shouldn't that be a priority? Family services are frustrating, well, it was in my circumstance. Here you had two helping, willing and able to work hard, caring people trying to do right by these kids and we were running into brick walls put up by the department. Family Services would bring quite traumatised young people, babies, to the shelter, sometimes with or without the details of the circumstances, to people without formal training, without counsellors on . . . just as well I could pull advice from my own life experiences. And my partner was a good man who was good with kids. A good attitude, not myall, you know, could talk up.

What's the hardest thing about this type of work?

The stories of abuse, one after another. The frustration of knowing you really can't do a thing—not enough information or couldn't remember certain dates, you weren't there, it goes on and on—too many walls to climb for both victim and workers. That left us really stressed out. It's not the physical work, it's the emotion that's the hardest. But just being there for those kids, you know, and showing them that you care, you really honestly care.

Do you take all ages at the shelter?

The kids that come to the shelter have to be five and over, or school age, but the majority of them have been traumatised nearly all their lives—there's nowhere for them to go. The best thing you can do for the kids in there is get them into really good homes . . . foster homes, finding the right people to foster them . . . but that's hard too. And some people will be thinking: But how can you say that with all the stuff now on the Stolen Generation and here you reckon you should give them away? But here, if they are not being looked after or protected in their family by their family, well you gotta do something. And getting them away from some of the shit that goes on out there has got to be a good thing . . . for a while, anyway, not forever. But to give them a chance to . . . rest and be normal kids and to deal with their pain. There are organisations starting up out there to try and deal with the issues but it all takes time and for that trust thing to build between the helpers, workers and the victims.

Not that it's just a job, but you're there because you want to help, you know. You really want to help them. You take on so much. It's frustrating and you get wild, true.

You said your favourite sense out of the five is touch. What touch don't you like?

Rough touch. Hidings. What sort of touch is that? Violent. Being bashed, that's not touching to me. All my relationships have been brutal in some way or another, not all the time, but it's present, mentally. The bruises heal quicker than the mind, that's what really fucks you up.

All around my head, jumped all over my back. Black eyes. Cut lips. Sore ribs. I limp. Broken jaw. Just laid into me. I suffer from headaches, the base of my skull there's a constant fluid dripping from somewhere in my brain, I hear it. I just say, the first hit you get from a man, even if it's just a slap, leave him because it always gets worse. Just gets worse. I'll do everything in my . . . everything in my power not to let that happen to my daughters.

The grog's the main instigator in the relationships at home. The drink fuels the fires in their bellies . . . it could be any-thing . . . it explodes from this to their fists. It's not right, we have to put a stop to the domestic violence through some sort of intimidation, but first they have to admit they are doing wrong. It's been going on for so long . . . it's accepted. And some of the hidings that have been happening lately are terrible. But we do have men's groups now out here working toward goals to help and stop it.

Why don't you leave Cherbourg?
I don't know. It's home. It's where I am comfortable . . . I guess. That's all the family I got. It's not easy to fit into white society, especially from the conditioning I'm from, and sometimes white people don't make it easy. It took them generations to break us and it will take generations before we are on top of our own lives again. It's a slow journey, but there has been change.

Having always lived on a community, do you connect to other Blackfellas from other areas?
Yeah. Especially if there are only a few of us around. But you know we all don't know each other. We are all strangers until you say hello to someone—anyone. But, you know, Blackfellas

Cilla in Cherbourg

always make that eye contact and that head nod, but we all don't know each other. The black community Australia-wide is big. And I only hang around the Wide Bay area or go to Brisbane and Sydney to you. Like the dinner, I didn't know any of the girls, heard of one or two, but you know we are always open to receiving each other, I suppose . . . unless they nuisance and want smoke or bingo price but that comes from the ones you do know, eh?! Anyways, I'm shy.

Being a fair-skinned Blackfella did you get, or do you get, any slack from the mob out there?
Not to ya face . . . nah, only in arguments they call you a yellow c— just to piss you off, but you get over it. It's just a colour and I like the colour yellow anyway. I was goin' to get my new house painted canary yellow.

Do you know much about cultural stuff?
No, not really. I'm the generation lost, I guess. We were the generation that had none passed down to us. We were trying to

fit into white man's society and we couldn't quite manage that. I know about hunting and little things, a bit of language and understanding of what our old people went through, and that all come from my last man. He was teaching me a little bit because he went back up to where his mob are from and they did some men's business with him. But I'm happy the way I am. Content to live my life as a contemporary community woman.

Do you know where your mum and dad were from?
See, that's the big fuck up there—we don't know. Mum and Dad were both born here at Cherbourg. I remember reading it in those papers [government documentation]. I'm not sure where their parents were brought in from. Mum's mother didn't bring her up; her grandmother did. I don't remember them. I didn't even know I had older brother and sisters, because of the dormitory. All the other ones were older, they were old enough to go and look after themselves, I suppose. I know them all now. I love all my brothers, mainly my brothers. It's the sisters that are the . . . rat-bags—different personalities, we clash, there's a big mob of us, you know. But they're my sisters and I love them. If there's one sister I am close to it's Edna, she's two years older than me. We did everything together, all the time we were little, growing up; even having my children. I lived with her most of my life. She's like my sister, my mother, my best friend, everything.

What's your relationship with your father like?
My father used to baby-sit. I think that's when I started looking for him, actually. Like, before that we'd go and cadge him for money and stuff, but really looking for him, to get to know him. I suppose, having my own child and not having his father for him, I felt my son needed some male influence and when I look back now it was my excuse to get to know my dad. I guess my baby broke the ice, made the first step easier.

Why do you think there had been a breakdown between you two when you were a child?
I don't really know because I'm sure he stayed on the community there. But I guess Mum kept us away because they had split up and I didn't really know him anyway; I was a baby when we were put in the dormitory.

Do you have an early memory of him?
I used to play with my father's ears. I remember that. Ngtali, my youngest, she plays with her father's ears. I used to always play with my father's ears, he had soft, long, saggy ears. They were really thin. I remember that, yeah. When I would play with his ears, Dad used to say, 'Go 'way!' But I'd still go back. That's a very early memory then, isn't it? It spins me out that Ngtali does that now. You know, if she can't find your ear in the dark, she'll play with your lip. I hate it when she does that to me.

Did you form a strong relationship with your dad?
I was only getting to know Dad just before he died, really, I don't remember him much when we were little.

Every time he was drunk . . . every time he was drunk he'd say he loved us and everything, he'd say it to our face. It felt good. I loved to hear him say it. He'd say, 'Do you love me?' I'd say, 'Yeah', and he'd say, 'How much?' and I'd say, 'Lots!' and he'd say, 'But how much?' You know, I couldn't say it enough, how much, to him. He'd say, 'This much?' and I'd say, 'No! This much!' I'd indicate with my hands and arms by trying to touch the back of my hands together behind me; I remember that, he always did that. I loved how he would ask us how much, you know. I drank with him, too. I don't remember any of it, he used to drink straight rum and you had to drink straight rum with him. He would go to the pub like clockwork every pension day for the same amount of hours. I'd just go there sometimes because I'd know he'd be there, just drink with him. I reckon he was about seventy when he died; he was going to the pub, I think, right up to the day he died. Every Wednesday, like clockwork.

I would go down and see him at the old people's home there. I cleaned his room out after he passed away. I've got his jumper, it's a big jacket. I won't wash it. I can smell him on that jumper. And that smell, I love it. It's just him, it's just so familiar, the smell. I got that and a bottle of wine he was drinking, still a little bit in it, and I just kept a pack of cards and his bottle of wine.

And that's about all I got from my father, but I know that he loved me and that's more than a lot of people got in some of the situation at home there. So I'm grateful.

How do you release your frustration and anger, besides drink, which you shouldn't do, Cilla?
I walk a lot from Cherbourg to Murgon and back when I'm angry. I just walk. I just really walk. And this day I was angry and when people offered to pick me up, give me a lift, I'd say, 'No.' I'd just keep walking. And this day, this whitefella, of all people, he pulls up and asks if I need a lift and I jump straight in, I didn't want a lift, but I just jumped straight in. Talking away to him and checking out this car as if I knew him. When I think back now, really that would be the last thing I would have normally done. I asked him, what was he doing? Cause I noticed he wasn't from around here. I asked, 'Do you work out here?' And he goes, 'No, I'm just sent from above' . . . he made a gesture with this hand indicating all around. He just went like that, but he didn't spin me out or anything by saying that, he should have, I reckon. But I just sat there asking him . . . and I said, 'Well, what are you here for?' And he said, 'I'm here to spread the word of love and just tell people to stop eating red meat from animals killed in anger, and start eating organic food' . . . and all this stuff. I went, 'Oh yeah.' And then, when he . . . cause he . . . what made me start asking questions was because he wasn't even going to Cherbourg, he said he was only going out

to take me out and that's when he started saying all that now. When we pulled up he goes, 'Oh, before you get out of the car, can I heal your chest?' I'm asthmatic, I'm really bad asthmatic, but I didn't tell him that. 'You've got something wrong with your chest.' I just said, 'Yeah.' Even that didn't spin me out and it should have by now. He put his hands on my shoulders and shook me three times and he said, 'On the third day, in three days, your asthma will be really good.' I was counting the days and on the third day I had the biggest asthma attack, but it's been good since. It's not as bad as it used to be. But yeah, that really spun me out that. He didn't really say he was an 'angel', he just said, 'sent from above'. I felt comfortable with him, whereas anyone else, I wouldn't have jumped in the car, it was a real flash car too. He lived out of it. He had all his stuff in the back. He looked tall . . . white hair . . . he was so beautiful to me and made me feel calm . . . because with the mood I was in that day . . . anyone else, let alone a whitefella, I wouldn't have got in the car for a lift. Haven't seen him since. He was my angel, anyway, I needed something to get me through that day.

Are you special?
Oh no! What do you mean?

Well, do you think you're special?
No. Not really. Not like . . .

Well, who do you think is special?
You!

Walked into that one, didn't I? Why? Why am I special?
To me? Because you're always, just always there for me. I don't ever ring you, you always ring me. You just have a lot of faith and trust in me. Not a lot of people do.
And sometimes the biggest culprit is me.

I hope Cilla reads her chapter in this book and looks back and sees that people have put their faith and trust in her. Then she can realise just how special she really is. What about the little boy she fought to get counselling for and the other children who were in her care when she was with the shelter? What about her eldest son? She gave him to her sister because, at the time, her sister could do a better job of raising him. It takes a mighty woman to admit she's not ready for motherhood; an unselfish woman to give up her child . . . And it takes a special woman to give the love she gives her kids now.

I don't mind paying for the phone calls; it's the least I could do. I just want her to know she's got a friend in me and I really am just a phone call away.

Where will you be in ten years time? What do you want to be doing?
In ten years time I hope to be looking after my grannies [grandchildren], smothering them with hugs and kisses and killing them with love.

But do you have dreams for your children? Do you encourage them to set goals and try to achieve them? Break that cycle of teenage pregnancy?
Yer, they talk about that sort of stuff . . . but, you know . . . I could encourage them a bit more to have dreams. I want them to do something with their lives. Well . . . make it twenty years until I'll have grandchildren then.

You mad bitch. And what about you?
And what I want for me . . . just a companion . . . who really cares about me and my children . . . companionship, just . . . someone who'll worry about me.

Fair enough. But you haven't had any luck yet, why don't you try a vibrator?
Oh, fuck off! Don't start talking stupid . . . and you don't wanna put this in the book either . . . thas shame, you mad bitch. I bet

you didn't talk like that with them other black chicks, hey? There, see, can't answer me so knock it off!

Serious now. If you had to lose a sense, out of the five which one would it be?
If I had to lose a sense, I suppose it would be . . . sight. Like, even when I'm intimate with a man, when we're kissing, I always touch the face. Always, I love it, it's my pleasure. I would still be able to feel and touch everything.

Well, I hadn't heard from Cilla for a while. Anyway, when I did finally speak to her, Cilla wasn't sounding the best—she was pissed and saying that she was fucked . . . just so fucked. She told me she loved me and we left it there. Weeks went by and I was worried. Then, I can't remember whether I rung her or she rung me . . . no, wait there, she rung me, because the bitch was giving me her new mobile number . . .
Yes, my new mobile number and I'm back with my man [the father of her youngest daughter] and I've got my learner's [driver's licence].

What the fuck happened to you?
Well, I went on a bit of a bender. So much so that I gave the kids to him now [father of youngest daughter] to take for good. Sis, I was just losing it big time. And I fucked off to Brisbane. I was gone a month and I hit it hard, drinkin' and dope. I just didn't want to live anymore. I was taken to a party and everything was there—I mean everything—and it was there for the taking . . . I was going to try the heavy shit but the 'thought' that I was actually thinking about doing it, that scared the fuck out of me and I saw one of the other women I was cruisin' with and she was bad; I didn't like what it was doing to her.

I actually bought an ounce and smoked the lot and I smoked myself to a realisation of what reality was . . . I saw my situation clearly for the first time in my life. Even to the point of understanding my mother's situation. You know, I don't hold anything against her anymore, like our relationship will never be perfect but I hope we make up. Anyway, there were other women with me that I looked up to but I saw them in this other world and they were losing it too and they were worse than me. I thought: I don't want this lifestyle anymore, it's this lifestyle that's actually making me tired.

So next day I was home in Cherbourg asking Ngtali's father to take me back and I wasn't going to take no for an answer. He wasn't sure at first but I told him this is what I want. I want you and my children to come home . . . I just had this new confidence, I don't know where it came from but I felt so good . . . I've never, ever experienced this feeling of confidence before in my entire life. And with this new me I got my learner's and I been cruisin' around—it's been deadly. And the girls are happy but they all fighting each other now. But it's so good to be with Boomi [Ngtali's dad]. He's helping me with everything and the girls just love him like he's their own dad . . . everything is really good.

You know, people have come up and asked me if I wanted to have a drink and smoke and said, 'We won't tell Boomi', but it's not him, I told them—it's ME . . . I don't want to do those things, it is MY choice. And I think that's what it comes down to: I gave up because I wanted to. I had to do it for me, and I did. And that is what is so rewarding. And if I drink again it will be in moderation, not desperation, because I been there and it really isn't that much fun. But I really had to go down—fuck, did I go down. I didn't want to live and I really was going to top myself. Leah, I was that bad, I even let my personal hygiene go.

What helped bring you around?
I kept seeing my girls' faces and thinking, Who would love them more than me? And when I knew that there would be no one that could love my girls more than me I decided to live for them. They're my strength. That's why I went home.

I went home to spend time with Cilla and man she was looking good, sending me text messages to say that she had to do a quick trip to Kingaroy and she shouldn't be long. She'd cut her hair and it looked great. She looked fit, although she reckons now that she's been driving she's put on weight. Her house looks beautiful—I'm envious, her views are stunning. The girls are happy. But even Cherbourg was great—the whole place is looking fantastic, a great change is taking place from community to individuals. I guess it's pride or something, I can't put my finger on it. I was going through my own personal stuff and what usually causes me stress when I do go home wasn't there and, fuck, I had a great, satisfying time. I realised how much I miss the place but also that I have grown up and I have come to really appreciate myself and my land of birth, my home town and family and friends and knowing that will always be there and that's so fucking nice. I'm nearly there with my journey—to where? I'm not sure; to be at the end would be death, but I'm feeling different, but it's a good feeling and what is even greater is that Cilla has begun her transition. I just hope she enjoys the ride.

I always had a fear that Cilla's story would be a posthumous addition to this book but it's not and she's here to have the last say to her chapter in this book.

About three weeks after going to Cherbourg to film Cilla for the documentary, I received a text message from her on my mobile. It read: having another 1 alls well e'bodies happy due in August! luv u. Cilla.

International Woman

Tammy Williams

lawyer

TAMMY: ONE OF MY MUM'S philosophies is: try and find your talents and live your dreams.

Ever since I was little I always had a dream. Just like I knew the sun was going to rise tomorrow, I knew I was going to meet Michael Jackson! Everybody's like, 'Oh, you ever going to stop gabbling on about that!'

Leah: You saw my room when I had the Michael Jackson posters up?(Yes, people, I was MAD on the gloved one! And Tammy and I are cousins.)

Oh, yeah! I was talking about it to Mum. In those times we had no money to afford tapes or anything, and I said, 'Mum, how come when I was at such a young age I was fascinated with Michael Jackson? Did you have a lot of CDs and tapes?' And she said, 'No, we had nothing. All I heard was what was on the radio!' And I had no pictures of him on my wall because I was really too young to have this fixed fascination with him.

I remember going to your place and I remember Mum and your mum, Aunty Flo, were chatting and so I'd get hoisted off to you. You would take me into your bedroom, and I remember just sitting on your bed, and you were chatting away, and the walls! The walls were just covered in pictures of this one face. And on your ceiling as well—Michael Jackson was on your roof! And I was just thinking, 'Wow!' I couldn't wait to have pictures on my wall just like you. Then we'd go out to Cherbourg ... because I'm the only girl in my family—I have two older brothers—I loved to play dress-ups when I was around my girl cousins. We would all pretend that we were married to the Jackson Five but we'd be all fighting over Michael! I remember going, 'That's okay, you can be married in a make-believe game because I'm going to meet him in real life anyhow!

So in 1993 when I was fifteen, that dream became reality.

In 1993 the circumstance that motivated me and helped that dream to become reality happened. I was in Grade Nine and someone wrote the word 'Nigger' over my school photograph that was in the school magazine. There was a copy that was held in the library, on show. I can remember my friends trying to tell me something, they were really nervous and they were looking at each other as if to say, 'What should we do? Should we tell her?' And I was like, 'Hey, what's up?'

And then one of my best mates said, 'Someone has written, in big black Nico pen, "Nigger" over your face in the photograph of your touch football team that's on display in the library.' I was in shock. I went and confronted the girl.

She was standing near the parade ground, and she's this big tall girl. I went up and I was a tiny little thing; I was just shocked, I was thinking, 'This girl doesn't really know me. Sure, we're in the same class, but ...' I kept to myself, I was into my sports, I was enjoying my school life, having a good time. I approached her and said, 'Why did you call me nigger? Why'd you write nigger across my face?' She just kept saying, 'Well, that's what you are!' She had this stupid little grin on her face like, emphasising, 'That's what you are!' and that's what did it for me. I was just so filled with anger and hatred, I jumped up and hit her!

I look back now and I realise that that incident of the 'Nigger' word was the straw that broke the camel's back. There were a lot of incidents that were building up in my young life. I was coping with my dad's death; he died when I was very little, I was six. Working at the school markets every second Sunday of the month, picking up rubbish and cleaning toilets four and a half hours for twenty dollars, while Mum hosed down the concrete walkways. And then dealing with the limited resources because of our lack of finances. A friend of the family had died of AIDS, a family friend with Downs Syndrome, and seeing all this as a child . . . it was like you were a front row audience member looking at all this discrimination, racism. I remember this one time I was walking along the road and this car full of white boys drove past and spat at me.

Seeing cousins going to gaol, deaths in custody, hearing about sexual abuse with family members, or people close, and also finding out from my mum about what she went through! Being taken off Cherbourg, in her early teens, made to work as domestics! She dealt with so much, being young and on her own. It hurt, you know? So the 'Nigger' incident was just . . . the anger was just boiling up, so I hit her; you can't justify violence but I just exploded and she was on the receiving end.

It wasn't until the next day, along the school grapevine, word got back to me that I was going to be sent up to the office. I didn't want to tell Mum . . . actually I was waiting for the office to ring Mum, but they didn't! And I was thinking, 'What type of game are they playing?' So I thought, 'Well, they're expecting me to be unprepared.' So I told everyone: 'Don't let word out that I know!'

That afternoon I went home and told Mum. Mum was just furious that she wasn't called up to the school. Mum has always taken an active role in the school, in our education. So they knew who Mum was. She was very upset about that. But more important for Mum was me, how was I feeling. How am I going to get over this?

So she said to me, she said, 'Tid', that's what she called me, Tid Tid for sister, she said, 'Tid Tid, there are two ways to fight racism. The first one is what you did with your fists! And you can keep on fighting everyone, but you're feeding into their stereotype. And that's what they want! They want to give you a reason to keep you beneath them.' So I was like, 'Okay, that's the first one.' She said, 'Well, the second way is you fight them with your achievements! With your talents!'

I started thinking everyone is born on this earth for a reason. We all have, like, a thousand little dilly bags of talent. But the key is for all of us to find our own talents, find what it is that we're good at and Mum said, 'You know, it's going to hurt them more. It's going to hurt that girl more. It's going to hurt those teachers at school who made you feel that you were dumb, that you could never achieve and be anything.'

So, that night in my room, I wrote out this big statement! Like legal statement! My future ambition started to kick in, unbeknown to me.

I just put down every incident and documented it. Then put it in my pocket, went to school the next day and then when I got called up . . . I even had some friends who were witnesses; we all got called up to the office. I was unhappy with the way that this particular teacher dealt with the situation, and I felt like I was the one who did the wrong thing. And sure, violence is wrong, but hey! I'm acting out this way because of what she did! I wouldn't have hit her if she'd respected me as an individual and not have written that 'word' across my face. I did nothing to her to have the word 'Nigger' put over my head! I was basically under the impression that violence isn't tolerated at school, and if it happens again I'll no longer be welcome. But what about racism?

This is my cousin-sister, blood. She is a lawyer. It was this incident that led her on her life journey to rectify the injustice and inequality done to those less fortunate. I am confident that she will become a barrister and she will eventually achieve her future goal to become the UN High Commissioner for Human Rights. It was a seven-page letter about inequality being one of the biggest problems in the world which she sent to Michael Jackson, yes, the gloved one.

I'd never really written anything before and, because I had been made to feel in the past that I was really dumb, I thought I would be wasting my time. Entering this competition required you to write or draw something relating to injustices in the world. I didn't think I could do either.

I told a teacher, Mrs King, who was very supportive of me through my schooling, about an opportunity with this competition I saw during the Jackson Five American Dream television program. It was a two-part series over two nights about their life. During the ad break on the first night, there was an ad advertising how Michael Jackson wanted to have this World Children's Conference. I wanted so badly to ring up, I had this strong overpowering sense to pick up the phone, we had just got the phone on. I knew that it was one of those 0055 numbers you've got to ring and pay a lot of money for, and I knew we couldn't afford it, so I went to bed that night but couldn't sleep because I had this hollow feeling—I just knew that going to bed was wrong, that I should have rung.

The next night I watched it again, and it just came on one final time, and I just went into the bedroom, Mum was half asleep, and I said, 'Mum, can I make a phone call?' She's like, 'Yeah, yeah.' And I'm like, 'It's going to cost a lot of money.' She's like, 'Oh, don't be long.' So I ring up, it's this tape-recorded voice and it's saying you need to write a letter or poem or draw a picture outlining the biggest problem the world faces.

I let it go for maybe one or two weeks, and the deadline was close. I had lunch with Mrs King, and she knew something was up. And I was like, 'Mrs King, what do you think about this?' And she said, 'Well, why don't you write to the competition and use the letter as a healing exercise for what happened to you, your experience of discrimination? Just write the letter, and if you don't want to send it, don't send it.'

That night I went home, I had a shower, and I remember just . . . like, I swear to God, I just knew exactly what I was going to write. I could see the letter in my head. Like I'd never written anything before. When I sat down and began to write, it felt as though the pen was moving by itself. From start to finish I had written this letter. I'm not even an artist and I drew little pictures, little Murri pictures around it. The letter turned out to be seven pages!

The only people I told about the letter, and that I was entering this competition, were my mum and Miss King. Mum didn't say anything. But she told me after that she knew I was going to win.

Mum took me to the post office, it was the final mailing! I gave the letter a kiss! And sent it. But I knew . . . I knew that I had won. Even before I sent it. It wasn't like a cocky feeling, it was just like I knew! I know this is it!

What was in the letter?
It was just a letter, talking about inequity in our society and about being discriminated against. About how the Jews were discriminated against because of Hitler's false beliefs. How we, Aboriginal people, are discriminated against. How our television programs are supposed to show society; well, it's a false image. So I wrote all of this as a fifteen year old . . .

This is pretty heavy stuff for a fifteen year old!
I got a phone call on that Wednesday. And it was the day before April Fools' Day.

Oh no!

Mum was over the back fence yarnin' to a neighbour and next minute there was a knock at the door, my brother comes rushing in to my room, he says, 'Tammy, there's a policeman to see you!' And I'm thinking he's joking. I walk out and there is this policeman there! He asks, 'Is this the Williams residence?' And I'm like, 'Yes.' And then he says, 'Can I speak to Tammy Williams please?' And I said, 'I'm Tammy.' He's like, 'I have a message for you, can you ring this number please?'

The neighbours, they're all looking through their windows. They're all thinking to each other, 'Now, they're good kids, eh? Surely the police must have the wrong address?'

And Belinda, a cousin who was staying with us at the time, jumps the fence to go get Mum. And she's saying, 'Auntie Les, Auntie Les! There's a policeman to see Tammy!' And Mum's like, 'Oh my God! What's she getting into now?'

So I look at the message and there was this number, 'Please call Gina Mandello'; I saw the area code, it was a Sydney number. I'm thinking, 'Hey, look out! This is a big Sydney police station! Now, I haven't really got into many fights. I haven't shoplifted. I haven't done anything like that.' So I ring up, and the policeman is standing there, because he didn't know what it was about either. He was just told, 'You have to find Tammy Williams and get her to call this number.'

So I ring up, and it wasn't the big Sydney police station but Sony Music Australia, Sony being Michael Jackson's music company. I get through and Gina says, 'Is this Tammy?' I said, 'Yeah.' And she says, 'Have you got a passport?' And I was like: 'Passport? What would I need a passport for?' And she said, 'Well, you're going to stay with Michael Jackson!' I was freaking out. I was thinking this is an April Fools' Day joke. But she kept telling me it wasn't a joke but for real. And I said, 'Look, you need to talk to my mother.' And Mum's like, 'What's this about? What's my baby done wrong?'

Was the copper still standing there?
Yeah, he was like, 'What's going on? Michael Jackson? What about him?'

Didn't you put your return address on the letter?!
I put my address on the letter, but you're supposed to put a phone number, and our phone number was silent and I didn't want to push the issue with Mum. I had gotten the phone call out of her. Mum was always saying, 'I don't want undesirables ringing us.' Michael Jackson couldn't even contact us!

They got the Gympie Police on the case. 'Bout the worst thing to send to Blackfellas' place, eh?
True! The hardest part was that I couldn't tell anyone I had won until the following Saturday. They wanted to announce it nationally on 'Video Hits' when Michael Jackson was to make the world premiere of his 'Heal The World' song. So the biggest dream of my life has just come true, and I can't tell anyone!

So when did you leave? How long after that?
Well, we were supposed to go straight after that. But, like, that year was the year when all the allegations against Michael Jackson started up so obviously we couldn't leave straightaway. There's thirty kids from around the world biting at the bit to see Michael Jackson and experience a flight to another country and meet all the other children involved, but we had to wait for things to settle. And wait we did. We had to wait two years—until 1995. And during that time I had received a lot of publicity, a lot of kids and a lot of people were teasing me, they were saying a lot of nasty things—horrible things. A lot of people kept telling me that the Michael Jackson competition, the letter that I wrote, it was a fluke. Everyone would say, 'You're just lucky!' But to me it was more than that and the lady who selected my letter, she said that even when she had the envelope in her hand, she had

this really strong feeling about my letter. There were 47 000 kids who wrote letters and I was selected to be one of the Australian Ambassadors.

While those two years of waiting were very hard and emotional, Mum continued to keep me positive and focused. She just kept reminding me that things happen for a reason. Mum was always good like that, ever since I was a little girl she has always had a way of putting things right or saying the right things at the right time or masking anxiety, grief or worry so we don't have to deal with the negativity.

I believe that everything happens for a reason. When I went to America in 1995 I met all these people who have had an influence on my life, my whole life has just changed from that one experience. Everything has just altered. And maybe being two years older I was really ready for the things I was going to receive from such an experience.

During that two year waiting period I had been involved in a lot of community work, not only for my people in Gympie, but I also did some work in Cherbourg—anyone who needed help. I try and advocate for child and human rights. So I did a lot of charity work during that time. Even though I had won, even though this huge great big event happened in my life, my confidence was still really low because I kept thinking of the racism in my life, and how people were treating me as though I was dumb.

So I went to America; it was the first time I've ever been in a big plane, first time overseas. And my mum was able to come too. And she was able to actually achieve one of her dreams: one of my aunties on my dad's side remembers my mum saying that her dream was to go on a big plane and go overseas. She told us it was her dreams of travelling overseas on a big plane that helped her get through her hard life as a young domestic servant. It was her dreams that kept her going. So it was good that my achievement was our family's achievement. So we went to

Michael Jackson's place, April 1995. And I came back a totally different person. And my mum did too. I went over there semi-shy, semi-low confidence. But to have someone like Michael Jackson, his Foundation, thirty kids listening to you . . . And I told them about what it is like being an Australian Aboriginal and of my ancestor's plights.

There were kids from Japan, kids from Africa—made best friends with these kids from all around the world. And to actually have those people listen to you and to value what you have to say, and believe in you! Your confidence just goes sky high and you think, 'Wow! If someone like Michael Jackson believes in me, wow there must be something all right inside of me?' And being there, yeah, I've never felt happier really. And to see my mum skipping at Michael Jackson's place!

Skipping?
Skipping! Running around! All these beautiful flowers and kids who've come from nothing, who've lived in rubbish tips, whose school was underneath a tree, in the dirt, Africa; or kids in Mexico who lived on the local rubbish tips. To see them so happy . . . there's a lot of love because there was a really good feel about the place. And out of all of that . . . for the first time in my life I got my understanding, my vision.

That trip took the blinkers off because I kept thinking what happened to our people was a unique thing. But by me talking to the African-American kids, the African kids, some of the Indigenous American or South American people, I realised that what happened to us isn't unique. That we're all brothers and sisters under the skin and that we all share a similar story. Sure the storyline differs a little bit, but we're all connected and just because I'm here in Australia and they're over there—they've got problems over there—we shouldn't isolate the fact that there's a bit of distance, it is all our problems. From that moment then I said, 'Well, I'm going to advocate for human and child rights, whoever. Regardless of where they live. Sure, being a Murri woman, Murri issues are always going to be at the centre of my heart, but it doesn't mean I should only focus on the problems in our backyard, my heart's big enough to take care . . . to help everyone, anyone who needs help.

That was your turning point? Your decision in life?
There wasn't really a decision being made, it was just . . . I just knew. Just knew that this was part of my journey and the reason why I was born.

One of the highlights for me was the bonds that I created and had with the other young people at the conference. In particular, the kids who were from non-English speaking backgrounds. I realised that to become friends you don't need to be able to speak the same language. But through touch, through eyes, through expressions we all became good friends. The only thing that we could say to each other that we could understand was our names. All I could say was their name and they could just say Tammy Williams. The translator finally arrived and the language barriers stopped.

Another special moment was when we were getting ready to leave the conference and those kids came up to us and said to us, 'Tammy Williams, my friend. We love you.' They wanted to be able to say that when we all left so they practised all week. Oh, Mum and I just wanted to cry.

One truly amazing moment which also helped to steer me in my chosen career path: one child was to be selected to represent everyone out of those thirty kids because in 1995 it was the fiftieth anniversary of the United Nations and all the kids voted me to be the representative.

I was to go to the United Nations World Summit of Children, and that was in June in San Francisco. So we decided that we'd stay in America for three months, Mum and I. Too bad about high school!

We stayed with people who we met at the conference. We got to travel around as well. I went to school there and we thought, 'Well, we're here for a reason. A lot of these people don't know about Blackfellas in Australia. All they can see is what's on *Crocodile Dundee*.' So we'd go in and we gave lectures, and went to places like South Central where the ghettos are, and Los Angeles, where a lot of African-Americans live.

And how were you received there?
Great, like we were sisters.

We went into schools and universities, but we just became friends with people. We'd just go into their homes: the best way to educate people is to become part of their family and meet their circle of family and friends and walk in the circles. We stayed with Chief Sitting Bull, great, great granddaughter of the Sioux Nation.

Wow! I'm in awe.
That was in Arizona. So I got to learn more about our Indigenous North American brothers and sisters, we did the circuit all around America. And here's us two Murries from Gympie.

Then Mum and I, we'd made this plan, 'Yeah, we'll go to New York City!' We caught this one plane, and we were all excited; next minute we started getting closer. It was midnight when we landed. The biggest city we've ever been to. I mean we were jammy when we came to Sydney and yet we had the cheek to want to go to New York. I remember flying and it was the dead of night, and then there was this sea of lights. We were like, 'Oh my God!' Our minds just kept overreacting and we'd exaggerate, 'Oh God, what could happen to us?' And then I remember sitting at the lights in a taxi in the heart of New York city and we were worried the taxi driver was going to take us off to some dark alley . . .

And do away with you . . .
But we eventually ended up in San Francisco for the United
Nations World Summit of Children.

What was the topic up for discussion?
I was with 130 kids and basically we had to come up with ways
in which young people can be involved: youth participation
within the United Nations. Then all the world leaders and
ambassadors were going to have this special ceremony and they
wanted some young people to be involved. And, out of the 130
kids, I was selected to be part of a small delegation to represent
the children of the world, to also be part of those celebrations.
So this coincided . . . just really bad timing, there was the
Oklahoma bombing, a federal building was blown up. They were
worried that another federal building was going to explode.

So were you in one of these federal buildings?
Well, this celebration took place at the foot, it was like in the
plaza area and it's surrounded entirely by federal buildings! And
all these ambassadors and world leaders being right there . . .

Well, it's a prime target, isn't it?
Yeah, so the FBI and everyone were worried. . . . So all us kids
had metal detectors passed over us—we're just kids, but they
were checking us. Sniffer dogs!

That would have been pretty heavy?
I was so nervous, we get called out to take our positions on stage
and there's Archbishop Desmond Tutu; the Secretary General,
Butros Butros Ghali of the United Nations; all these high
profile, prominent leaders in the audience. And I remember
standing up there, getting ready to read and I looked up and in
the distance there's all these skyscrapers, and there's men in

black, they were snipers, strategically placed on the opposite buildings with their guns!

So, when you were reading you were seeing all this?
Well, I'm just about to read and I see this, and then I'm like, gosh, you know, I'm here for business, here to do a job, and then I just blanked that out and got down to business. We had to read out the UN Charter and some other youth issues. Fortunately the Michael Jackson conference had prepared me.

Michael Jackson's righthand woman! Bitch. So did you meet the gloved one?
Yes. I did meet Michael Jackson.

Biiitch! What was he like?
I felt so comfortable and warm in his presence, he has such a warm presence, you could tell. Like he has the most incredible eyes. And highly intelligent.

Was Michael Jackson married to Lisa-Marie Presley at the time? Did you meet her?
Yeah, oh she's such a beautiful woman, and tiny too.

True?!
I remember looking at her high heels and thinking—I had never seen platforms before—and I was thinking, 'Wow! I want a pair.'

And what were they like together? Did they seem in love?
They were holding hands and giggling, they were newlyweds. And how I presume newlyweds acted.
    When I was selected to be a spokesperson at the Michael Jackson conference, there was a media launch in front of Michael's place. There was a helicopter buzzing over top, and all of this media. I'm standing there as this seventeen-year-old Murri

girl from country Queensland, in front of his house and all this media around and cameras. I'd never, ever, ever been in that situation before. So that incident had prepared me for the snipers, metal detectors and the sniffer dogs at the United Nations forum!

After the United Nations World Summit of Children I networked with a lot more kids and learnt about health issues—AIDS, issues about the high incidences of sexual assault in Africa and how fortunate we really are . . . you know, I used to grumble about my high school in Gympie, 'Oh, it's a boring high school, and we've got nothing and we live in housing commission, we've only got a little green Gemini, and oh we haven't got much.' But going over there made me realise how blessed I am. Sure compared to, at that stage, compared to other people's standards we struggled like hell, but we were healthy. And our family was together.

It is amazing: one little act like that can just alter your entire life's course. Changed my entire life.

Do you reckon that this little path was planned out?
Yeah, I do. All of our journeys are. It's just a matter of us remembering what we're supposed to do. And sure, our paths; I believe spiritually that we all have a destiny, but there's also choice. I believe one individual's achievement is the entire family's. I don't like to use the word sacrifice. It's all about choices. And they made a choice. They went without some things, so that I can do some things. So therefore what I do is theirs, and likewise for them.

Tammy comes from a country town—small country city, it does have traffic lights and all the fast food outlets—if you were bored in Murgon you would go for an hour's drive to Gympie to get a feed. I got the feeling that Gympie was very feminine, something to do with the mountains?

I always look forward to, ever since I was a little girl, the spring time, the summer rains and the late evening rains—everything was so lush at home. Like the flowers would start blossoming, the horses come into season, the sun just seems that little bit brighter. It makes me so excited, just energised and very happy. It's also very gentle and yet there's this sense of strength, determination about the place.

So what happened when you came back to Gympie after this huge adventure?
When we got back to Australia, Queensland ... Gympie, and then I'm thinking, 'Yeah, okay. This was a wonderful journey and I'm back to a normal school girl now. I'll try and live with that for a while.' Then this express envelope arrives saying I've been invited to go to the United Nations in Geneva, that's where the Human Rights headquarters are. They wanted me to represent the young people of Australasia and join a delegation of thirteen young kids from around the world representing different regions. So I travelled to Switzerland and gave my speech to the UN High Commissioner for Human Rights, with the thirteen other delegates.

Did he listen?
Oh, yes. He inspired me to go on and to one day take his job. He came in and truly listened; he didn't write anything, he brought someone else to do that. He gave us his full attention. This is the man who is the head of human rights in the world. And he just sat there and listened. He made us feel so comfortable. He wanted to hear what we had to say.

Did you tell him that you wanted his job?
I didn't tell him that. I was thinking, 'Yep, this is what I want to do! I want to be just like him.' Obviously you can't walk in off the street out of high school and work in the UN and be a

Tammy at one of her many conferences

high-ranking UN official; so, more school, university, more study, on-the-job experience . . . It's just merely a stepping-stone and so is being an international human rights lawyer. And then when I'm forty or fifty, when I have enough qualifications and enough knowledge and wisdom, then get into the UN.

What issues did you speak about?
I spoke about deaths in custody; I spoke about racism here; I talked about sexual abuse of people; and particularly about young males, how there is not enough facilities for young guys. The members all spoke about a different issue that they could relate to. One of the speakers was gay and spoke about how when she confronted her family and friends—finally to let out the secret, to be able to live and not hide, to be the woman that she is—some people tried to slit her throat, they tried to put her on fire. She naturally broke down in tears when she was telling her story; and this man, the head of the UN, he went up, regardless of the amount of money that he might have or his position, he went up and gave her a hug and held her. Held her and said,

'It is okay.' He thanked her for sharing her story, for having the courage.

His assistant continued to write down every problem that we had. And then they sent off letters, to our leaders and to other leaders. Raising their awareness about the problems of the youth. Every country must report every four years about human rights violations.

Have you been asked for your input in those reports?
No. Well, see, obviously the government has their own processes, but the United Nations tries to invite other individuals, or bodies, to come and make a complaint. And so that's what we did.

It's just been one step at a time. That Michael Jackson conference gave me confidence to say: yep, I'm good enough to finish high school and to go on to university, go to law school. And then going to speak at the United Nations, and as I have become a part of the Anne Frank Exhibition, or going to the President Jimmy Carter conference, I feel like my dreams are . . . I feel like I'm getting a foundation to enable me to take off from. A bit stronger in the legs, so I feel brave enough to reach up and grab for anything I want.

I am so proud of my little cuss! She blew me off my chair. It actually has brought a tear to my eye. I'm just so proud.

So tell us about the Anne Frank Exhibition?
Well, while we were in Geneva . . . Michael Jackson's Foundation had offered to pay for us to go to Switzerland but I thought, well, hang on, this man has already changed my life; I'm representing the young people of Australia, surely there's got to be a company that would sponsor me from home. No company in Australia would sponsor me. I got a little bit of money from the government and different communities, philanthropic foundations, but most of my fundraising came from kids in the community or

pensioners sending me a hundred dollars out of their pension. We had managed to rake up enough funds, and because I was still a minor I needed a chaperone. So Mum came too. We got the cheapest airfare.

So, after our work at the UN in Geneva had finished, we still had a couple of days up our sleeve and we knew we had to go to Amsterdam for our return flight home. So we caught a train through Italy, Austria and Germany and then ended up in the Netherlands. And Mum kept saying, 'Anne Frank!'

All I knew about this girl Anne Frank was that she lived in an attic, and she was Jewish; I didn't know anything more. We wanted to try and track down her 'house'. So we just asked people in Amsterdam and we ended up getting there. We were just fascinated. It brought Mum to tears because she could see some of the parallels of what happened to the Jewish people according to their race and what happened to our people, living on missions—they were like mini-concentration camps.

We were in the bookstore at the end of the museum and we had a little bit of money left, so we thought we would buy an Anne Frank diary for all those school kids and communities who had sponsored us, and donate it to the library. So there we were, big armful of this huge big pile of books, and this man just kept looking at us. And we're thinking, 'Oh, this is a security guard. He thinks us Murris are going to steal.' We forgot ourselves, he didn't even know what a Murri was, but he just kept looking at us. He eventually came over and said, 'Hello, how are you?' And we're like, 'Yer, all right.' We're just thinking he's just trying to worm his way in. And then he just said, 'Look, I don't know why I've been drawn to you, for some reason I feel like I have to talk to you.' He said, 'My job here is to . . . see we get millions of people in through the museum, and I need to just ask a couple of people about their views on it, and for some reason I need to talk to you?' So we get led out to this other room, we started talking and talking about life on a mission and racism. And he's like, oh wow! He said, 'Well, we realise that not everyone can come to Amsterdam to see the Anne Frank Exhibition, so we're thinking of taking an exhibition around the world.' Later it turned out they wanted me to be a part of it.

I'm the only person who's not a survivor of the Jewish Holocaust to be featured in it. And obviously the only young person to be profiled and the only Australian, the only person from the Southern Hemisphere. So for the last five years it's been travelling all around the world with my profile.

Princess Margaret and Tony Blair launched it in England, and apparently Nelson Mandela launched it in Africa—it's been too hard to believe. People in Japan have seen my profile, know a little bit of my story and it arrived in Australia for the Australian premiere in Melbourne in May 2000. That was the first time I had seen it.

What did you think? Did it blow you away?
Yeah, it did. It's a photograph and a little bit of a blurb about me. I remember thinking when I was being interviewed for it, I knew that it was coming in the year 2000, that was five years away, and I remember thinking, oh God, I'm going to be so old! I'm going to be like twenty-two and what am I going to look like? They put my profile right at the very front of the exhibition and I remember just sitting there going, wow! It was surreal. It just amazed me. So, when I looked at my profile and what I had said about certain issues, it was good to see that some changes have been made for the better. Talking about issues that are so rele-vant, still relevant today. And I kept thinking about the journey that Australia has taken with the reconciliation process . . .

Any progress?
I've always got to be positive. I am unhappy, very unhappy, with the way things have been on a political level, but I'm very, very happy, very proud of what has happened and inspired the grass

roots level. And I think it's important for people . . . it's easy to lose . . . get disheartened by what's happening at a political level. But reconciliation's bigger than just one man.

What other famous shoulders have you rubbed up against?
I went to the 1996 State of the World with Gorbachev. I was then sponsored by the Australian Youth Foundation to go to the State of the World Forum in San Francisco. There were world leaders—leaders from different areas, like political, scientific, philanthropic, entertainment industries, just to name a few— were there. So, 750 world leaders, present, and about thirty so-called future, potential world leaders. So I was selected and went along proudly. There was Mikhail Gorbachev, the Queen of Jordan, John Denver, Dr Jane Goodall and all these other high profile people. So, to be able to be mentored alongside and to engage in international debate on international issues such as nuclear disarmament, the right to the girl child, rights of Indigenous people; to be around a table with all these people— it was mind blowing, but very challenging.

I was chosen by Dr Marianne Wright-Addledman, who is a prominent child rights campaigner and very close with Hilary Clinton, to speak at an international press conference. I was given this opportunity to say everything we needed to say about youth issues around the world.

Wow! That's huge, isn't it? But how much . . . like all these confer-ences that you've gone to over the years, have you seen progress in issues that you put forward?
It frustrates me with the politics they've been playing. Whenever I go to a conference or a meeting, I always go back to the com-munity that gave me money to travel overseas. I go back to report to them, just so I'm accountable to what I do. I've spoken at the Cherbourg State School, Murgon High School and Gympie schools. I took it upon myself to travel to all of those commu-

nities and the schools because I feel that there's not enough self-appointed leaders who do that. They aren't accountable. There are some that do put in the effort, like for instance the UN High Commissioner for Human Rights had, up until his retirement, kept me up-to-date with the issues. He would copy all of his letters that were related to Australia and youth to me, even the letter he wrote to the Prime Minister he sent to me. So I knew exactly what was happening.

Obviously we can't get everything our own way, but what I have seen is a lot more youth participation. When I first started on the scene we were just a tokenistic thing, in some respects. Having young people is still seen as being tokenistic; but now I'm seeing more and more young people on companies, as directors of boards, seeing the government wanting to engage and consult with young people. You know, Indigenous issues are being . . . sure no action's, very little action's been taken, but there's a lot of media attention. And so you have to know the different forums and the different platforms, and canvass—not just the one, but using all the meetings, using contacts in the political arena. But the most important element that I got out of all the conferences I have been involved in is the networking: being able to see, like, the President of the World Bank at lunchtime, make a beeline for him to just yap in his ear. You know, if you're on the circuit long enough you're continuously seeing those people; you just keep talking to them and sooner or later you make an impact and change happens.

Is that something you hope to do? Stay on that circuit and make a change?
Yeah. I do a lot of volunteer work too.

Why do you do volunteer work?
For two simple reasons. One, I love working with people. And two, there are a lot of opportunities out there, but unfortunately

not everyone knows about them. So by working with the communities I can share my knowledge with them. I believe it's important to share any opportunity that may come my way with others less fortunate; I know what it's like to be on the receiving end of nothing.

What are you doing at the moment?
I have just finished my Law degree and am working as a paralegal at the Commonwealth Director of Public Prosecutors in Brisbane. I will be undergoing the Bar Practice Course to become a barrister.

Why did you choose Law?
Law is such a versatile and important degree to have. Once I pass my Bar and become a barrister I will practise for a while so that I can get experience and solid legal knowledge. Ultimately I intend to use my degree as a stepping-stone into social justice areas. I am proud of my level of education as it was never easy to acquire.

See, my mother, through no fault of her own, only received limited education. In her day, living under the Aboriginal Protection Act, she was not given the opportunity to gain higher education; some people of her time only received Grade Four education. There were very trying times when it sometimes came to maths or science homework, but nevertheless we did our best. So my brothers and I are the first generation in our family to receive a higher education. Mum always knew the importance of education. She supported and encouraged us wholeheartedly. That's one of the reasons why I've always been so determined to seize every opportunity that comes my way; especially educational opportunities.

Then there is all my invitations to conferences; I've tried to stop going to these conferences, I'm studying. You know, I've tried to stop going to these conferences, but I just keep getting

Graduation day: Tammy and her mum

invitations. I keep getting led into that arena and I just thought, well, why fight the tide? Go with it. I don't get paid for what I do, it's voluntary. Some people will make a donation, help out with transportation costs, but other than that I do it for me because I realise I'm where I am today because I had support. I had people surrounding me who believed in me, and who helped me. That's what I'm all about: wanting to empower young people and individuals.

You go to some of our communities all over Australia and you see kids there with more potential than I've ever had; more talents, they'll probably go faster than Cathy Freeman. It's just that some of us, like I guess most of the women in this book, we were all given support, we've latched onto people who believed in us and we believed in ourselves and some of us were raised with that sense of belief. And that's what I want to do, give young people an opportunity.

So where did that belief come from in you?

My family, who are so supportive and loving. I was raised thinking that I could be anything if I set my mind to it, irrespective of our family's situation. My family, they were just so unselfish. For me it's about giving back. Michael Jackson changed my life; the United Nations and the UN High Commissioner helped me along.

Not many people can say that.

Now I'm on a board: the Foundation for Young Australians. I've been given opportunities, so it's about reciprocation—making sure that the flow doesn't stop with me, that other people benefit from it. That it's more than me, it's more than my family, it's about everyone.

You had an opportunity just recently to work with the Federal government.

I didn't want to accept it. I was offered a position on a government task force, a Youth Pathways Project. It's like an independent task force to basically investigate and study the transition of young people from youth into adulthood. It's commissioned by the Federal government and I was concerned, because I don't agree with their policy and, in particular, the racial policies of the Federal government, so I didn't want to be involved. Initially I thought it'd be a whitewash. I thought I would just be perceived as a token young black person on the board.

But then I thought, well, change has to come from within, and you can't be judgmental without getting involved. So I thought, well, I'm going to take this challenge and whether I was appointed to be a puppet is another thing. I thought, well, I'm giving up a lot of my time, my study time at law school, to be here, so I'm not going to sit on the board and be a yes person. And so I contributed.

This is a task force about youth, so how about we find out what the views of the young people are? Let's not ask the experts, the academics; the experts are those young people. So I made sure that they had consultations with kids all around Australia, up until the age of twenty-five. I was concerned when they did the consultations there were very few black kids on it. The only black kids that they had were black kids in the cities. So I came up with a venture to send a team to remote communities like Cape York, Tiwi Island, then to Alice Springs, working with and having active consultation with those kids up there.

What has been the outcome from those reports?
All I can say is that the people who went on those trips with me, they've come back and said that a part of them feels like they know more; they have been enriched by this experience.

It made them see that the issues of education and housing were only some of the important factors; that education is not made accessible to the children in those communities. They have to leave their own community, move to a city like Cairns—which is in some cases eight hours drive away in the dry season, inaccessible in the wet season—in order to go to high school. Sometimes it's the first time they've been with so many whites. I mean, they're used to being in a majority in their black community. Having to deal with the racism.

So these so-called experts that sit at their desks and decide our futures, they had no idea until this trip. They've had no idea about the poverty on the communities, about the designs of the houses. Sure, they might design a house a certain way ... they might look all right, but the thing is they're not appropriate for the area, the people, the climate etc, etc. They're said to be designed for the people, but with no consultations of the people. I don't know what's going to happen from this report, but I hope they have learnt from it.

In your already busy schedule are there any other pet projects?
At the moment I'm with a newly formed company. It's an Indigenous business institute. Noel Pearson, the owner of the Body Shop, a professor from the Harvard Business School in the US are all involved. The company is about fostering entrepreneurship within the Aboriginal community. Our people are stereotyped into achieving in categories of just sport or entertainment. Instead we are about getting businesses into our community. Because all the money, it gets sucked out of the communities. They employ non-Indigenous carpenters to come into communities and build their houses, but the carpenters then spend their money elsewhere. Instead we need to keep the money in the communities and give the work to the locals.

And then helping my mum with her campaign.

What's that about and how's it going?
It's going good. It's to do with the payback issue of unpaid wages of Aboriginal people.

For those that don't know about this, back in the early days, and right up to the late '70s and early '80s, the government would take part of the Aboriginal person's pay—in most cases most of it—and put it into this so-called 'trustee account'. The Aboriginal person believed that eventually they would receive it later, or be able to draw on it at times of need, but this never happened. Tammy's mother was affected by this and she has been doing research to try and retrieve this money, not only for herself, but for other people and communities. She has been successful, but there is still a long way to go.
It was like slave labour of Aboriginal people that were sent out west to work as domestic servants. They didn't receive their money, it all went into government trust funds, and to this day our people never received the money for their work. So Mum is working to get those funds to the people.

When did your mum leave Cherbourg to work?
She was sent out when she was like sixteen years old. Went out to work at Taroom, Condamine and then to Brisbane.

She was a maid?
Yeah, basically. Looked after the kids, did the cleaning and cooking, only being a child herself. She had to eat meals on verandahs and sleep outside in a shed, and had to cook and clean for white people but wasn't good enough to sleep indoors. But then when she came to Brisbane she had a really good white boss and she became part of the family and was treated with respect. That was to be her last job, with Mrs Robert, and to this day Mum and Mrs Robert are very close. And then she met my dad.

Where did they meet?
They met at the Ekka! The Brisbane Exhibition Show.

Dad actually went to school in Murgon and he was actually really good friends with our Uncle Donny and Uncle Claudy.

Mum had heard that Uncle Donny was down in Brisbane; Mum wasn't working this day so she thought she'd go and see him. She caught up with him at this one meeting spot where all the Blackfellas hang out and there was this handsome white guy there next to Uncle Donny and, yeah, it was like love at first sight. They ended up getting married and having us three kids and moved to Gympie.

Your dad died when you were young. How do you think he would feel if he was alive today?
I believe that he's still with me. He's helped me a lot, he's taught me a lot in the short time that we had together, he continues to teach me a lot more in death, his spirit. All the old people that have passed on, they're all with us.

So you believe in them as our guides?
Yes, I do. They're a part of my soul.

Do you think your father's death made you stronger?
Oh, definitely! Everything happens for a reason. Some things are more painful than others and you wish that they didn't happen that way, wish that you could have learnt the lesson through another means. But the one thing it taught me was to make sure you tell people how you feel, because you just don't know what's around the corner; your whole life could change tomorrow. And it's important that. Like, if you really love someone: tell them. Sometimes we don't like to say things because we're worried— oh, what will they say or think, or that'd be shame. We must overcome the fears before it's too late.

And if your dad was alive today, what do you think he'd say to you?
I don't think it's what he would say, I think it would be a look. A feeling of security—to know that, whatever I do, my family will be there for me. I'm very lucky to have that and to get that from my family. I guess it's unconditional love.

What was the last happy memory that you've got of them two together?
The laughter. My dad used to always laugh at my mum's laugh. Mum describes her laugh as an old witch's. She's got this really prominent laugh. They had pet names for each other, he'd call her like Lello, she'd call him Willy because of the family surname: Williams.

If I could fill a little bottle of cherished moments it would be with the everyday fun and humour that they shared together. Of Dad teaching me to ride our horses, we had a lot of horses, we had about nine horses all up over the years. Being outside, with my dad leading me on the horse and then watching him ride. That feeling of safety when Dad would have a hand just behind my back, making sure that I wouldn't fall off the horse; bareback. Leading me around and making sure I was holding the reins right, don't dig your legs in; it was my horse, you had to treat them with respect. Just really enjoying the silence of two people . . . just being together. Sitting on his lap, he would sing, 'Two Little Dicky Birds Sitting . . . One named Peter, One named Paul . . . Fly away Peter, Fly away Paul, Come back Peter, Come back Paul . . .'

There is a moment of silence as Tammy reflects on this moment.

What's the first memory of your mother?
One of my first loving memories of my mother would have to be her cooking in the kitchen. My mother is a really good cook, I'm sure everyone's mother is a good cook! But, being the youngest, everyone else would be off going to school and Dad would be away in the trucks, he was a truck driver, and we were out on this little farm, out in the middle of nowhere, just me and Mum. I can remember seeing the back of her. Seeing her legs underneath a summer dress, and her cooking in the kitchen. The kitchen was . . . It was a big old Queenslander house, high set like an open plan, high ceilings house. There was no distinction between the kitchen and dining room, it was just one big room. I had scribbled on the back of each dining table chair. I wanted to write everyone's name on the back, couldn't write, it was just scribble.

I remember her darting around the kitchen. And the smell. I remember watching her putting the sultana cake mixture into the oven and I remember every now and again going to the oven, because I love heat, and touching the oven, and looking in and watching the mixture rise.

I had a lucky upbringing because I felt so safe, so happy, so contented and so loved. A very special time, I just wish that every child in the world could experience that feeling.

What about a memory of your brothers? What have they done for you, for love? Sister, brotherly love.

Tammy and her mum

We all have very different personalities. One's shyer than the other, and one's more diplomatic. That brotherly love, just them being there for me as big brothers should be. When I was little I got a Barbie doll and Barbie house, they didn't play with Barbie or anything, but they loved building. My oldest brother would help me construct Barbie's house. He couldn't give a damn about Barbie! Which reminds me, Ken wasn't good enough for Barbie! The only man for Barbie was Michael! So Santa got me a Michael Jackson doll.

And did he live in Barbie's house?
Yes. But they weren't married at that stage. So he'd come over and just visit.

And did the Michael Jackson doll sing for Barbie?
Oh, yes! He moonwalked and everything, he was a sweet charming, young black man.

So Barbie has had a black man!
Yeah! And she's still got him! Because they lived happily ever after.

Back to my brothers—they are both really very talented.

One of my brothers has a degree in Built Environment Industrial Design, so designing like product-based things. He's now doing his postgraduate. My other brother, who is always being the diplomat, sort of the father figure as I grew up, he went on to work in the Defence Department and wants to be involved in politics and become a political adviser.

Apart from your busy business life, do you see children? Do you see marriage? Are you in looooove?
I see my soul smiling happy. All I want is to be truly, truly happy; spiritually happy. I'd like to achieve, and I will achieve, my law degree's one thing, get my Masters, study overseas and International Human Rights Law, practise as an international Human Rights lawyer. Work for my people, not just my people as in my Indigenous, my Murri people, but just 'people' in general.

I would love to be with someone special one day, a man who can be a partner in life and in my journey. I'd love to become a parent, but not necessarily my own kids. You know, I have lots of cousin's kids and, regardless of what I do, I will always want to take care of and help children, whether they're mine or not. It's the Murri way, taking care of everyone's kids, we're not fixated with little miniatures of ourselves.

Sure, I'd love to maybe have my own, but I believe children are a gift, you don't own them, or you don't own your partner or your husband. If I was blessed to have children, I would want them to have the commitment and the love that my mother gave to me. And you know she set a high standard.

There's one song that I really identify with, especially with my mum, and that I think sums up our relationship. Celine

Dion's song, 'Because you loved me'. My mum, she's my best friend, she's my soul mate, she's my mother. When I say she's my mother, I say that with so much pride. Being a parent is the most important role or position in society, and I'm not going to take that lightly. I am the woman I am today because of her love.

There's a lot of things that I want to achieve and they are things that require a lot of energy, I will need to invest a lot of time and energy for those things and I wouldn't want to compromise my children for that.

Spirituality?
I believe in souls. I believe that we're all here for a reason, that there is a path that's created for us. It's a matter of remembering we also have choices. There are more than just physical characteristics that come with being human.

I think the key is an internal examination. I think the answer is within us. I mean, our lives are so external: I mean, we need to travel to the moon, we need to travel to Mars; as if that's going to give us some big divine answer. People think that we need to fall in love, or be with a person in order for us to become complete. In order to be loved and to love, you have to love yourself. Exploring your soul, your innermost parts.

I believe our souls go to another place. I believe in the life-death-life cycle. The more that I learn about my culture, and the culture of other Indigenous peoples, the more I believe. Our whole culture is about cycles. There's time for everything. And that's all that life is: a cycle. And when people die, it's not the end.

Out of the five senses, which one do you most relate to?
There's not really one sense, it's more of a feeling. The feeling I had when I was going to meet Michael Jackson.

Intuition? That sixth sense.
Yeah.

You've jumped them all! Straight to the sixth sense.
I believe in it. A knowing. I've always been in the knowing, I think. I think everyone's in the knowing. It's just whether you want to acknowledge the knowing, or whether you cloud the knowing with ego. Sort of, 'I wish, I wish this would happen'. It's more than a wish, or a desire, it's just the knowing. You know it's going to happen.

Is it something that Blackfellas or Indigenous races have more strongly than the other races?
I think our culture plays a big part in it. It is spiritually based, and I think the knowing is within all of us. It's whether we choose as individuals to listen. There are some of our white brothers and sisters who are . . . who want to explore that, are in tune with that, whereas some of our own people are like, 'I don't want to know that.' So I think it's everyone that wants to listen to that gut feeling.

All of the senses to me are involved in the knowing. One of the individual senses will trigger that sense of the 'knowing'.

It is difficult to explain, no one understands it, maybe because it is hard to understand. People find it hard to believe but I know it exists and that's all that counts. It has taken me on this incredible journey.

Life's an individual journey, and you're the one who has to wake up tomorrow and face the consequences of what you choose to do, no one else. It all comes down to you. It's a matter of you being strong, I think that's what spirituality is. It's about grasping this thing, this 'knowing', because if you don't have something to hold onto, then you're just an empty shell. So just follow your dreams. You need to have that dream, that vision, that goal, and then work out, how am I going to go about this task? And once you have got that dream, then you're open for opportunities, to see opportunities and grasp opportunities, making those choices that are going to get you to achieve your goal. And that's why I don't like to use the word sacrifices. Because when the work becomes a sacrifice, it's a negative thing. Like you're giving up something and then it's like, oh, I don't really want to do that. Rather make it a choice. I choose to spend less time socialising because I want to get this outcome.

Everyone's got potential. Every seed is meant to grow into a beautiful flower. Who is anyone to say, no, this flower's more beautiful than that one. Because that's what people tried to do to me. They tried to make me feel like I was dumb, that my dreams of going to university were ridiculous. I tell them, I'm a young Murri woman, and this is what I was able to do. But I did it with support, and I'm willing to try and support you, if you want me to.

Do you think enough of our people are wanting?
I think our people do want, it's just being okay with asking.

Shining Light

Kathryn Hay

former Miss Australia

KATHRYN: MY MUM'S MOTHER—and I think her mum—were Aboriginal or part . . . I'm a sixteenth, so my mum's half-caste . . . yeah, and then her . . .

Leah: Hang on a minute, I'm going to stop you right there! You've got to stop that talk, Kathryn!
But that's how they categorise us or classify us.

Hey, don't be boxed girlfriend! You're a black woman and that's it.
Australia must accept that Indigenous Australia comes in all shapes, sizes and colours. *Being a Blackfella in today's society has got nothing to do with skin colour, it's about what you hold in your heart and soul.*
You know what's really sad? We've had one of the family in-laws come up and say, 'Would you mind not telling anyone that we're part Aboriginal?' We were all fine about our Aboriginality until that little scene happened.

When I became Miss Australia I wanted everyone to know that I was Aboriginal. Mum beat me to it; she told everyone.

When I was having my first media conference after winning Miss Australia, the media was asking questions and they fired this one question that I was not prepared for at all. I was all set for all these other questions on the monarchy, republic, GST, taxation reform and all these other things, but they asked me about my Aboriginality. So I had to think on my feet.

They said, 'How do you feel about being the first ever Aboriginal winner for the Miss Australia Awards?'

Without thinking about it I said something really good: 'Oh am I? I didn't realise.' Which is saying anyone could win the Miss Australia Awards, I wouldn't have been surprised if other people of Aboriginal descent had won it before because there are a lot of wonderful people from our culture. Then I said, 'Gosh, I feel so privileged to have been the first.' People remember that, and being the first is almost like you're setting the scene for what can come after. I feel privileged to be the first one. But it was the media who brought light to the Aboriginality, it wasn't an issue for me because I just am. But I am proud of the fact that I was the first to win the title.

It was an exciting time for both of us, Mum and I; her baby girl had become Miss Australia.

But that same in-law rang a family member and said, 'Why did Kate have to let everyone know that you all are Aborigines, you know one of your siblings isn't comfortable about that.' I thought, well, that is their problem! I'm not going to ruin what I want to do because they've got a problem with being Aboriginal.

Kathryn and her family's issues with loss of identity or loss of culture, or having no understanding of your Aboriginality, is really essential to this book. There are thousands of, dare I say the word, part Aboriginal people out there who would prefer to remain unknown to their people or community. Fair enough, that's their business. But, while this denial of their Aboriginality might not affect them (but I bet it does, I bet they think about it, when they're alone), it could affect their children. I witnessed this situation with some of my family members: that feeling of being lost, the confusion caused by a yearning they hold in the depths of their stomachs. This sense of being lost happens all the time to our young black people and that's why most turn to drugs, alcohol and suicide, because they have a yearning inside that they don't understand and it is the yearning for culture, wanting to belong, finding your place in today's society. Culture, or an understanding of it, equals strength and identity. If you have those elements to make a strong foundation you can move forward in life.

I also chose Kathryn to be part of this book (aside from being absolutely proud of her for being the first Aboriginal Miss Australia, let alone being Miss Australia) because when I was crowned as Miss Murgon in good old Murgon town in 1987 one of my sisters, Lesley, said: 'Miss Murgon today, Miss World tomorrow!' With that she gave me inspiration to go after my dreams. And Kathryn's title, Miss Australia, has opened many opportunities for herself and others. So, ya see, Kate and I have this other connection and so she just had to be in the book.

Tell us what your title of Miss Australia allowed you to do?
There are so many people out there with disabilities or who are homeless, abused and underprivileged who I could help with my title of Miss Australia. Predominantly, I raised awareness, and money, for the Cerebral Palsy and Spastic Centres of Australia. When I say I will do something, especially if it's for others, I will do it; I have to do it.

How did you raise your money for the appeal?
One way I thought I could raise some money was by walking. 'I'll walk, everyone can walk.' But it's, well, no, actually, no, not everyone can walk. It's something that has become very real for me since working with people with disabilities and I've learnt to be really appreciative of everything I can do.

[To raise money for the appeal] I walked from Hobart to Launceston, 245 kilometres over four and a half days. It was painful, it was monotonous, it was horrible; but it was something that I had wanted to do for years and years. I thought, people reward endeavour, people reward things that they wouldn't like to do or know if they can do themselves, but if 'you' do it and it's for a good cause, they'll give you support and, importantly, financial support for the cause. It's too easy or uninteresting to just say, 'Look, I'm working for this cause, can you give a donation?' People are sick of it; the market is saturated. You've got to do something a little different. It was a great way to raise money and to get the whole state behind me. And people are still talking about it. Like some ask, 'Why did you do that?' and 'Didn't you know that buses were running?' I wanted to do it, it took a good cause to make me do it and to have belief in myself. Doing things for other people, you really learn what you're all about and then you can give a little bit more. So being hung up on whether you're Aboriginal or not has no comparison to what some people have to go through in life living with a severe disability.

But being Aboriginal was considered a disability.
Only by those that are naive and can't see beyond their narrow vision.

The sad thing is there are some people in this country from both sides, black and white, who still think like that. It's a shame that they haven't experienced the beautiful side to something that is very special and unique to this country.

So how did you really win the crown and title for Miss Australia?
I'm happy to say that there were only two male judges and five female ones. It was legitimate. There is no actual talent side. There's no parading around or any of that stuff. It's how you

Miss Australia meets the Queen

carry yourself, not merely posture and poise, but confidence, openness and strength.

The infrastructure of the Miss Australia Awards—the coordinators, or administrators, or whatever—they were really great when you went in there and talked to them, or they had ideas for you. Or they'd be willing to help you in some way because they had the passion as well. And then when you get to meet the people that you're working for, your motivation just soars, because you know how much . . . how important it is, how needed you are, and that your efforts are making a difference. So, yeah, I think when you realise, when there is a dependence on you, you can often do things you never thought you could.

It's an awesome thing, I mean, Miss Australia!
Well, I don't know, I mean, I couldn't get a date in Alice Springs! Miss Northern Territory said, 'Look, do you want to come out,

there's a free ticket to a ball, usually 125 dollars a ticket, all you can eat and drink, dancing if you want, sit down, it's whatever you want to make of the night. Let's take Miss Australia!' 'Oh no, I couldn't do that!' I said. 'I don't have a date.' She actually found me a date in the end and he was just so quiet for the first half hour; didn't say hello. I said 'Come on, don't you talk up here?' And I was just really talkative and wanting to have a good time and after a while he said, 'I can't believe what you're like, it's great.'

So I suppose people expect something or even a clone of the previous Miss Australia, which upset me at first because I'll never be her. I'm not scared to let people into my life. So why not open up to people? Just be you. Blows their expectation out of the water, and more than likely for the better.

And do you think you may have put a little bit of soul into this Miss Australia situation?
Yeah, I think so.

It was funny, when I was in Alice Springs I went to . . . it wasn't part of my tour but when they knew I was part Aboriginal: 'Oh, would you like to come and see the cultural centre in Alice Springs?' I said, 'Yeah, of course I would.' It was really funny, I arrived at the centre and I tasted some food and things like that. There were Aboriginal dancers, two of them, and they asked people to come up and I was like, oh yeah, I wouldn't mind doing a bit of dancing. So this man, Aboriginal, could see definitely Aboriginal, and he said, 'So, sis, come up and dance with us?' and I thought he must know that I'm Aboriginal.

Later when I was talking to him and they said, 'Oh, Miss Australia. Oh wow! An Aboriginal Miss Australia!' I said, 'Oh, I thought you knew when you called me sis'. But he was working, of course, trying to be friendly, and was calling everyone sis. But because he called me 'sis' I felt special, like I belonged to their family, welcomed already and he didn't even know who I was, or what title I held.

We had a real great time chatting and then, later on, everyone had a chance to throw the boomerang or the spear. I went pretty well with the boomerang, but the spear—first time; I used to be really good at javelin, you see. So I threw the spear and this other person came round from the other side and said, 'Gosh, who threw that?' And they said, 'Oh, it was this lady', and they said, 'That's really good.' I thought yeah, I must have been doing this in a former life or . . . I've just got the swing from my ancestors long ago . . . I thought that was pretty cool.

Has anyone held you back from anything that you've wanted to do?
My mother, in some situations, has held me back in a certain sense, in a protective, loving way. My mum has always been so loving and understanding, when maybe what I needed was a bit of a push! Mum being so loving actually put all these inhibitions in my head, stopped me doing certain things. Funny though, when I think about it, Mum got me into a modelling course to build my self-esteem because she could see I didn't believe in myself.

The modelling course included the catwalk and photo shoots . . . it was the whole kit and caboodle. I never looked at modelling as a career choice because I've never . . . I've always loved chocolate too much. I did the course when I was fifteen. She didn't recommend it to me to get me on the covers of magazines but she could see my potential—I had lots to offer people. I just needed to believe in me. So I did the course for confidence. I ended up doing two courses and was fairly successful in both of them. I guess you could say I have found my confidence: I won Miss Australia. But there is always room for improvement because I still need to learn to believe in myself, I don't personally feel like I'm there yet but it has been a fairly huge transformation in the last eight years.

Kathryn as a young girl

What was your childhood like?

When I was little I would lie in bed awake at night and listen for Dad to start on Mum. Dad would go to bed at 9 pm and Mum would go to bed at 1 am, so he would be asleep. But there were times, once Mum had settled for the night, he would wake up and then I would hear Mum say, 'Stop kicking me.' He'd be just kicking her in bed. I don't know how hard, or where on her body, but I would hear her saying, 'Stop kicking me', and that was enough for me. A lot of the time I would go in, but by this time Mum would say, 'Just leave it, I can cope with this.' Other times I would just say, 'You're sleeping in my bed.' I'd be making up the top bunk for me at whatever time of the night or the early hours of the morning . . . or the couch . . . as young as five years old, ringing the police, running next door or running down to the phone box in the dead of night. Dangerous for a little girl to be outside on her own . . . it's really weird to re-visit this.

Do you want to go on?
Yes. I think it's important to tell some things . . . and maybe, hopefully, help others.

Dad was an alcoholic and that really has shaped our lives because, say, four out of seven nights he'd be really drunk and he wasn't a friendly drunk. We didn't have a lot of money so there was the resentment that he wasted whatever on alcohol, he just made our lives a misery. He sat and read the newspaper and watched telly; when he was drunk he never interacted with other people or his own family. Most of my life he was like that, but the other sisters and brothers have really nice memories of him, he wasn't always in a state of drunkenness for them.

I sort of kept him in his place. I was distant from him because he used to upset Mum so much. So, instead of doing homework, I'd be at the kitchen table, sitting at the table with Mum and she'd be trying to watch . . . like she worked so hard, my mum, and she'd only watch one or two shows a night—'Sale of the Century' and the news. But Dad wouldn't let her watch it, he'd be in front of her all the time pointing at her, but when I was near her he would be more respectful to her. So instead of doing homework, I'd be Mum's little protector waiting and ready to pounce.

He mentally abused her. Didn't hit her . . . a lot . . . but he did get the jug cord, the adaptor bit, hit her in the eye once and she had to have stitches. I once got hit; Mum moved and it connected with me, I had to have an X-ray. That incident surprised even me because he never usually hit her, never around me. I was the mediator, the buffer zone for my mother. My brother would just retreat into his bedroom because it was too hard and I think Mum felt better with it like that, one thing less to worry about.

He hardly ever hit us kids, never really, just pushed us and we'd push him back. It was just a horrible situation. Once we pushed him just because we were so annoyed that he was ruining our family, he fell and hit his head on the corner of our oil heater, which is situated in our lounge room. He was unconscious for a short while. As we were standing around him, Mum said, 'What if he did die from something like that, that was accidental, what would happen to you kids?' She didn't want to lose us.

We had to spend time in women's shelters, and on one particular occasion I was really upset because one of my brothers reached an age where he was too old to go into the women's shelter. Where would he go? What would we do?

I'm making Dad out to be this really bad person; well, I'm speaking the absolute truth. My truth: what I saw, what I experienced. Dad was weak . . . I'd written a story, just a page about how much I hated him, and last year I was tidying up and found the letter again, and reread it. After, I thought I should rip that up, that it is too painful and horrible, even nasty, of me, his daughter. Then I thought, no, I want to keep it, it's my memory of him. It was also part of my coping with it and, in a sense, my healing too.

He started off as a social drinker and you know how most people leave the pub and finish? Well, he never did, and he didn't even need a lot. So in the end he'd just be topping up every day. He'd walk down to the pub, buy two bottles, come home, play that patience game . . . cards . . . over and over and over again. I hated it, it frustrated me. I just wanted to shake him.

But, then again, in some way I can see why Dad turned to drink. You could use his life as an excuse, but why turn to the drink when he had a great wife and children? Dad had a fairly hard life. His mother died quite early into his childhood. He had to look after some of his family. He's been to war. He smoked a lot and then he got emphysema. When he died, I was relieved.

And yet, I hate myself because I can see a lot of him in me, and I think what I hated about him, I've got in me. You can't blame your parents though, because acknowledging that you've got problems is the first step to recovery. I probably am too hard on myself, yet I've got so much to do, so many people depending on me, and sometimes I just want to do nothing, or sometimes I feel like I'm lazy, and I hate it because I think that's Dad.

I can't honestly say I loved him. He was . . . I wrote this down in my story . . . 'Father–provider'. Provider is like this person who makes sure you've got a good schooling, food and shelter. And that to me is not a father, but he was a provider. I respect him in the sense that I had a good education, always food on the table, always had everything . . . not spoilt, well, material-istically, anyway! But always had everything I needed. So to me he wasn't a father, and he wasn't a loved one, but . . . I should always be thankful that he provided me with those important things.

I've always been able to talk to people about my feelings toward my father, not wanting them to feel sorry for me. I feel that I had one of the best childhood experiences, it's just that that happened. I've always been able to talk about the stuff that went on between Mum and Dad and the family. It's sort of like therapy.

If your dad was alive when you won Miss Australia what do you think he would have said?
I don't know if he would have said anything to me face to face. I know he would have been really proud and happy and . . . chuffed is the word. And he would have talked about it over a beer with almost everyone in Launceston and every taxi driver in Melbourne or wherever we travelled cause he used to talk about the boys and their sporting achievements, football achieve-ments, all the time to perfect strangers. So I feel he would have been, and is, so proud. But I don't know if he would have said

anything to me directly. Same as Mum, she never said anything to me directly.

Does she say stuff directly to you now ... ?
One of the biggest things was yesterday, I said—when I was making some phone calls, to the media—and I said, 'Oh, why can't other people do this?' You know, I don't have time for this but it's very important, and it probably would come better from someone else. And Mum said, 'No one else could do it or should do it because no one would do it as well as you', and that's ... I'd ... I was ... I didn't know what to do. Mum said that and I was like, 'Oh, are you joking ... you know'. She goes, 'No, no, that's what I mean, that's how I feel', and I was ... I couldn't believe it. And then I thought—I actually replayed in my mind the conversation I had to entice the media to come out—and I thought, I didn't do anything extraordinary then or anything I don't usually do, and yet Mum still rated me for it. And I guess I'm still thinking about it now. And, and if people are thinking I'm unappreciative there as well, Mum's just never been directly praising me, but I again know, and especially as an adult know, that she's happy with how all of her children have turned out and she's proud of each of us for different things.

Because of Dad's drinking and behaviour, Mum was never used to welcoming people into her life. I've got this thought or fear ... I guess it's really terrible because I don't want her to meet anyone else. Not that they will do the same to her, but I look after my mother—I'm the one to look after her. I'm the person who makes Mum happy. But then you think, surely there is enough space in people's lives for another person? But I feel that is a real challenge ... for me to accept that she could have some-one new in her life, because this person could take my place; be to her what I am. Being the youngest in the family, she's my responsibility. I suppose all the family feels that they need to look after Mum. Like, so many times the family has wanted to all put money together and get her away from Dad in her own place but she was too proud for that. She's got this big old Kingswood car, it's really hard to drive. 'We'll buy you a nice little car!' Too proud for that. Our mum deserves to be spoilt, we just want her to say, 'I've done a lot for my kids and I can see by their offers they are just repaying me.' But she's too proud for that.

Mum left school in Grade Eight, she was fourteen years old, there weren't that many opportunities in Western Australia for Aboriginal women. So she went to work in the local hotel in her home town of Kwolyin, Western Australia. A very small place, that's where she wants her ashes scattered over the rocks; I don't like to think about it, but if it's what Mum wants it's the least I can do for her.

So she worked in the only hotel in town as a cook and cleaner and that's where she met our father. I think she was twenty when she left WA. Just before my father came on the scene—he was fifteen years older than Mum—there was another man very interested in her, but Dad swept my mum off her feet. She was going to Tasmania to marry and live with this man. But her mum wouldn't approve of it. My grandmother didn't even go to the wedding. That old woman knew this man was no good for her, she liked Mum's old beau and she just wouldn't go to the wedding. Funny how old people know things, but I guess it was Mum's chosen life path, otherwise she might not of had me and we wouldn't be here today.

My mum's one of the smartest people I know, she'll watch 'Sale of the Century', for instance, and get almost every question right. And she's a good one to talk to because she's very objective. I'll come to her and I might have had a misunderstanding with someone and she'll let me see the whole picture. And that's what helped me to create that power of seeing other people's point of view, and not being so selfish or biased toward people's opinions. So she's had a huge impact on my life. She's my backbone, my

Kathryn and her mum

bone, my rock of Gibraltar. She's just amazing. She's taught me selflessness. She's just unbelievable, like she spoils me, she'll iron all my clothes, sends me away when I have to go somewhere and she'll miss me. And when I come home, she's done everything for me so that everything's fine, she knows how hectic my life is.

She's always been there, but I think we became a lot closer in 1998 when I was a participant in the Miss Australia Awards and that's because she wasn't just a mother anymore, she wasn't someone I just relied on, she learnt to rely on me. We became business partners, best friends, comrades, everything like that. And our relationship has so many facets now.

What's your earliest memory of your mum?
I don't know if I have an isolated memory of my mother. She has always been there, and I guess that's even nicer than saying my memory of Mum started at a certain age because it's just been; it's like she's wrapped me up, let me see the world but I've

always been in a safe place with her. She's the most important person in my life and always has been. Though she wasn't very . . . she didn't really give us cuddles and affection. I've often questioned her on that because I really like it, and I guess because I like the cuddles and kisses, it highlighted how much she wasn't into that sort of thing. I'd say 'Mum, don't you love me?' And she'd say, 'Of course I do.' But again that's another thing, she can't really say, 'I love you.' I asked her for probably two years about why she didn't freely cuddle or kiss us and say, 'I love you.' And once she broke down and said, 'Well my mother never showed me any affection so I find it really hard to.' So I guess there was a bit of limitation there with her, but I think she's really trying to get over it. I'll go over to her to give her a cuddle, there's no barrier between us at all, but she's still a bit jittery when it comes to showing affection, but we're working on that!

Yeah. I think love's like soup. You know, it's soup to everyone, but if I see love as chicken soup and Mum sees love as tomato soup, she'll give me lots and lots of tomato soup; but I don't like tomato soup, I'm always yearning for chicken soup. Both soups are full of nutrients, they're both hot, both served in a bowl with a spoon, but I want chicken soup, I like the flavour of chicken soup. But Mum doesn't know that chicken soup is my idea of love and, and, she doesn't know that her tomato soup is never quite enough. So she gives me gallons and gallons of tomato soup, but I probably only need a bowl of chicken soup. But that's the same the world over.

She's a wonderful mother, but for her . . . she doesn't seem to think that she needs . . . or . . . she doesn't need any accolades, or anything like that, and she can't take them. Or if she's done something really good and people say it, she's like, 'Oh, but anyone could do that.' I've learnt so much from her and she has learnt from me as well. Through the Miss Australia Awards she's learnt to send faxes, ring people who are . . . Mum's also got that mentality . . . I've read a couple of Aboriginal books, how the 'Bossman' and 'white man' is the important man, it's like Mum's still with that olden day thinking, whereas I've always seen everyone as equal . . . but now she can ring people—mayors, managers, whomever—and talk to them on level footing. I have grown so much through this experience, but Mum has grown much, much more.

Do you know where your mob is from?
Yeah, Mum is a Nyoongar from Western Australia.

We used to go to Western Australia a great deal. Always to the beach, I guess I remember that from the peeling skin. I'd usually just go brown, but sometimes you're a bit silly, you stay out for too long. I can remember that feeling of peeling skin and the beach towels and then just . . . hot, you know, the heat that stays under your skin after you've been out in it all day. It was so hot being in the Western Australia summertime. We've got over two hundred relatives there so . . . Mum's got a big family. I still don't really know each name for every face! And we're also doing family research.

Is your mum much help in that area? Because around that age group of your mum's, that era and earlier generations, was when you didn't talk about your Aboriginality, which makes it extremely hard when you are trying to find out about your past.
She doesn't talk about the past much; she used to. The family was poor, there were about ten of them. Her father died when she was four and her mother was a very strict woman who had very strong beliefs and was very hard on the children. One story Mum would always tell: there'd be a peddler and he came twice a year, he sold clothes to the families in the area. If the shoes didn't fit you still took them, you'd grow into them. And there was no 'I'd like a red sweater', if there was a sweater then it didn't matter what colour it was, you got it. Mum would speak of little

things like that. Mum doesn't see her brothers and sisters much as they are in WA.

Were you born in Tasmania?
Yeah.

Do you know what they call the Blackfellas down there?
Coons?

No!
They do though!

No, that's a person with narrow vision of the world who needs to take off their blinkers and get with the times.
I call them, I say, 'Oh, you Wadjalla', because that's about the only language word I know. That means 'white man' from Western Australia. It's not degrading or anything but I get frustrated with some of their comments so I say that with a little bit of bite to it.

Palawa. That's what they call the mob down there in Tasmania.
Oh, okay. Thanks!

You're a Palawa woman because of your birthplace and your strong connection to Tassie but your roots lie in Western Australia so your ancestral connection is to the Nyoongar.
Thanks for that.

What do you remember about growing up in Tasmania?
How cold it can get. So remembering how to get and keep warm. The warmest place in our home, it was probably in bed with the electric blanket on. No, it would be the kitchen/lounge room. We've got a fairly small house. Our lounge room is part of the kitchen. There's an archway, a huge archway in between, and

Mum's always out in the kitchen and Dad was always out in the lounge and the good old oil heater would sit in the wall in the lounge room and the heat flowed into the kitchen. Mum would be cooking, so it would be all the smells from the kitchen—she's a great cook. Um, my body shape is evidence of just how good a cook she is. I guess it's the whole sense of the warmth from the heater and then the stove, and then just the family atmosphere. So it all happened in the lounge room or the kitchen, so it was nice in there, on occasions.

Mum would have been in that same house for, I'd say, twenty-nine years. I think it was the sixth house on the street, and it was possibly the fourth street in the suburb, it's quite a big suburb now, Ravenswood. And I'm still living there.

Same bedroom! I've still got bunk beds, but now I'm the bottom bunker! There are three bedrooms and the master bedroom used to have to belong to the four boys, Mum and Dad were in the smallest room, and the girls were in the other one. Very small bedrooms, we used to be able to open the door only three-quarters of the way because the bed would be there and then we'd have to squeeze around that to either get in or out of the room, but it was still nice.

Are there any other siblings at home with you and your mum?
Siblings grow up and they have families and of course they move out. So I've got a bedroom to myself. My brother just bought a house for himself so I have somewhere else to go and sleep over. I'm very proud of my brother Matt. Instead of having an obstacle course to my bed, I'm able to put all those things in my brother's old room. It's horrible though because I don't want him to go. He's twenty-six and he would be one of the closest siblings I have, we went through all the stages of hating each other, you know throwing mud at each other, hitting each other. Hard, too! He's number six and I'm number seven.

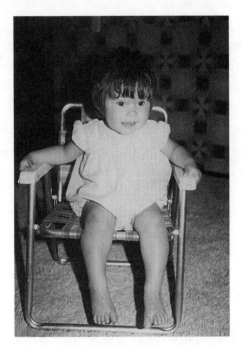

Baby Kathryn

I don't know how many times . . . we had so many fights and bashed each other with anything that was in hand's reach—tennis rackets, anything. If anyone were to attack my brother I'd stand up for him and it would definitely be the same if the situation was reversed.

What is your relationship with the rest of your brothers and sisters?
I was fairly young when my eldest sister moved out so there was only ever two in the girls' room, which is still my room today. My eldest sister is like the head of the family and she's really responsible, she's always there, she's there for advice and she tries to help you out. She's like another mother. My eldest sister is now a mother of three children so she's in a different role to just being my sister. I remember my oldest sister, I just love people stroking my hair and my sister used to do that all the time, but

now I guess she does it with her children, so the affection she exhibits to me now is different because of what she has to give to others. My relationship differs with each of them but we all feel fairly relaxed with each other. The family circumstances have changed throughout my life, we've all gone into different aspects of our lives now. We've built up a bit of a wall between each other because one lives in London and one's in Hobart, so geographically we lack a bit of contact.

You said before that your older brothers and sisters had happier memories of growing up with your parents, is there a memory from them that they would share with you?
The first five of my family have got different memories of their childhood than us last two. This memory or story they would share with me is before I was born, I was told this by my older siblings and I just love it, just a little story they would share with my brother and I around Christmas time.

On Christmas Eve, nothing would be up, no tree, no decorations, there'd be no Christmas cooking, no presents, nothing. But Mum would stay up all night, like she'd kiss the kids asleep, and then she would start her surprise for her children on Christmas day; she didn't have loads of money so she made do with what she had. She'd put up the stockings, fill them with some little things, and then all the rest of the presents were specially, lovingly wrapped. My brothers and sisters would wake up the next day and truly think Santa had come and just waved his magic wand. There'd be a tree, beautifully decorated, stockings filled, presents wrapped and everything perfect. All Christmas day she'd have to be working, working, working, after not much sleep at all, until once again she would bid her children goodnight and they fell asleep, content and happy from their special Christmas day. She would clean up and then she rested. What a mum!

Considering your childhood experiences, what gave you joy, like in those times for yourself what did you do for enjoyment?

I used to dance, as an escape in a sense. Made me feel really good about myself. Absolutely loved it. And I haven't thought about it for years and years until we're talking about it today, but I can see me prancing around, probably looking really silly but having the best time. I don't know if I needed to escape anything in particular but it was just . . . it was my outlet that let me be who I wanted to be, to express myself to myself. If you saw me play squash or tennis you wouldn't think I was that coordinated. I'm very much a 'flowy' person, not properly technically based but a good dancer more than anything. I would put the music on really loud, go out in the backyard, this huge square that is more or less just grass, and I'd take a scarf out with me and I'd just dance. And not like a normal dance, it was theatrical.

In the backyard you could see the road and people would walk past, so no doubt they could see me. Sometimes I'd look over and someone would be looking, so I'd run away for a while and wait for them to go. How embarrassing! I used to go out and dance quite often, I don't know if other people really knew what I was doing. The first time one of my sisters saw me she actually laughed, but she said I was pretty good. After that my brother asked me to teach him how to dance. Dancing was a really powerful thing that I needed. I loved the music and I really loved dancing. It's a huge part of my life—music and movement.

I had the passion for dancing way before I took on anything like gymnastics. I actually went really well with gym until we had to start learning to flip over backwards with no hands and things like that, it scared me a bit. And, you know, it's just amazing . . . I think back to my life and so much of it was held back by this non-belief in myself. You know, it wasn't just the technical side of gymnastics that was scary. It wasn't until I was to go down to Hobart to actually pass my Fifth Grade, Fifth Level . . .

You went to Fifth, I only got to Third.
Fifth Level in a year.

In a year!
In a year, but I gave it up. I didn't want to do something in this foreign place, in a stadium. I'd never been in a situation where people actually watched you. And you know, that is so sad to think that I'd given up something I really loved and something I was good at because I didn't have a belief in myself. And I guess that's how much my life's changed. I really didn't like being the centre of attention, but being able to stand up in a room and share a part of myself and take that challenge and that step, and be vulnerable. It is a huge achievement for me.

If I was to say, 'I look at you and I see you've got a "dash" of some-thing in your make-up.'
Yep. You know everybody says, 'Are you Italian?' I reply, 'I'm part Aboriginal', and when I tell them they always say, 'Really?' and I say 'Yeah, from Western Australia', and I give them a bit of a rundown. I always share that I am part Aboriginal. I've always been happy to acknowledge that I'm part Aboriginal.

Culture hasn't been a huge part of my life, I must say. In Tassie it's just not confronting. We're isolated from our cul-ture from Western Australia, so it hasn't had a big impact. But I still like that I am Aboriginal, and I feel that I am as well. I mean, if your friends can't handle that you're part Aboriginal, which is nothing to be ashamed of, then you're not even showing your true self to your friends. How short-sighted.

Do you think you have to say 'part'? Why do you put 'part' in front of it?
Probably because people don't know I'm Aboriginal so if I said 'Aboriginal' and then they wanted to know more I couldn't give

them any more information. And then I'd feel like I was letting them down . . . I should just say, yeah, I'm Aboriginal.

So how will you describe yourself from here onwards if someone says you've got lovely skin?
I could say I'm Aboriginal or I could say I'm part Aboriginal—

And what are you going to say?
Well, I don't know. If I say I'm Aboriginal, I'd probably say on my mother's side a few generations ago. And then I'd go on to say how fantastic it is and how proud I am about it or whatever. If I say I'm part Aboriginal, again it's more or less saying, I sort of still don't see anything wrong with saying part Aboriginal—

Well, what part are you? What part Aboriginal are you today?
It's probably in layers more than parts, I see your point though. I see your point, yeah. But I guess I'm still torn because of what people would expect if I said I was Aboriginal. Because say an Aboriginal community said, 'Are you Aboriginal?' and I said, 'Yes, I am', and then they ask me all of these questions, or how I . . . tangible evidence that I'm Aboriginal—

And they'll say, 'Where you from, sis, where you from?'
And I could say somewhere in Western Australia. But 'Where?' and 'What language?' and 'What words?' and 'What did you used to do?' . . . Nothing of my background is, is that way inclined to be able to answer them. I guess I know I'm not letting them down because that's just where I was at, but when I say part Aboriginal it's almost preparing them for me not having all of the answers. I don't want to pretend; I don't want them to think I'm pretending for my own means or anything.

It's a very fine line for the fair-skinned person but it's simply about being confident and being able to stand up and go: 'Well, I'm

Aboriginal, but my knowledge is limited.' That shouldn't mean that you're not able to say I'm Aboriginal. You know there's different . . . like in society today, we come in all shapes and sizes and colours.

I guess I probably think it's like if someone said, 'What do you do?' and I said I'm a librarian and then they said, 'How do you classify books? How do you arrange them?' and I didn't have any answers, I'd feel like a pretty bad librarian and I guess I'm likening it to—

But then aren't you feeding these people that go, 'Ha-ha, you're not sure of yourself, about your blackness'? They don't deserve anything. Isn't it like . . . so you've got a job as a librarian and you're work-ing your way through levels of understanding, like it's up to the individual to go back and find that knowledge to be the librarian. Okay, you want to be a librarian, you get out there and you've got to start at the bottom, you make connections, you learn, you read books, you ask people, you talk and then you put that into practice. I'm not saying that you've got to go out there and do a corroboree, run around this field in a lap-lap, it's about you turning up at your job and just being who you are and being confident with an answer: 'I'm Kathryn. Hey, I'm an Aboriginal woman. Yes, I'm very limited in my knowledge, but this is who I am, and this is how you accept me.' So by those people being pushed that, here I am, this is it, don't you think they're learning something?

I guess I've got to come to that point myself. You can lead a horse to water but you can't make them drink. People can say exactly what you need to hear a thousand times, but until your ears are open to hearing it . . . I'm just not quite there yet.

I was brought up very much with my black family around me and, although it only had a small amount of culture, it made a difference to my person.

I do feel a little bit like a fake in the sense that I don't know a lot about my heritage. I'd love to . . . and I know it's not my fault.

I don't want to let . . . or be a bad representative of Aboriginal people. Like, how can you say you're something and not know a lot about it. I'd hate to let people down by saying, 'I'm Aboriginal' and then I couldn't spin off tribe names and language and culture, because I couldn't. So I'd feel if I presume to be Aboriginal, people will ask me those questions, whereas if I say part Aboriginal, they sort of expect less, I guess. It's like, 'So what's your tribe?' I couldn't answer them. It'd be like I'd be letting everyone down who said they're Aboriginal. Whereas if I say I'm 'part' Aboriginal . . . you know, no one's ever asked me that question before, so maybe I will change how I cope with it. I'm Aboriginal and very proud of it but I lack the knowledge of my culture, I don't know a lot, but I'm willing and wanting to find out more!

That's all people want to hear, it's what comes from the heart and soul.

Did you spend much time with your mum's family, being Aboriginal?
Well, not in that, like the traditional Aboriginal sense.

When you say traditional, what do you mean by that?
Well, when . . . I guess in Tassie if someone said, 'Did you go over to Western Australia and spend time with your Aboriginal relatives?' they would imagine me going over and almost shedding my jeans and stiletto shoes or whatever else to much more casual clothes, sitting down in the earth, having like a bonfire and maybe a corroboree. That's what I think that they would be viewing that as.

Is that what you think?
Is that what I think traditional is? Probably . . . probably traditional, yeah, I think. But being involved with this project has challenged my thoughts as well, and the other girls being so accepting of me and who I am and how I live my life and the limited knowledge I have, of my ancestry, I guess has challenged

my whole idea of traditional. Traditional in the twenty-first century could now mean just getting together and sharing a meal and still talking and that whole love bit. It's just geography or it's just different clothes, or instead of someone playing the didgeridoo someone could be playing their guitar and we're all singing round, so I guess it's just different tools and different ways, but it's the same feeling.

So why can't you be Aboriginal and wear your Nike shoes, your Nike top, your earrings, your engagement ring, your lipstick, your eyeliner, why is that . . .
Well I can . . . I guess I've answered my own question. Being Aboriginal is not about . . . not just about what it was back then, because if it was just about the traditional life, the corroborees, the . . . the culture as it was . . . If it was just about that, then it wouldn't exist anymore. But it does still exist, and I guess it exists in people like me. I guess I didn't realise that I could be Aboriginal if I didn't do those traditional things but . . . well, I know I can and I know it's me. I can wear whatever I like and do whatever I want as a career, nothing will hold me back. I'm not in a mould, if I want to wear these shoes or go barefoot, it doesn't make me any more or any less Aboriginal, maybe in other people's eyes or perceptions, but importantly now not in my own.

But you know what I've been disappointed in myself about? In Grade Eleven there was this real bitch in Grade Twelve and she was talking about some black issues and she said, 'Why should Aborigines get this, this and this?' Suddenly something just stirred inside me. Why attack us? But I didn't have the answers. I couldn't fight her because I didn't have the answers.

But you have an opportunity to make a difference now.
Yes, I do.
When I was little, probably eight or nine, I said to Mum, 'I have to do something with my life.' She said, 'What do you

The black chicks' portraits were painted by Robert Hannaford. Here, each chick talks about how it felt to see their portrait taking shape.

leah purcell

'I saw the whole process and it was really scary at one point because I was watching the painting and I had to stop for a moment, because when I looked back at myself in a mirror it didn't look like me. I said to Alf: "I've got to get up, I think you've captured my soul in the painting, I'm not seeing me in my reflection in the mirror".'

rosanna angus

'I love the finished product; it's just deadly. And I enjoyed being painted but it was tiring. Man, sometimes I would go to sleep and Alf would say, "Go have a lay down and when you're ready come back". Alf was great like that and I'm glad that I stayed at his house because I got to know him. I felt welcomed so it was easier to sit for the portrait. I love it because he captured me, real nature way: that's me.'

sharon finnan

'I like the expression he has captured of me—he's very good to get that. I can really see me in the portrait. But it was very trying and strenuous to stand that way for so long. But Alf was great; he picked that up and gave me breaks. But I kept on wanting to look at it and see the process and progress.'

cilla malone

'Alf was lovely—gentle. He made it enjoyable to sit there and be painted, and he was crazy too when he did his handstands. I love my portrait, it's deadly and Alf's deadly. I like what he captured. When I finally received it I went around at home there showing everybody and they reckon it's deadly too. Nah, it was really good to get that done. I feel proud.'

deborah mailman

'To sit and watch my portrait take form was incredible. To see Alf work and to such a speed…but the detail that was forming on the canvas was amazing, to say the least. But I liked the fact that Alf spoke to me as well; it was like he was trying to paint through our conversation. I love all the portraits — I think Alf has captured this great strength in all the women.'

liza fraser-gooda

'I wanted to show the raw beauty of us black women and that we should be proud of our bodies, so I decided to go bottomless. But I added my favourite little denim jacket to show my contemporary side. And then, in respect of our ancient culture, I wore my traditional shark necklace and carried my treasured dilly bag. And my side stance for dignity. I often think that maybe I was a little too daring, but I am proud of the portrait and love it.'

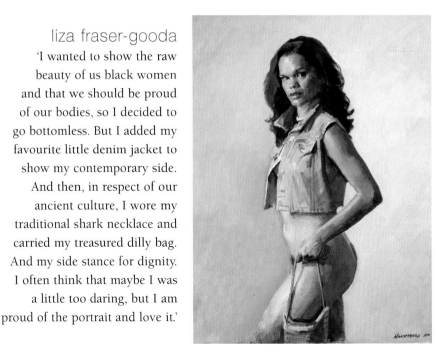

the portraits

'I love painting people and I love painting people from different parts of the world. When you study a face and are fascinated by them the way I am, or the whole personality, the way they sit, you can see so much. You seem to see into their background, their history, their everything. I love looking into someone's eyes and finding those things to capture on the canvas.'

Robert Hannaford, 'Alf' to the chicks, is one of Australia's most distinguished portrait painters. He has painted a number of prominent and illustrious Australians (mostly men), so naturally he leapt at the chance to paint these gorgeous women.

'I came to Sydney to paint the black chicks and was impressed with the culture and vitality of the people involved and of the sophistication that smashes all the stereotypes that we are taught of Aboriginal culture in this country.

'It was interesting talking to these women, personally finding out their stories and their culture; and seeing some on the journey of rediscovery.'

Alf painted some of the women in Sydney at the studios of Bangarra Dance Theatre and Accessible Arts. Deb Mailman had to be smuggled into the back gate of the Governor of NSW's residence at night to get her portrait finished because Alf was painting the governor's portrait at the same time as Deb's. Some of the women also had to make the journey to Adelaide to be painted in Alf's studio. All the women spoke highly of him. Some of the women found it hard to deal with a white man staring at them so intensely, but as the stories of both artist and subject unfolded they became comfortable in each other's presence, which is why these portraits are so powerful and capture the amazing presence of these women.

'I don't consciously set out to capture someone's amazing presence; with the women of this project, it was just there in all of them. The different energies and powerful personalities and their differences as women… And that all comes through in the paintings.'

rachel perkins

'It was weird to have someone stare at you for that long… we are talking a couple of days of intense staring. But I found the process interesting— another type of documentation. Documentation of yourself being captured in a point of time. Alf was a great fella to hang out with; him and his funny little whistle. And I like the portrait, it's just hard to see myself or looking at myself as the image. I'm used to putting other people in that situation.'

tammy williams

'Alf is very professional and has a beautiful charm that eases you into trusting him with his work. It was hard work to sit still for so long, but to watch and then see the progress of the portrait was amazing. I saw a photograph of the finished portrait and I was amazed at what Alf captured. I can't wait to see it in person.'

frances rings

'The portrait was very trying for me; to sit still is a challenge and to be sitting in my rehearsal space at Bangarra was an even bigger challenge because in that space I'm moving and creating. It was, however, therapeutic, almost meditative. It was the end of a busy year and it allowed me to reflect back on what was. I love the outcome.'

kathryn hay

'My dress for the portrait was going to be my red dress, but Alf liked the blue so we went with that. But it was weird because you think, "Doesn't this happen to important people? But, oh my god, it's happening to me". It was a proud moment. It was a unique experience. Alf was great. I just had great faith in him and knew that he would do a great job. And he did.'

dinner at edna's table II

What would nine black chicks talk about when they get together? You'd be surprised. Nine of the ten black chicks (Rachel Perkins was unable to attend) got together for dinner at Edna's Table II in Sydney and talked until the wee hours.

Eight of the chicks are pictured (Liza Fraser-Gooda was still in the air).

The chicks clockwise from bottom left: Tammy Williams, Frances Rings, Kathryn Hay, Leah Purcell, Rosanna Angus, Deobrah Mailman, Sharon Finnan and Cilla Malone (centre).

mean?' I said, 'Well, I don't know, I have to achieve something.' And you know what scares me? It's that I don't know what it is, and I know that if I don't make it I'll never be happy, I'll never be satisfied or fulfilled. I'd cry because I just knew I had to do something. It's not that I have to be great at sport or anything like that, it's just that something is out there that I know I have to do. It's like this haunting feeling and when . . . heck . . . when am I going to know what it is? Because how can I get there if I don't know what it is? You don't know the path of how to get there if you don't know where 'there' is. Scary feeling! It used to really upset me. I used to cry and cry and Mum would say, 'Look, you need to talk to someone, maybe someone you don't know.' I've tried that as well, but no one can help me. So I've just thought, well, that's life. Maybe it's here and now . . . those years looking for something that I should have just accepted.

Could becoming Miss Australia have been that 'something' that you needed to do when you were young?
I don't think it was, but it may have been the decision to enter the Miss Australia Awards because it has changed me so much. Winning has been a big turning point in my life.

Look at all the goodwill you have done, raising money for the Spastic and Cerebral Palsy Centres, making the Aboriginal people of this country proud. That's huge. You make a difference in people's lives; we need people like you out there, unselfishly working for others. There are not a lot of people out there who are willing to do that. But, you know, all the women in this book are people like that. I think we are special in our unselfishness to give to others. That requires a special human being. And to all the other special beings out there devoting their time to 'causes'—thank you!
I've been receiving letters from people of Aboriginal descent that I've never met before and one in particular, she said, 'We're so proud of you.' And I thought, gosh, but you don't even know

me or the person I am; but they have a belief that I'm a good person, and I've achieved something and it means something to the whole Aboriginal race. I can remember one article from country Queensland, they actually called me, 'Our Kate'. So they've taken on this ownership and I don't mind that at all. Someone sent down the clipping to me and that's really nice.

That's what's nice about us Blackfellas because, no matter where you are in Australia, if you do something like . . . deadly . . . they will claim you. You've got an extended family and it's fantastic, the show of support.
But they're so accepting.

We are, and it's nice to have some success. We want to relate to that and be proud. Positive reinforcement is so important.
It's a shining light.

Yeah. Showing that it can be done.
I think the shining light is a good way to say it because it's not that you're special in yourself, it's that you're shining a light that shows others the way, and it doesn't mean they have to be exactly the same—but look what's out there. There's opportunity for all to succeed. It may have been veiled to them before, but it's open to them now. And to achieve.

Do you believe in spirituality?
Yeah, very much.

Do you think black women are more in touch with that side?
From what I've read and seen, perhaps so, but I wouldn't say that I'm a specialist on that and I don't know if I could comment. But I feel that the whole Aboriginal people have, are renowned for, their inter-reliance with the environment, and not just their dependence or exploitation of it. And that's not

categorising all Aboriginal people or white people, because you can't do that, you can't stereotype anyone. But I do feel that we have a sense of belonging, with community values, and to the land. I often feel that, because I haven't really grown up with it, I feel I've missed out on certain things.

Culturally?
Yes, definitely, and I feel that a lot of my relatives in Western Australia feel the same. It's only now that people are going back into family history doing the 'tree' and wondering where we came from and it's now that people think, 'Oh, we've missed out on that.' But it's not too late to recapture some of it.

And do you think that was part of your goal when you were eight or nine, when you needed to achieve 'something'. Do you think that might be part of finding out who you are, so your belief in you becomes stronger?
Yes, definitely, because it's like when people are adopted, the majority have a very happy family life and yet when they realise that they are adopted, they don't know who they are anymore. They go and chase something they have never known, but they have to do it. Lots of people who are adopted want to know where they came from. They still love their people who cared for and nurtured them, it's nothing against them at all, and they still really love them, but they have to know where they came from before they can move on. So therefore I'm trying to reconnect culturally.

The spiritual ancestors work in mysterious ways. Do you believe they are working for you?
This may be the start to my journey for that 'something' that I'm looking for. I would say that I am open to it. Maybe the ancestors will show me my calling.

Do you understand yourself? Do you understand you?
Well, I feel I do, I feel I'm really in tune with myself as well, but then what do I have to do with my life? Like why sometimes am I 'up here', and other days 'down there'. Is it nicer just to be on that level plane and never really be 'that happy' or 'that upset'? I'm very up and down, very confused still and yet happy. Like a lot of emotions always going, bit of turmoil.

Where do you want to be in ten years from now?
Well, I'm hoping Mum will still be here. I don't know how I'll cope if anything happened to her. I hope we are happy, together and happy. She's been a wonderful mother. She's been a mother, a father, a whole family and she keeps everyone together.

Mothers do that. You see families fall apart when their mothers die. They are the cores and we all gravitate around them.

It's not until I sit and talk to other people and they talk about their mothers that I realise how much I miss my own mum. And oh, how I do. I would have loved to have bought her a new dress and been able to do things for her. To actually have a drink with her, I wonder what that would have been like. Take her all dolled up to one of the many 'opening nights' I'm invited to. To experience her delight in my success . . .

I had the pleasure in feeling that with one of my mum's sisters at a performance of the Aboriginal musical Bran Nue Dae. *Aunty Nessy came to see it and she was sitting in the front row. When I sang my song I sat down at the very front of the stage and I actually heard the conversation she was having with her daughter. She wanted to come up to me and sing with me! I saw her pride in me and that sort of stuff is something you don't forget.*

Looking at the future . . . the future is an idea in the present, so what ideas do you think we should be talking about? In a personal, community and national sense?

Oh, it's just amazing that you're asking me this question because I recently had to submit a story, just a few paragraphs, about my hopes for the future as part of the Miss Australia Quest. I didn't know what was really expected, so my mum and I worked on it together. I had read a few other Miss Australia's comments to get an idea and it was like, 'I want to do this, I want to go into this career, whatever.' Whereas mine, and I guess because of how my mum is, was for Australia, which encompassed the reconciliation, the acceptance of people's disabilities and also people from the different cultural backgrounds. They all encapsulated one in that I hope we all come together because how wonderful . . . wonderful . . . Australia is a brilliant place. What wonderful people, excellent things to do, so lucky a country, but how wonderful would our country be when we all appreciate our similarities and differences, and learn from each other. We value our similarities and differences in cultures, beliefs and way of life. But because we all have so many different things to offer we need to tolerate each other and respect what they have and appreciate it. Take it on board and try it. Be open. It's about how we treat other people. And I'd like to say that that's something about being Aboriginal. We all live together in harmony, there's self-improvement but we're happy as people and I think as people that's when you make the real difference to others.

I'm trying to make a difference with my home community of Ravenswood. It's not the best at the moment, high unemployment and crime, but there are people working hard to improve its image by doing things for the community. I have offered my services as Miss Australia; if they can use me to get some extra help then that's great. I want to help.

I think the youth and the new generations have a lot to offer, they have a lot of great new ideas, and a different way of seeing things. But I think as we grow up and especially after maybe having families or being married, then you realise not everything is centered around you, that there's other people relying on you and the decisions you make today affect others tomorrow.

Having a balanced view, living for yourself and your family but also thinking about others. Decisions made at the grass roots level and further developed at the highest point. It will be those who weren't thinking of themselves, but were thinking for the benefit of everyone for tomorrow's generation who make the appropriate and correct decisions. Like one of the biggest words now is sustainability and, you know, is it viable? I'm thinking really of an environmental basis—okay, we'll do this to the planet, we can get everything out of it, it won't affect us because we won't be around. 'What about my children?' Even those people who are making these wrong decisions will have links with other people who will be around. Although I think the young generation should be heard, and should be a part of future decision making, let's compromise, the elders know too . . . wisdom.

What now for Kathryn Hay?
Keep pushing myself. Be less down on myself and don't cry about things anymore. I still believe that I have to do something, and I don't know what it is, and maybe it will take someone else to show me. But I'm pretty happy with my life at the moment and what I've achieved.

I'm this person who is still learning every day. Who loves meeting people and learning from people. And sometimes I don't . . . it's funny, I don't tap into other things that I need to know, like street names and things like that, but I can remember a lot about a person. I take so much from meeting someone . . . unbelievable what knowledge, insight you can get from people. I'm someone who's really caring, sometimes a little bit too much so and I get a little bit hurt. But I'll keep on believing in the human race and keep giving out love and attention. Before, I couldn't really see a lot of good things about me, and even now it's hard to take a compliment, but I'm starting to realise that I'm a special person and everyone else is special in their own way.

I remember this woman who was present at one of my speeches came up to me afterward and said, 'Have you always been this positive?' I said, 'You know, I've always considered that I've been really lucky throughout my life, but this year I've really changed by winning the title of Miss Australia and it's for the better because I have pushed myself to all sorts of extremes and by doing so I have discovered a little more about myself and I have helped others, just by knowing myself.' And she said, 'Look, I'm going to go to work and I'm going to say everyone should just have a great day, because that's the effect you've had on me.' So that's really nice that I've been a little bit infectious in a positive sense.

As you can see, its life's experience that makes you who you are, look for the positive in everything and make it work for you!

Well, I caught up with Kathryn recently to see how things were going. We've had a couple of chats since the original interview and got to know each other better. She has made some big changes to herself.

So, Kathryn, what have you been up to?
Finding myself—there's been personal growth that could have taken ten to twenty years to discover, but because I had this challenge as Miss Australia it just sped up my discovery process. What I've learnt from being Miss Australia, I can now look back on, for instance, what I once looked at as something negative, I have now found positive outcomes for; from wondering 'can I' to 'I have done'; things that were so daunting have become just little challenges and empowering learning experiences.

From the moment I became Miss Australia, there were immediate changes: confidence, strength, power. There were frustrating, tiring and wonderful moments. I came to appreciate myself more and family and friends. And I've found the love of my life, he proposed nine minutes into the new year and I said yes. I really know what love is now, from all aspects.

I also hope, I feel, that people have benefited from my efforts as Miss Australia, and through this journey of discovery I have found my calling, and that is to go into politics. At present I am a selected State candidate for the Labor Party of Tasmania in the seat of Bass. This journey so far has been very encouraging from all people involved and I am happy with my choice of career path.

Has the family member who didn't want the secret of being Aboriginal out changed through what you have done as Miss Australia?
I think that they will have to go on their own journey of discovery to really appreciate what they have. But I have made the conscious decision to, and because I am in the public eye, to be proud of my heritage . . . I guess they have to deal with it. Maybe I was meant to be the person to shake or stir the issue. But this is my journey and I have every right to discover whatever I want and it's my decision as to what I do with it.

We have actually started the family tree, but it is a very slow process and we have sort of come to a dead end. But I want it to continue. You know, after the dinner [nine of the chicks got together for a dinner after all the interviews] and the offer from Rosanna [Angus] to go to her country and spend time, that's what I want to do. Her traditional culture may not be directly connected but it's an opportunity to get in touch with that part of me and to live the life, to just experience it. Just like when you go overseas to other countries you experience their lifestyle, well, I want to experience my culture here.

So do you still feel that you're a fake?
No.

When did that change for you?
Talking to you made me explore how I was feeling but probably not until the dinner when I asked the question—

What was that question?
How can I sit here with you all around me and . . . and you love me and accept me when I'm the lightest skinned? I don't know anything. Am I . . . am I not embarrassing you as a group of women, proud women who have all the things that I don't have, like why, why, how can you accept me? And they were unbelievable and I, I was crying and that was a big thing for me, a big move in the right direction.

We did. You still felt like that right up until that moment?
Yep.

And were you expecting the answers that the women gave?
Ah, no. I guess, you know, sometimes I sit back and think about how things come about and I'm amazed. Like, me saying that was almost like me sitting at an exclusive card table on a train in the days of the cowboys and Indians, playing cards and, taking people's, all of these people's money and then saying, 'Oh, but I cheated.' You know, I was coming out saying: 'I don't know if I should be here', but I was sitting at the table and was sort of in the home straight and I said: 'I don't know if I should be here.' I guess I didn't really think about what I was saying, but it had been on my mind for months, maybe years, and it just fell out of my mouth. But God I'm glad it did because now I feel so different; it's because of the people that were there and I don't feel that anybody said that just to be nice to me, I know they didn't.

Have you got one hundred per cent belief in yourself now?
No.

Why not?

I don't know. Maybe I will when I'm older. No, not one hundred per cent. I've really improved like out of sight to what I was, but I am fearful of the unknown and whether I can do things, or, if I can't, whether I'll let people down. You know, there's this weight on my shoulders which only I put there, nobody puts it there, I feel like they do but I know deep down they don't. I guess because I haven't done everything and I never will, and I know this, but because I haven't done everything, there's that unknown factor or element of whether I can or can't. And I think that'll always be with me, it's just how I am, like it or loathe it. Whatever, it's there and I can't sort of change it. I'm just attempting to control it, you know, this fanaticism with getting things right and doing so much and being so busy and yet enjoying life as well. I really am searching for a balance, and it's coming together.

Golden Holden

Rachel Perkins

filmmaker

RACHEL: WE WERE BORN and we lived and breathed Aboriginal politics from day one.

One of my early memories as a little girl was when I would get ready for school. I would have to sift through Dad's cupboard and he had all the placards and demo essentials in there and I'd sift through all this political paraphernalia to find my shoes and coats. It's funny the level of political stuff that went on in our house.

For me the 'Aboriginal cause' is like a primary motivating influence for me, so I'm thankful for it in my life because it gives me something to believe in, to strive towards, and it gives me meaning.

Leah: It must have been amazing in your lounge room at home as a kid?
Yeah, yeah, yeah. We used to have everybody there . . . every week. We'd get Chinese takeaway and we'd have forty or so Blackfellas around; it was just constant. It was Aboriginal politics twenty-four hours a day, seven days a week. The house was just full of Blackfellas, because it was Canberra, a big meeting place, that's the meaning of Canberra in Ngunawal. And the bush mob used to rock into town and just say at the airport, 'Take me

to Charlie Perkins' house.' They wouldn't know the address; they'd rock up and come and get clothes, have a feed and then cruise on. So we always had like carloads of Blackfellas arriving outside our house, 'Dad, another load's here!' So it was always full-on.

I don't know whether other people would have experienced that so much, but the amount of traffic that used to go through our house! And every issue that came up was discussed in detail. Whether it was the Tent Embassy; Queensland Lands Rights Act, trying to get that repealed; the Land Rights Act; National Land Rights Act; all of that stuff was the topic of discussion in our house, all of those issues of the '70s and '80s—we lived and breathed them. We'd have to watch the news and everyone had to shut up while it was on. So it was full-on twenty-four hours a day, Black Politics!

Did you participate in any of the demos with your father?
Did I? I've been to . . . gosh, more than I can remember. My job, along with my brother and sister, was to make all the placards; draw up all the placards; make our T-shirts, sitting around with red, black and yellow textas making up slogans; bringing out all of our 'demo' clothes; and then going to all the rallies. I've been to so many rallies in my life! There's nothing like a demo! Love the adrenaline rush for demos!

Any one in particular that stands out from the rest?
There are two demos that really stand out in my mind. The first being the Tent Embassy, I must have been about five or six, I remember . . . oh, it was exciting! We camped at the demo sight. Sleeping in the tents on the lawn of the old Parliament House, smoky tents at the Tent Embassy, and Dad mowing the lawn. Trying to make it look respectable! And then having to get away quick when the police came, we'd have to run. We were trained in that . . . 'Police coming, quick run!' And you do the bolt.

'What do we want? Land rights!' and all of that. We did all of those things. Dad would be up the front leading the demo, so we wouldn't see him, we'd just be in the crowd somewhere. Trying to keep track of each other.

Were there any really scary times?
There have been lots of demos where I've been quite scared. It can get full-on and violent. I mean when all the Blackfellas get really wound up. I remember one I went to recently, a couple of years ago now, we stormed Parliament House, old Parliament House, and they decided to storm the doors, to try and get in, and there must have been more than a hundred people! Trying to bash the doors down. They called the riot police, and I was taking photos and we all just had to bolt! There I was trying to run, doing the bolt and taking photos at the same time. I've grown up with demos. Love demos!

So there's a bit of a rush, hey?
Yeah, yeah! Absolutely! I mean there's such an adrenaline rush. It's the one time when Blackfellas really get unified together, at a demo. Nothing like the feeling of unity, moving together, fighting for the cause. But I'm a bit of a connoisseur of demos now!

The second demo that has made an impact on my life was the '88 (Bicentennial) demo. That was amazing. There were 20 000 people, this was just before I went to Alice Springs, and at that time I was about sixteen or seventeen. Why I went to Alice Springs was because I didn't really know anybody from there, and that's where my dad's mob is from, and I felt really strongly about all these social political issues but I didn't know anything about the cultural side. So at the '88 demo we were like 'Where do we stand?' in the demo itself. Demos have their own little structures of clans. There was the Territory mob, so we stood with them. I actually got grabbed in with the Territory mob, and I felt a real strong sense of belonging and identity, and that's when I thought, 'Yes, I'm going to Alice! I've got to find out about this!'

That demo was amazing. It was the true sense of strength and unity. I'd done Aboriginal studies at school and was destined to go on to do uni and do Aboriginal studies there, but I thought, 'Well, I don't want to regurgitate some white academic point of view about this. I want to keep my own people's version of it and actually learn it for myself, rather than studying it as some social political subject.' So that's why straight after that demo, I took off for Alice.

And how long did you stay in Alice Springs?
Three years. At that stage in my life I was trying to stand on my own two feet and didn't want to take a handout from Mum and Dad to get me to Alice. I was just trying to get up to Alice, I didn't know how I was going to support myself or get there. Then this job came up at CAAMA (the Central Australian Aboriginal Media Association) as a TV presenter. I was like, 'I don't want to be a TV presenter!' But I thought, at least I'll get the airfare for an interview and I'll get up there to Alice Springs. So they flew me up for an interview. I didn't get the job, but they offered me another traineeship in the film and TV section, and so I decided there and then to stay, and stayed from then on.

It wasn't my first trip to Alice Springs; I had been there before with the family when I was a small child, I did pre-school there. It was the time in the '70s when my dad got kicked out of government for being too radical. We had nowhere to go so we headed for Dad's country; he had been taken away by a priest from there as a young child and he felt it was a good time to go home. So we took off in this 'Golden Holden' we used to have. We drove from Canberra to Alice and that was when there was no bitumen road through, it was dirt all the way: three thousand k's. It was full-on summer, we were in this beat-up old car... one of them deadly Kingswoods with the round tail-lights.

The Golden Holden

It was forty degrees, we had wet towels on the windows, and I got chicken pox on the journey, and it was fucking hot! We had our big black dog in the back and he kept spewing up on us, it was a hell trip really! I remember just travelling at night a lot: the stars going past, the coolness of night . . . and then I remember by day just wet towels and the heat and the red dust that kicked up at the back of the Holden as it fishtailed through the red dirt everywhere. It felt like we were travelling forever, an endless journey, but for a kid quite exciting because we made our own little camp in the back of the car and would fall asleep looking at the stars.

Then when we got to Alice Springs, it flooded and that was a really significant experience. We hadn't spent much time there before, this was to be the first and last time as a family we spent a whole year there. So that was a bit of a blast after Canberra, and actually being there with the flood was a special time.

Why was the flooding of the Todd River such a significant time for you?
The Todd River's a really significant place, because it's the main river that runs through Alice Springs, which is where we're from,

Swimming in the river

east of the Todd River. So I suppose that's why it's such a strong influence because it's got such a sense of home and place to it as well. So to be there when it was full of water was just great. There's something so special about it.

The water is . . . is red. It's like red and thick because it brings up all the desert sand, it comes rushing through the country and takes all that's there with it. Mum, Dad, my brother and sister, me and the dog swimming in . . . just this redness. I remember just the luxury of it, because all that water in the desert is such a miracle when it happens. It's such an extraordinary sensation to see this desert full of water, and so much water! Coming from nowhere, going nowhere! Being amazed by it. It floods every year, and every year you've gotta put your foot in it. When it floods in town the whole town stops cause it gets blocked off. Everyone comes out of their houses and gets wet, gets in the river. It only lasts for like two days and then it's back to the desert again, so it's really significant, being from the desert, water's such a big thing. Even now when I go to places I've got to get into the water from that place. It makes you feel like you've been there, gives you a connection, I guess.

I went to school there for a year, spending time with my grandmother and family. It was a hard year. Dad didn't have a salary so we were pretty broke. It was hard for my parents but good for us kids. So that's my strongest first visual memory, of swimming in that river, all this red water, and of Alice Springs, I suppose.

Our place was situated on the other side of the river and there was this bush mob living next door and they were really poor. And then on the other side, closer to town, there was this white family. They had a swimming pool and we, as the Perkins kids, were allowed to swim in the white family's pool. We'd go over there after school, but on this one occasion we took the kids from next door with us. Then the white mother arrives home . . . this was my first experience of racism . . . We got in so much trouble from her for swimming in the pool. But actually it all boiled down to who was allowed in the pool—we were, but not the bush kids. And I remember all those kids having to get out and we could stay in there and I was thinking, 'Oh, why is that?' That was an interesting experience from a childhood perspective. When it's just all kids having fun in a pool, we as kids didn't understand.

Did those other bush kids understand?
Yeah, they understood that they were the untouchables. And we were . . . the accepted Blacks.

So did the other kids say anything to you?
No, I just remember that it was like, well, they have to get out and we don't, how weird! How wrong! It was a glimpse of this adult world where there were these rules that you couldn't justify

in your mind as a child . . . why? 'Why are these people not allowed and we are?' Where's the logic? And then, from that sense of disbelief comes . . . and then all the layers of social views come in. 'Oh, right, because they're that and I'm this and they're white, so therefore they have this upper hand and they can do this to us.' And as a child you start to make sense of it in those terms and that's what leads to social acceptance of those circumstances. Structuring of that social difference, it begins with little circumstances like that.

The kids that got told to get out of the pool actually turned out to be relatives of ours. We still talk about it today . . . and laugh.

So, when I finally got back up there to Alice I was at the age were I was open, really open, to learning and wanting to know about culture, so it was a great age to go there. I was seventeen. I didn't realise how much I missed the place. That bush smell, that smoky fantastic campfire smell. The smell of the bush mob from Alice—they carry this certain smell.

I've experienced it. If it was a perfume in a bottle you would call it 'nature'. It's a very comforting and protective scent.
It's a distinctive bush smell. After you have been out bush for about three days or so you pick it up too.

It's like an acceptance from the bush itself.
Alice Springs too has a special smell like those pepper trees. They've got those pink peppers on them. Peppercorn! Peppercorn trees, they're called, now that's real Alice. When I smell those, that's Alice Springs and I yearn for home.

Do you have any connection with the desert up there?
What I love about the desert is the silence. There's not a lot of sound in the desert. When you go out in the middle of the desert, there's actually no sound at all! There's just nothing, and

when you're on your own there's just . . . nothing. It's the sensual nature of the bush. I mean you don't even hear bird calls that much. It's just so hard to describe, you've just got to experience it . . . it's just . . .

Beautifully amazing. Especially when you see a kangaroo bounding off in the distance, you look at it and think: that is a weight hitting the earth at a high speed with a large force behind it and you hear nothing. Even when it is beside you, you only hear the loose rocks being disturbed. The ancestor just made things so right, to fit in with the environment, for peace and harmony.
. . . really quiet, you don't get that here in the city . . .

(As we sit on the patio of a hotel in Crown Street, Darlinghurst having this conversation.)

So you went to school in Alice?
Yep, I went to school in Alice. Just a year, pre-school.

And then from there?
And then from there I think we went to Adelaide maybe or back to Canberra or . . . we travelled a lot of Australia. Wherever the work was, in the deadly Golden Holden!

And did you like those times?
Yeah. Swag in the back. It was good, I mean . . . there were all these adventures and we'd set up house in a new place and it was just the way we lived our lives for a lot of time. I remember just spending a lot of time on the road. Distance. Dad and Mum shared the driving. We'd sing country and western songs everywhere we went. And everyone had to sing, otherwise you'd have to get out and walk! You'd know them all! 'Crystal Chandelier', 'Green Green Grass of Home', 'Freddy Fender', 'Charlie Pride' . . .

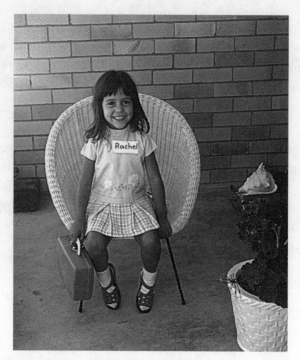

Rachel as a young girl

Are you a good singer?
Not particularly, but we were forced to sing.

You were backing vocals in Mixed Relations?
Yeah, but that was just for fun more than anything to do with a career move.

Did you all enjoy the sing-a-longs on the trips?
No, we all hated country and western. My brother didn't sing and I remember once Dad got so pissed off with him, he's like, 'You sing; otherwise you have to walk!' And my brother went like, 'Right! I'm walking!' We actually stopped the car, he got out and walked and refused to sing. And since then he has never sung! He can't stand singing!

Before Mixed Relations, I started singing with a band from Alice Springs, but that was just more for the fun and something to do, cause it's so boring in Alice Springs, you know it was just a muck around thing. And then it suddenly got all serious!

And were you backing or lead vocals?
Mostly backing vocals and they'd throw me a song or two. Much to my embarrassment! Yeah, but that was just more fun really. No girls used to sing in Alice at all, so it was quite a radical thing to do. Everyone thought I was a bit 'out there' really.

Where did you get your gigs?
We got gigs at the local pubs, but we couldn't get many gigs.

Why's that?
Oh, because we'd bring the 'dark crowd', as they say, so we couldn't get into many places for gigs. When I think back, there's only one venue in town that will let black bands play, black bands can't play in Alice anywhere. You'd have to rent out the local boxing shed or the local football hall yourself and put on the gig. So as the 'band' we'd hire these places and put on a dance. Once a week, pension week, so the mob could come in and everyone ran amuck. It was good fun. And if you happened to score a pub gig the bush mob wouldn't be allowed in . . . they just won't let them in . . . into the pub. So that was always really hard because you'd always have relations trying to get in, and you try to get them in and you'd have a big drama at the door.

Are you still singing with bands?
No, it's definitely not still happening. I mean, it was never a career for me. I love music and had a great time just touring around with the band and it's fun and they were like all my brothers, you know, the band. So it was more like a family/mate thing and we'd just go cruising around and play a lot of the

outback community gigs. Got to travel and see the remote places of this country.

Do you think by you travelling with the band, going to the small remote communities, did that open you up to more politics?
I think probably the political issues didn't come from the bands much. So, really, the band was like a bit of a relief. Just music. Although the band was quite political in a lot of its songs and the way we really tried to break through into town gigs and stuff like that, and trying to stand up for ourselves within the music industry. We got a lot of shit for that, as all Black bands do. I suppose the political stuff was intrinsically a part of it, anyway.

Although I was up in Alice having a good time, I was also up there to learn. There were two jobs that I wanted to complete while I was up there. There was the job that paid my way and got me to where I am today as a filmmaker, but the most important job for me was to learn my culture from my people.

I got thrown in the deep end. It was like, 'How do you hold a goanna properly?' I don't know! 'How do you hunt, how do you track? What's the proper way to boil a billy on a fire? How do you roll your swag properly? How do you do this?!' Just a huge set of social etiquette that I had to learn. You don't look people in the eye. It was like kindergarten all over again. But luckily I was at that age—I was young enough, I was into it. I learnt basic stuff to survive in the bush. Just really fundamental stuff.

Any of it scare you?
Well, I don't know about scare, but it did freak me out a lot because you're just completely unaware of that way of life and living, and I didn't know many people there, although many were my relations. But I didn't know who was related to me, but they all knew me, because of who my father was, and here I was! But people were really warm to me, because they'd say, 'Oh,

you've come back!' It was scary at times, especially ceremony business and Law. It's real serious stuff. During ceremony time, when you're dancing out bush, and there were times when I didn't know quite what the rules were or what was really going on, it can be really scary and it's serious shit you know! But you just followed the elders and didn't ask too many questions, if any at all. The singing, it just goes on and on . . . you go until dawn. And all night, and just that repetitive singing . . . the thumping on the ground . . . that clapping. Just being in a whole group of people just singing and singing and it's at night and there's smoke and the people gathering under a big sky blanket of stars, the thud, thud of people dancing by the firelight—it's very powerful! There's nothing that I've come even close to that's as strong as ceremony. It's just the strongest quintessential experience!

Do you have your own designs that are used in ceremony?
Yeah, well, we belong to a couple of Dreamings. So, yeah, whatever the song cycle that you'd be doing, you'd be painted up in that design. There are certain levels of understanding and I'm still so much at that early stage.

Is cultural awareness another sense for us Blackfellas?
Blackfellas just have this whole other spiritual sense to them, and I think that's what we have that makes us different. And it's connected to land and other levels of existence. That's hard to quantify, but is very tangible and I think that during ceremony time, it's evoked—that sense—it's evoked really intensely and that is what people might describe as religion, which it is, it's a religious experience—it takes you to another space and level. And I think that that's what really does distinguish it! I think there is a real tangible essence of something there that we all tap into because of who we are, as Blackfellas. That's different from white people, who live on this other level. But I think in terms of the deeper religious or spiritual experience, I think that that

has to be nurtured really carefully, and I very much see it as our personal responsibility. Like, it's up to every person to try and maintain it as much as they can, because that's what it comes down to. It comes down to you!

Or go back looking for it?
Go back and look for it, try and build it up and then pass it on. Like, it's actually every person's responsibility to try, and I'm very conscious of that.

I'd hate for those things that I've witnessed out bush, with ceremonies, the really traditional stuff, to be lost. Those songs have to be embedded deep within our souls to sustain it. And you've got to be able to sing those songs to keep them stories alive, to keep that Dreaming alive.

I started in the film industry about ten years ago at CAAMA in Alice Springs. Really my work has been politically motivated rather than inspired by art. I suppose the visual stuff's grown out of me because of the political necessity of making television, so the love of visual imagery has come as an after-effect of politics, rather than being the primary reason you get involved in the film industry. But there's a constant fork in my career path. One is the mainstream, and the second, recording the culture stuff with my family, is a pet project I have been trying to get started for some time.

To really properly sit down, like I know a little bit of my language now, but to learn all those songs in language, to learn all the moves to the dances and where they connect and to which country, and what the stories are is a long-term commitment. It is a lifetime commitment, but to even get the information that I need, which is my stories, my inheritance, is a really big job. That's what I went to Alice Springs to do, but I fell into film and television and it took me on this other path, but I still want to go and do what I set out to do all those years ago. But it's a constant battle, and then I think very consciously of, 'Well, what am

I going to tell my children?' I want to bequeath something to my children. Because Dad was taken away when he was young, so really it was up to us to find out about our cultural heritage. I don't know whether I want it to be like that for my kids? So it's a constant battle and . . . and it comes up in work all the time. That decision whether to go white mainstream studio way, or keep doing what I'm doing. Like being a black filmmaker.

It's about how you shape your life and what you want to do in your life. And what has meaning to you. And I see people who are successful in the movie industry and I think, well, what meaning does that have? They do another film and another, and they do another film, and what do they actually get out of that? They get fun and good times. They get to travel around the world, meet people blah, blah, blah, but actually what does that mean?

But as I see it, there's two paths and at some point I'm going to get off this path of commercial filmmaking, which is going to be probably quite soon. I've done the feature film, *Radiance,* now, I've done that so I don't have to do any more now and I can go back and sit down and do the oral history recording for a while. And my family all tell me, 'When are you going to come back, sit down with us?'

Do you think that's where your real passion is, with community?
Yes, very much! That's why I got into filmmaking. It was that political influence. Documenting the ceremonies and our political movement. Movies are movies, and films are films, and they're great fun to do and there's important messages in some, but actually there's this other stuff, the oral history, that's really important to me. It's about doing things for the community, doing stuff for ourselves, giving back to the community.

But regarding the professional career side, I also think, and my father would say to me, it is a continual battle about which to do, and he would say, 'Look! Not everyone can do what you can do. Like, you are in a special position where you can do this

Fox film, you can do *Radiance*, other people don't have that choice. So because you have that option, you should do it!' I'm at a crossroad at the moment; I'm trying to make a decision about which way to go. What's more important? But I certainly feel like, after doing *Radiance*, like I spent ten years battling in the mainstream as one of the only few Blackfellas going to the stupid SPAA [Screen Producers Association Australia] conference, the stupid AFIs, and all these stupid things you go to, to get further, and I feel like, well, I've done *Radiance* now, I can sort of relax and think about the oral history project. So maybe I will; maybe I won't.

Is there an interest of going into politics like your old man?
No. No. It's a hideous game and I don't think . . . I don't like it. And I don't like what happens to people because of it. So I don't want to do it. But you do get sucked into it, it goes with the territory. I am my old man's daughter.

What's the reaction from people when you introduce yourself as Rachel Perkins?
It affects me really significantly. Like Blackfellas, they always, as soon as they meet you they immediately place you. I'll say, 'Rachel Perkins', and they go, 'Are you a relation to Charlie?' And I'll say, 'Daughter', and they go, 'Right! Okay.' They're either going to love you or hate you. It can be great or bad because with the ones who love him then I'd immediately get a lot of respect and a lot of generosity because of that. And the ones that hate him I've immediately got to jump hurdles to prove myself to them. And with some I'll never get them to see me as a different person to my father or judge me as an individual.

Does that happen with many non-Indigenous people too?
Doesn't seem to be as much of an issue with whitefellas as it is with Blackfellas. Sometimes the whitefellas, they're like, 'Ohhh,

great! Charlie Perkins' daughter!' They think that you're some part of this black elite. Like I once had my dentist say to me, 'You know, I think really as Charlie Perkins' daughter you should form a black elite. You need a black elite.' I'm like, 'Oh yeah, mate, just do my teeth!' But I don't know how whitefellas really react, I haven't really noticed that much, as much as Blackfellas. I always get a big reaction with them.

And did you believe everything your old man said?
Of course! No, no, he had a lot of really strange views which we disagreed on a lot.

But as a father?
No, he's been a really good father. He was a very strong motivational force, really inspirational and provided good guidance. He would pull me up and I'd talk to him about something and say, 'What do you think about this? Do you think that was the right way to go?' or 'What do you think about that?' and he was really good that way. Both him and my mother are very strong that way.

How would you describe your upbringing?
We had a very protective upbringing. I know how fortunate I am to live in such a protective environment. Compared to what a lot of our people went through in their childhood. Drunks were strictly kept out of our house and we were really cared for, a nurturing environment but still very stressful in terms of the professional stuff happening in our lives. Both my mother and father, they were reasonably strict. Keeping things under control. My parents didn't drink or smoke and they were really strict about that.

Where did they meet?
They met at a soccer dance. Mum got dragged along with a friend. Dad was working on the railways then as a fitter and

Rachel's mum and dad

turner, but he told her that he was the manager of the railways, and she rang up one time and said, 'Can I speak to the Manager, Mr Perkins?' and they said, 'No, he's not the manager.'

She thought he was Mediterranean and then realised he was a Blackfella. But she really supported him and put him through uni. They moved to Sydney together and stayed in this church house that didn't have a floor in the kitchen and to get into the house you had to climb through the window; Mum was pregnant at the time. They didn't have enough money to get a key cut to open the lock. Like, they were dirt poor but she supported him, she seen that as her role. Like, she talks about that as her job, like, 'My job is backing him up.' And she's done an excellent job of it! But she ran the business side of things. Mum does up houses herself, paints them and redecorates them and re-sells them. Looks after my sister's kids, great nana, mum, wife and friend! Just a hard working labourer.

What's your first sight of your mum?
First sight of Mum? I can never remember these things when you need to! There's so many.

That's nice.
I remember being sick, and my mother and her cold facewashers on the forehead sitting next to me in the dark. I used to get migraines a lot. And she'd be there for that, her soothing presence, I suppose.

Yeah, did she sing to you?
No, no. Dad was the big singer in the family.

Mum's very funny too. I'm living back at home at the moment with them and my sister and her husband and the four kids . . . in this big house! All raging around! I think the good moments are when me and my mum and my sister are together. When we're all just being girls together. And it's really good moving back in with them. I left home when I was fifteen, but I moved back when I'm thirty! It's pretty weird! But it's really nice too, because now I'm actually enjoying them as people much more, as you do when you're older.

Does your mum come from a big family?
Yeah. Nine kids.

Do you see much of them?
Not really, no. I think about them but we've taken more the Aboriginal side, I suppose. Or I have, anyway. Mum always said to us, 'Whenever anyone asks you what you are, you say I'm Aboriginal!' But she's always been staunch that that's how we should identify ourselves.

She's a very staunch person. Like she married my father in the '50s when no white girls married Aboriginal men. Quite ballsy really. And I think for her to do that, like sometimes I think, 'Did you know what you were getting into? Did you realise the step you were taking?' She's always had that clarity of what she was doing, this was for a reason. In fact, it was my father's family that didn't want him to marry a white girl and my mother's family really liked Dad.

What was your favourite side to your dad?
I don't know. He was quite inspiring when he was in a meeting with a big mob of Blackfellas. I'd never seen anyone work a meeting the way he did, or speaking publicly. He was a really good public speaker and really motivational and really got that fire and brimstone and he could see the crowd being moved by him and he would give a little more. And that's when he'd be in his finest moment. When he was really talking about what he believed in. It's the ultimate. He had that amazing quality that not a lot of people have! And that's when he was at his quintessential best. But he was really very funny too! He was totally hilarious and funny. Big soccer player too, legend in his own time. He played soccer a lot through his life, but that was before I came along. I may have been to a few games as a baby. Dad was pretty good—he was picked to play for English club side Everton in 1957 for first grade with Everton. On his return to Australia he was captain–coach for Pan-Hellenic in Sydney.

Do you play soccer?
No, I would have liked to. I did play one game, my first and last, thirteen goals, but no one saw it.

True?
I did! Thirteen goals! True's God! Forwards, I played in the forwards. But only had one game, I was a legend for one game.

Was there anybody else in your life, apart from your immediate family, that you remember as being rock solid or somebody who was there in some way for you?
No. Our family is very close. It's a really strong unit and we are very much there for each other.

So why did you leave home at such a young age?
I left ... must have been when I was about fifteen or sixteen, actually. I left and lived in a squat for about a year, and then I went to Alice after that.

And what was the moment of leaving like?
Oh, I can't really remember, but I ... it was just sort of like ... you know ...

Were you rebelling?
Yeah, very headstrong. Didn't want to have my life ruled by my parents, and so I was going, thank you very much and I'm out of here—as you do!

I'm a strong believer in fate. And I think that things happen for a reason. Everything I do I think, 'Yes, that's happening because of this, and that's happening because of that.' So I think that things happen for certain reasons and you've got to follow those things through. And there are destinies and pathways that are there and you've got to follow them.

You are so used to being the one in control of interviews and cameras and things, so how does it feel to be the one being interviewed?
Well ... I must say I'm a bit nervous!

As a filmmaker what is the creative process for you? Don't rave on about it forever, but give us your insight.
Well, I start with something interesting like a moment or something that is of interest. And then piece it with visual references. Just remember images, like snapshots, images of things. The thing with filmmaking is that it's told visually, so you've actually got to visually connect all these pieces to tell the story. So you think of the moment, like there's a moment in this film that'll I'll be starting soon, where the mother finds the remains of her child five years later and she's going to put the bones in her skirt and carry the bones of her child across this paddock, that's a

visual moment. So I see the woman doing that, how she's holding her skirt, how she picks up the bones and places them in
her skirt. So you understand what she's feeling at that moment.
And then there's the music to go with it. You see it in your mind.

For instance, when we were doing *Radiance* I had to go to
the place first and find my location, to physically see it with my
own eyes so that I could imagine the film in that place. It's really
hard to write a film without knowing where it is—so that you
can plot what the shots are going to be, how it's going to look
in the landscape . . . So by seeing the landscape you then write
scenes around the landscape.

You've got to construct a visual framework for the film.
A film is a set of visual pictures, so a sequence has to be designed
visually as well as written. There's script lines, but you've got to
write the vision of the film that's in your head too, try and write
that into the script somehow.

How do you recharge?
I spend leisurely time with people I like hanging out with, you
relax, go bush, enjoy life and appreciate what you've got. Sleep.
Have a few social drinks with friends. Go dancing. Run amuck!

Up to the Bourbon and Beef?
Beef and Bourbon downstairs. Discovered that. It's good down
there! All the Blackfellas go there.

What are your weaknesses?
Doing too much. Not being able to say no, but, you know, all
Blackfellas have that problem. I don't know? Mmmmm. Acting
too quickly, not thinking, all that sort of stuff.

Just explain that a little bit. All Blackfellas have trouble saying no!
Well, for example, all these women you're interviewing. People
put demands on you besides having your own business and

personal matters, and you get asked to do stuff like this, so we take on the extra work; we're trying to save the world. Just doing too much. Like, at the moment I'm trying to finance a 4.5 million dollar feature, a 1.2 million documentary fund, a 1 million documentary fund and I'm writing the 'Black' book [Aboriginal entertainment industry information book]. I'm also setting up an organisation called 'ISA' [Indigenous Screen Australia], it's like a cooperative for Aboriginal Filmmakers and practitioners. So I'm establishing that, and starting up a distribution network for that, writing the newsletter, writing the constitution, negotiating with NIMA [National Indigenous Media Association] to get it financed and at the same time I've got my oral history project to finish. What else am I doing?

What does the word 'cause' mean to you?
Well, I suppose the 'cause' is a word that we don't use much now. It was a blanket term for a whole movement of a people to try and improve our life. And it covers everything, you know. It's just the 'cause' that we are born into and we struggle towards. It's a good word because it means a lot of things. It can mean anything from working on a radio station doing a program to try to maintain language, to giving Indigenous mentorship schemes for sporting kids, to building a pool, to making housing, and much more. It's a movement of a people towards improvement for our people. There's something different in terms of Blackfellas because we're all born with this motivation towards this 'cause', which is our lot trying to get justice in a whole lot of areas.

So I suppose that's the thing I talk about when I talk about motivation, that's where it comes from, that 'cause', I suppose, to try and strive towards things. A lot of people are saying, 'Why do you do this stuff?' It's all about that 'cause'. I suppose for me ... like here I am sitting doing all these films and stuff, but I appreciate why I'm doing this and it's because of people like Freda

Glynn and Mick Miller, who wrote the AEDP Strategy, which was an Aboriginal Employment Development Policy, which I got trained under, and it's only because he wrote it that I'm here where I am! And so I appreciate where that's come from, so that's why I'm trying to do the same thing—so that other people can benefit. Like I don't . . . like a lot of filmmakers, they go, 'I'm just a filmmaker and I'm just here because I'm talented!' Well, it's not! It's actually because all these other people spent all this time working towards the fact, the possibilities, so that you could do this! And I understand that, so I'm trying to pursue that movement. You know, people, they don't think, they think you're trying to do it for power or money or gain, but actually it's . . . it's about a social movement that you've got to play a part in.

How do you feel about the progress of reconciliation in this country?
Well, I think there are different levels of it. Like there's a surface level . . . like when we were in Wee Waa, now they've just renamed this highway the Kamilaroi Highway! And I saw it and just went, 'Excellent! I'm on the Kamilaroi Highway!' And I just thought, 'How deadly is that!' And it's just a surface thing, but immediately it places the country in a certain framework, that you're in Kamilaroi country. It's so small but it is a start of something that will acknowledge this country's culture! So there's things like that I think that we'll . . . as reconciliation furthers, people can more strongly identify with our cultural significance. Like, even the new airport, they're putting in a reconciliation bridge and they're acknowledging the custodians; they're putting a Dreaming story on the bridge that's going to be in the airport. So it's small things like that that actually make reference to our culture.

Acknowledgment is a huge leap forward in the reconciliation process. I believe it's a great start.

Is there another side to you? Is there a place that is not political?
Oh yeah! Yeah, yeah, yeah, of course! I mean, the political is the easiest and most obvious to talk about, I suppose . . . I'd just like to sit down and live just like everyone else! Not run around like a lunatic and do all these things; but that time will come when I have kids, I'll sit down then.

Has there ever been a time where you just wanted to say, 'Stop, I want to get off! I've had enough!'
In a work sense, yeah, because I've worked ever since I left school, solidly. Like, I've never not worked. So in a work sense, yeah, but certainly not in the Indigenous community development work that I do. I still really enjoy that, whatever it is. End of last year, I went back home to my father's country to help organise a big festival up there—it was great. It was the 'Yeperenye' Festival and it is all about the Caterpillar Dreaming story of the Arrernte people. Communities brought music and dance from all over Australia and we kept true to using local talent as well. It was televised on the ABC. I'm basing myself up there now.

And then there was the film project *One Night the Moon*. It's an opera, the idea came from a documentary about a black tracker finding a lost child. It should make for an interesting journey but I'm looking forward to the challenge, it's pretty heavy subject matter too. And then there will be a documentary series with SBS. And in between all that it's back to Alice. And to see those achievements made by other Blackfellas and sharing in their success!

I think that's what keeps us going—that we are making progress.
Yeah, absolutely. Yeah, you do get these little achievements and they are great, so satisfying.

So my decision to look for my identity and wanting to go home to my father's country and get that from my old people, I know it was the best thing I ever did.

Natural Woman

Rosanna Angus

community police warden

Rosanna: Being a descendant from my grandfather, who had a high status in the tribe, well, that gives us status as well. Makes you feel good.

I am a strong woman and I get my strength from my grandparents, my aunty, my mum, our family; we're very strong in our values and the way we think as well. Family values. Our family's big on our culture. That plays a big part in the way you think and behave.

Respect is the number one value you should always have, whether you're black or white. I mean respect for other people. Respect in our culture is important, respect elders, and that respect can only come down from generation to generation.

Like respecting my uncles, I have got to talk to them in a special way, like around them, not at them. Your brothers and that, you don't talk down to them or anything. They tell you to do something, you do it. You don't question it. That comes from customs, culture.

In our community it's really strict with the traditional laws and the ways of doing things for elders. I mean, if there was a group of elders sitting down and some young guys were walking past and they were just laughing, the elders would get offended and start throwing boomerangs at them, because you're not allowed to laugh around the elders because they think you're making fun of them. But nowadays people are . . . that sense of respect has moved on . . . different ways now, you know. Like, I teach my kids, if your uncle tells you something, you listen; if I tell you something, you listen. And that sense of respect will stay with you throughout your life and you become a better person for it. Like you, say your mum told you to respect someone the way you want to be treated as well. How you want to be respected. With respect it should go both ways now.

In our community meetings . . . I respect and understand that you don't talk down to the elders, but being a strong woman and one that has left the community, gone away for schooling and work, I have an opinion on things and I think they need to be heard. Most of the time the old people don't like this, but I say respect got to go both ways now. I give you respect if you give me respect. In the early days it was the elders who made the decisions for the people. Elders were right about making decisions. When we have meetings now the elders make decisions, but I tell the elders, you know, I'm not going to sit back and let you make a decision for my future, and the future of my kids, if it's going to affect me in a negative way. They don't like it, they don't like it, because there's a young person coming in and having an opinion. They say, 'Oh, you don't know nothing!' But still, times are changing and we need fresh ideas about the future of our community. I want the best for my children and for the community. The elders have all the right to make decisions about community things, but they must listen to the young people's views because if you want the young people to still respect, not only the elders, but the community and themselves, they have to voice their concerns.

My community is called One Arm Point. The population is about four hundred to five hundred people. Small community. But it's home for me.

Leah: You've been there all your life?
Most of my life. Just had to go away to study or work.

And where did you go to study?
For study, I went down to Perth to study. I was only about twelve when I first went to high school, so I was away for four years, boarding school down at Perth, and the first time being around a lot of white people.

What was that like as a twelve year old, going all that way from a community of five hundred people to the city of Perth?
It was scary really. Because, you know, you're leaving your family, your home, your comfort zone and going to a new . . . like a city is . . . a city is too big for me. I mean, leaving my remote community to go and study dozens of k's away, it was hard. I was homesick. Whole different style of life. Boy, that's when I saw the white man's world. We really are different people, in ways of thinking and doing things, belief and just everything.

So what made you decide to go to the city for schooling?
Well, that decision was made for me because there's no high schools in the community. So instead of going to Broome, I decided to go further. Mum decided to send me further away, actually. She thought I had potential.

I was Year Eight. I went to an all girl school but we had to travel by bus, a half hour every morning, to get to the school. We boarded in a Catholic boarding school called Pallottine Mission, in Rossmoyne.

There were kids from all over the Kimberleys there, like from Broome right up to Darwin, the Top End. They were all there, boarding down there. It was co-ed at Pallottine Mission, boys down one end, girls down the other, of course. On weekends we'd go places together. To the dams or to national parks or to the beach. It was like a family environment there at Pallottine.

Rosanna and her sister at boarding school

Did you get up to mischief?

Well, everybody gets up to mischief when there's boys! I actually got kicked out because of boys! Well, I got accused of sneaking out one night.

The priest... so funny! Father Carney.

I jumped off the bus from school one afternoon, I seen him coming across, we called him Clint Eastwood because of the way he walked and the way he looked. I seen him coming across the oval and I reckoned, uh oh, here's trouble! He just came to me, straight up, and he said, 'There's stories that you were sneaking out last night. I've booked your plane fare. You're going home this afternoon at four o' clock.' I was so depressed because I didn't know how to tell Mum or what to tell her. I didn't know... I didn't know what was going on. I couldn't explain myself because my ticket was already paid for. But I went home for a week and then Mum sent me back to another boarding school.

So were you guilty?
Sort of, I was one of the ones on guard. I wasn't the one actually in with the boy.

I was sent back to a boarding school in Mirribooka. It was
a co-ed. I was used to being around girls all the time. Then going
to a co-ed, I couldn't hack it. So I used to wag school.

What couldn't you hack about it?
I didn't like being around boys. But you could say I was a tomboy
in Year Eleven. But I used to wag school.

But why did you wag?
I don't know, I was shame for boys, I guess. I don't know, I just
didn't like being around boys in the same school environment,
you know? Because being around girls, being comfortable
around girls all the time and then changing from four years being
around girls to going for six months to be around boys, they
make schooling harder. I didn't know how to react in a class-
room with boys around.

So what's your opinion on co-ed schools?
Well, I'm going to send my sons to a boy's school. I don't want
them learning about girls too early.

Well, I'm sending my daughter to an all girls school.
I think it's a good thing. I mean they can focus more on learning, not on the opposite sex.

You know when you get boys around you get distracted.

*Yeah. Because I went to co-ed high school and was extremely dis-
tracted. I wouldn't have gone anywhere else because I was a hard
head but I managed to pull my head in and buckle down and do the
schoolwork, but I was still distracted. Murgon High ruled the South
Burnett.*

That's probably what happened to me, I mean, I must have been distracted, all them deadly Nyoongar blokes around.

I didn't complete my senior but I furthered my education through university. I came to the Northern Territory in '91 and I did a . . . what do you call it?

Equivalent to Year Twelve course?
Yeah. I did that to get into uni. So I was able to move straight into like my diploma in primary teaching. In '91 I did that.

You're a teacher? You can teach?
No. Not yet. It was incomplete because I had . . . we lived there for about three years, me and my ex-boyfriend.

We lived in Darwin for three years. My son was born in Darwin, Jessie. And I went straight out of the hospital, straight into the lecture theatre—just two days later!

Really?
Yeah!

Why was that? You just didn't want to miss out on school?
I mean, it was the first day, you know, I didn't want to miss out the first day.

Fair enough! That's determination for you.
I guess so. Straight out of the hospital with my baby. Oh, it was funny.

The baby came with me. He was in a capsule. I had him in the lecture theatre. And I used to take the baby to all the classes until I eventually got a babysitter, he was only like a week old when I put him in babysitting. But, like, I got homesick, especially with a newborn, so I went back home. Personal problems too, that I was having with my ex, so I left and didn't complete it [the degree]. We moved from Darwin back to One Arm Point.

I tried to come back this year to complete it, but I couldn't do it externally. So that's why I'm doing my Bachelor of Teaching, Adult. That's the only one that's been offered externally.

Excellent. So at the end of it do you want to teach or is it just to have the diploma?
Just to have a diploma. Just to say I completed something!

But one day I might teach, you know I'm not getting any younger, so one day I might.

How old are you?
Thirty.

Plenty of time, sis.

Would you ever think about teaching in One Arm Point?
Yes, I have thought about it. Because there's a need for more Aboriginal teachers in the schools, to be teaching our own people. You can understand better, the kids can understand you better and relate to you better. It helps their learning. But I do a lot of tours see, so I'm always around groups of school kids, groups of tourists, and it just gives me more confidence in what I want to do.

When you say tours, is that tours around One Arm Point?
They call me the Coral Princess—it's really the cruise boat's name but I'm the princess up One Arm Point—I do cultural tours. Like a couple of days or two-day tours here and there, just cultural education. To mainly wealthy, elderly white people or people from overseas, but I don't care how much money they got as long as they listen and learn. And they do, hey; they really get into it.

Where do you take them?
Sometimes we take them on the island and show them the old mission so they can understand how the Bardi people lived and

survived on the island for so long. We are probably one of the oldest families, with our family line going right back, deadly unna?!

There were five groups of Bardi people. Four on the mainland and one on the island. So there were island Bardi people. That was my grandfather. We've got land on the island, traditional owners . . . we're traditional owners of half of Sunday Island.

From what I know of the Kimberley region I could only imagine that One Arm Point would be paradise.
It is. On the island itself, there's a beautiful place there called Running Water. I take tourists into that because it's a coral reef, it's a bay. You have to go in with a boat and then there's beautiful white beach, then you've got a mangrove on the left-hand side. So you walk through the mangrove and then there's a big spring in there.

So there's fresh water, running water all year around.
Banana plants are there . . . plantains. Looks tropical.

It's surrounded by salt water, it's magic, I don't know where the fresh water comes from but it's beautiful water. There's a lot of variety of fish that we can eat. We're saltwater people. So our diet is basically seafood. And that's because we've lived by the sea.

Convenient, isn't it?
Convenient, exactly! Oysters, crabs, you name it, we got it. The beaches are covered in sand as white as white. It's bleachy white. It just hurts your eyes. And the water is so blue. Crystal clear.

Wow.
Lovely.

Paradise!
It is paradise, I say. Home is . . . it's a beautiful place One Arm Point, but people have got to learn to appreciate it.

You don't know how pretty it is until you go away and live away for a long time. Go to big cities, then you go back home and then you think, yep, I missed this kind of life. I'd never swap anything for it. It's so flexible as well. In the community, the work, it's so flexible. It's not like you work from nine till five. It's really flexible in how you work and how you want to work. You do your job, but if you wanna shut up shop and go fishing, that's okay too.

It's on Blackfella time, eh?
On Blackfella time all right!

What are you doing with your grandfather's land?
We don't really go back. I mean, we go onto the island to do tours and educational stuff, but we're not going to like actually move back onto the island. We just want to leave it as it is. Leave it to nature; our roots are planted so deep in that country, we just gonna leave it alone. We don't want to and there's no need to 'do' anything with it. We just need to know that it will be there for us and for our future generations to come.

So can you describe your community?
It was a dirt community, as in no bitumen road, but now we have proper roads. But it's like a five minute walk from one side of the community to the other.

The community is set out in the family groups. There's one group where you've got my family in a row of seven houses— that's my family. The next street you get another group of family and so on and so on. So it'll be easy for you to find me. Like, I couldn't live on the other side of the community anyway, because I've always grown up with my family group around me.

I'm very family-orientated too. We've got quite a large family—the Chambers family, that's our family name. But I make it my business to try and stay in touch with them, either by phone or when I go home. It becomes a bit of a chore when you only have a short time to see them all, but I make sure I see the elders, it's important to see the old people.

You've got to go out of your way to see the elders.

So you'd say that you grew up with a happy childhood?
Yes, I would say I had a happy childhood. I haven't come across anyone who was really prejudiced or discriminating. If I did I'd feel really upset, I've never been faced with that.

In my life, you know coming from a very cultural background going to live in the city, then having to work in different areas, like in the towns and the cities, I'm proud to say I've never been faced with racism.

If it was there you learn to avoid it, you learn to listen to your *ly'rhn*. My best friend in school was a white girl. She'd come to the boarding school for the weekends, and I'd go to her place for the weekends. So it was just lovely. You learnt, their parents take you in and you feel good about yourself. Not just you're black, it's about just being you. By going to that boarding school I also learnt to get on with all walks of life, from Aboriginal culture to mixed race mob from up that way. I mean, people are different, yes, that's how you learn to respect, and that's why that respect came at an early age for me. Respecting different cultures in our own Aboriginal culture. That's what the white man must also do. Us as Aboriginal people are multiculture, I guess you could put it that way.

You're giving the impression that you don't have any hang-ups about anything?
No, I don't have any hang-ups about nothing. I'm a pretty flexible woman. I go with the flow and I learn to adapt to different situations, and if I don't like the situation, I'll go. It's best to

avoid it before you get hurt, or before you get too hung up with something.

How many people are in your immediate family?
There's six. Six in my family. I'm the oldest of six. Three and three.

Your mum is Aboriginal?
My mum's full-blood Aboriginal, yes. My dad's Malaysian, pearl diver.

When the pearl luggers used to come in—and there was a big thing in the '60s, the pearl fleets—my dad was a pearl diver. He was the last of the hard hat . . . hard hat divers. With the helmet and suit. The hard hat divers. There's a documentary with him on it called *Follow The Sun*. So he's on that, my dad. He's in books as well, you know, for diving.

My father lives in South Hedland Community, South Hedland town. He's a taxi driver there.

Do you see him much?
If I take time to go down to South Hedland, yes, I would make time to go and see him. But other than that I don't see him that often. It's hard.

I mean I can go to Dad's, we go around there for dinner. He'd sit down there and bring out the curry puffs and satays and things like that; it's really hard to have a conversation with him, not only because we are strangers, but he's Malaysian and, like the way he speaks, I can't understand him sometimes.

Oh wow, that would put an added strain on the relationship!
But emotionally it's . . . it's very . . . hard.

Is he a good cook?
He's an excellent cook! Of course, I only go there for the curries! Dad, I only want your curry! And mangoes, he always saves a bag of mangoes for me every time I go there.

But I went there one time with my boys when they were only little and we were sitting down at the table and I told my children, 'You know, this your grandfather.' And my kids said: 'No, I know he's not my grandfather, my grandfather back in One Arm Point!' Because my aunty lives with a Malaysian bloke as well, like, I call her Mum, that's my aunty mum. My mum passed away five years ago. So my aunty mum's been living with him for about twenty-three years. Oh, even longer than that. So my kids grew up knowing him to be their grandfather. But I said, 'This is your grandfather'; they said, 'No he's not!' I think he was . . . I'm sure he was offended by that, but what can you do?

He would ask a lot about my sisters and brothers and my family. My family always talk about him in a good way but, like I said, I can't remember much about him. But my mum, yes, I can remember a lot of things about her.

Relating to the five senses which one do you like?
Touch, I reckon.

Can you remember your first loving touch from your mum?
Oh yeah, I can remember it.

I haven't got a really good long-term memory, but I'm just remembering the cuddles I used to get from my mum. Yeah, I can remember that. I was about three or four and we lived in Broome on Kennedy Hill at that time. Mum used to give us hugs before I'd run off to school.

What was the first time you remember giving touch to someone?
I remember when my little brother was born I'd kick him out of the bed and go and lay in between Mum and Dad, my stepfather. And I'd just sneak in there and just lay in there and Mum would have to put my little brother on another bed, because I'd always want to be laying down next my mum.

Yeah, why do think that is?

I don't know. Maybe because I'm the oldest in the family so, having all my brothers and sisters after me, I missed that attention from my mum, that one-on-one contact.

You've got other sisters and brothers to look after and you're giving them affection, but they forget you need a little in return. That's why I just had to chuck my little baby brother off the bed and jump in with Mum. Or I'd go in there really late at night and gamin cry at the door just for her to come and get me.

I'm an affectionate person and I like to feel comfortable. I like to touch and I like to hold, I like to be hugged.

I have two children, two boys. Eleven and thirteen. Bradley's a thirteen year old, and Jessie's an eleven year old. They're at One Arm Point at the moment with my mum. My mum's looking after them.

I guess you touch them a lot?

I hug them a lot, yes, I do. And I miss hugging them. They're pretty good kids, my kids. I don't have to use that other touch, smacking them, because they listen. Being a single mother is hard work. So, you know, they only grow up with one rule, but it's a good one: to respect their mother. I raised them up; their father was around for the first few years, but you know what it's like. They leave and it's hard. You have to struggle on to grow your boys up the way you want to grow them up. And I guess I did a pretty good job because they're very good kids.

So do they like to be touched?

No, my oldest one, no. He doesn't like to be held or touched or anything. But my youngest one, he's just starting to want Mummy's touch again. He's still a baby to me. I always call him my baby. And he'll say, 'I'm not your baby, we're grown up now!' He's gorgeous. When I'm away he'll ring me up, like yesterday, to tell me how much he loved me and he missed me. And I was

Rosanna and her sons, Jessie (left) and Bradley (right)

in tears! He had me in tears, yeah. I miss them when I'm away from them. I miss their touch. Because my youngest one, he still sleeps with me. He'll sneak into my bed all the time.

What is life for a kid like, growing up in One Arm Point?
My brother and sisters and I grew up mostly with our grandparents, because Mum travelled a lot. Even when she was around we'd spend more time with our grandparents. All us cousins mob too, we'd just hang out with our grandparents and every weekend we'd go camping with them. Every school holidays we'd go camping with them. For two weeks we'd just go camp on the beach somewhere with our grandparents.

You got any scary yarns from camping with your grandparents?
Oh, all the time! Plenty! We called this thing the *Liared*. *Liared* is a devil, kind of thing, you know? *Liared* that lives in the mangroves or just wanders along the beach. It's this white figure.

When we'd go camping out, we'd be hanging around the beach and if my grandparents wanted us near the fireplace or wanted us in bed early, they'd say, 'If you gonna keep muckin' up, the *Liared's* gonna come and tonight he's gonna take you from your bed!' And we'd just run and lay down and we'd all be asleep in twenty minutes, within twenty minutes, you know. She'd always tell us things like that.

Yeah. And did you ever see the Liared? *Was it real?*
It's real, it's real in our culture.

It's like the Yeti or something like that, but it is the *Liared* you know, and it's real but I've never seen it and I don't want to!

If we'd go wandering off on our own, they'd tell us, 'You're not allowed to go wandering on your own, because you know that thing will make you' . . . *gurringee* we call it, meaning stupid, you know. Then it'll just draw you to where it wants to take you, into the mangroves or to a cave or something like that, you know. So we have little *Rye* men as well, little men. They live in the caves and rocks, rock edges.

Isn't it funny, like we've got little men too. We call them junjuddi. Yeah?

Yeah!
But sometimes when you're a kid you have your own little *Rye*, and that *Rye* protects you.

Yeah, that's the same with our one, same sort of thing.
Yeah. Well when we go camping, the *Rye* would come out and it'd tickle our feet . . . the only people who could really see it were my grandparents. My grandfather, he's like a witch doctor, a spiritual man.

Recently I was coming back from fishing and the motor cut, ran out of petrol. The tides were high and there were actual whirlpools in the water. We have the highest and most danger-ous tides up here, but if you are a proper Bardi fisherman or woman you know how to work the tides.

Anyway, the motor cut out and we started drifting back with the current to one of the big whirlpools and the driver panicked and told me to throw the anchor over and I argued that that was not right, but in the panic I did it.

Well, while I was doing that he got the motor started and didn't realise the anchor was still over and at that stage it got caught on the rocks below. He just kept going with the boat, caus-ing the rope to be reeled off at a speed. The boat, it was going for it, and the rope started to wrap around my leg before I realised what was happening. When the rope ran out it pulled me over, there was nothing I could do and I knew I was gone, going to die.

There is no way of surviving those waters, even if you were Dawn Fraser.

I had hit my head on the side of the boat, knocked myself out. My family filled me in on the rest.

I was under for four minutes and drifted about ten metres away from where they were looking for me and when I did sur-face my arms were outstretched above my head, as if someone had pushed me up from underneath. I know someone did. I had this feeling. That's when I came to. Then I realised I was in the water and the boat was a long way off and the rip was behind me and if I'd got caught in that I was gone again.

I tried to kick my legs but the pain was too great—I had broken my ankle and there was blood. Then I remembered, on the way to our fishing spot, we had seen sharks here chasing tuna, 'Oh god,' I thought, 'I'm live bait.' So I just started swimming with my arms. They brought the boat back and pulled me in.

It wasn't until I got back in the boat that I panicked and then I went into shock and cried all the way back.

When I got home and into bed my grandparents came to see me. My grandmother told me the night before she had had a dream I was supposed to die. She saw that accident happen and I was dead in the dream. I was in a great deal of pain and my grandfather, being a healer, pulled some magic from his stomach and laid his hands on my pain and I went to sleep.

Before I drifted off to sleep I whispered to my grandfather that I thought my brother, who passed away a couple of months before, saved me. That night my brother's spirit came to my grandfather and told him that he saved me: it wasn't my time. The spirit of my dead brother saved me, that's how strong our belief is, and thank goodness, otherwise I wouldn't be here. My grandfather told me this.

That's my mum's parents. They're full-bloods from One Arm Point. Strong in beliefs and culture, you know, proper way. In the early days when people lived on Sunday Island, they belonged to that tribe, tribal area there on that island, there was an old mission on the island and they were looked after by missionaries. Then the people moved to the mainland. We lived along the beach in tin shacks; right along the beach until I was about seven years old, then we moved into our house. But it was good kind of living because everybody was together.

Do your grandparents still have the language?
They speak their language very well and they're both still around to teach us and keep us in check.

So do you speak any language?
I speak language, yeah. *Bard* or *Bardi* language.

My grandmother speaks the language all the time to us. But . . . because I went away for five years of schooling, I lost the ability to speak fluently. I can't speak fluently.

And does that annoy you?
It hurts me, it hurts me. We're trying to keep our culture alive and language is a big part of your culture. Language is your

culture. It identifies you and where you come from. So you should be able to speak it fluently.

And what about your boys? Are they learning?
It's in the schools now. So language has come back. Say they get elders come out from the community, go into the school, they teach the kids language so it's very much alive. They sing in language and it's so deadly when you hear it! My son will say, 'Sing this one in language', and I'll sing it in language with them because they are teaching me.

They make up songs with the elders. It's deadly because they . . . oh, it's funny! Like when we're cruising in the car, and, come sing now, you know. And all the kids will start singing. I will sit there trying not to laugh. But it sounds so deadly! I'm so proud that they can actually sing in their language and speak in their language. In school they have language classes. My son's pretty deadly, so I hear, in the schools. And when I tell him to say something to me in language, he gets shame, you know. But I always encourage him: you shouldn't be shamed of that, you're lucky.

Yeah, very lucky.
The strength of your culture and your language is so important and something to be so proud of. When I did a music gig in Alice Springs—the best gig ever, they love their rock 'n' roll up there— one of the women that I had met up there said to me, 'Where do you come from?' And I tried to explain it to her, but she didn't understand. A couple of them have come to the city for their art-work, and then this old woman, she said, 'I want to know what's your language?' That just cut me! I said, 'I don't know it.'
I guess language places you and tells others what mob you come from. But I've found my grandmother's people now and ran into a woman that knows my family and was very close to my nan and mother. She's got a book, them old people, they wrote down some of

the language on paper. Aunty Ruthie reckons she's going to give it to me. She said, 'We don't give this to everyone, but we're meeting with the old people, and they said that you can have this because you're a singer. And because of all the hard work you do.' So it's something I am looking forward to receiving. Today we are trying to reconnect and language is one way, but the hardest; some may never redis-cover it. I don't think it makes me less an Aboriginal if I don't have my language, but it's something that I am personally interested in and for me it will make me complete.

I used to sleep with my grandparents until I was twelve, thirteen.

Yeah, I slept with my mum till I was fourteen. I loved her smell, kept you safe.

It makes you feel good as well. Like if you're sick and you sleep with your mum or you sleep with Granny, it makes you better.

Yeah, I would sleep at the foot end of my nana's bed to feel safe. Even now I long for the smell of my mother and the soft touch of my nana, especially when I'm sick.

    Tell ya yarn now. I was twenty-four and I got the chicken pox off my daughter Amanda, who was about five, I think. She was over her bout of the pox in about five days; I was in bed for three weeks, I thought I was dying . . . anyway, I must have been going through the horrors, I was calling for my mum and all I wanted to eat was chicken soup, just the plain old watered chicken broth. But my part-ner Bain, bless him, brought me everything but . . . there was cream of chicken, noodle and chicken, creamy chicken, chicken and corn . . . you get the picture, so in the end if the can wasn't right I was just throwing them out of the room. I was that buggered I looked up at him and said, 'I WANT MY MOTHER!' He was so cute, he knelt down beside me and took me into his arms and said with the most heartfelt emotion, 'Darling, your mum's dead.' I turn to him and if looks could kill he was dead there and then, 'I know that! At least she would know what soup to get.' Poor fella, he was trying so hard. But it's so true: mothers know best.

Yeah, my granny be at home there now worrying about me, wondering what I'm doing in the big smoke! Because they're always so concerned when I travel around, they worry about me, so far from home.

So what do your two boys get up to there on the weekend in One Arm Point?

They go fishing. My kids love to go spearing, you know. There's a normal kind of life on the community where the kids go fishing on weekends. It's a group of them, get together and they go and collect their little brothers and their friends, and then they go off spearing down to the fish traps, or just along the water's edge. They get crabs and squid and just fish. They're pretty crackshot with a spear.

All done with a proper spear? The proper hunting one?

Yep. They make their own spears. They go and cut their own wood, strip it and put a wire in it and then they take off!

So what else do you do up in the community? Single mother, Bachelor of Arts for Teaching.

I work as a warden in community aid.

What is a warden?

Warden is just like a community policing officer. Just keeping the peace in the community, and just enforcing the bi-laws. Because community have different laws to the town groups, see, community have their own set of rules so we're just making sure that the community upholds the laws that they set—you people made these rules, we're going to charge you people under these by-laws now.

Woman in uniform

Are they pretty hard?
Yes and no. The trouble is the community don't know them so
we are trained to not only uphold the laws but to tell the community about them. See, it was community people that set the
by-laws in the 1960s and '70s. But I feel that the by-laws need
to be updated. I'll set curfews for the kids that hang around late
at night at the schools, so they can't get into trouble and things
like that. But that's basically taking the responsibility away from
the parents.

Exactly!
And, like I say, I love my sleep, and I'm not going to stay around
the school ground prying around there looking for kids to send
them home.

Fair enough.
    *Do you think that the community people need to swing the
responsibility back to the parents? Do they need to be reminded of*

their responsibilities as parents? Do they need to be educated in parenting?

Oh yes. But the parents know, you know. But as soon as you want to do something like ... if the kids get into trouble, and the parents are not around, they're probably at cards or somewhere else and don't care, you know, and like when we go and approach the parents, and say, 'Look, your kids were caught here doing this and that you know, like something may have been broken at the school grounds and your kids were there', parents say, 'Oh no, that wasn't my kid. My kid was home.' But the parents don't know, they was at cards. So they know, but as soon as the kids get in trouble, they're up us. 'Not my kid! You're always picking on my kid!' It's like, snap out of it!

It's a hard one to deal with, I think, for every community. It's something that should be addressed. For not only the children's wellbeing but for the future of the communities. We don't want our communities to become ghettos. They need to be safe and thriving, positive energy.

The kids become so bored and they think that their parents don't care, so if their parents don't care where they hang out at night, then the kids lose respect for their parents and themselves and they start drinking and smoking. That's when the harder stuff starts to happen, like petrol sniffing and other hard drugs, but not a lot can afford that stuff so that's where petrol comes in, because it is easier to access. This is not such a problem in our community but I know of others where it is really bad.

I was telling the community this at a meeting and one old grandmother come up to this meeting and she said, 'Oh, what do the wardens do? Where were the wardens last night when the kids were hanging around the school at eleven o'clock at night, swearing and carrying on!' I said, 'Excuse me! Do you ever think: where were the parents at that time?'

I just put it straight back onto them. See, only community people can do that to one another.

I think that's exactly what's got to happen: strong people have to stand up and voice their concerns. Too many people turn a blind eye or don't want to deal with the issues. You may become the bitch of the community but I bet you there are people there who would back you as soon as the topics were up for discussion, because they've probably wanted to say something for a while but are just not game. I'm pretty strong with my views because I'm a strong woman, so I make sure that my views are heard. I've got two kids of my own and up until the time that they grow to be teenagers, I make sure that they're home with me. But my kids are good, I mean they're home before sunset, so I don't have a problem with them hanging around school grounds, or being influenced. They're not easily influenced by kids in the community.

You're seen as a community spokesperson for the young. Do the young kids come to you for help and stuff?
I get on good with the young people, yes. We all sit around, you know, I talk to them. Give them advice, but sometimes . . . sometimes the young people in the community think that you don't care, so you've got to show them that you do care.

And how do you show them that you care?
Like, just the way I talk to them, and in the way I do things for them. Like, I took them for basketball, a group of under twelves, under fourteens and under sixteens. Like, there's two teams of girls and boys in each age group. Into town for basketball. I had about fifty kids. Showing them that I believed in them and it showed them that I cared by arranging this trip for them. That they can do good and achieve something for themselves as individuals and in a team sport. As in life as well. So I took them in to play basketball.

Did they win?

Yes. Our teams got in and to be winning made them feel even more special. They knew I was there supporting them, I was their coach as well as their organiser. I cooked for them and took them around. Made sure they got to the games on time. But just giving them . . . giving them a bit of time, showing them that I really cared made a difference in those kids' attitude.

So there's still problems in the community? Like with the young? Same old same old?

Same old problems in every community, anywhere really. It's because they're bored. Bored and their lack of self-esteem. So what do they do? They just turn to drugs and alcohol. Some kids start it at an early age. In our community it's getting better because the young ones, they're playing sports. So you get them into basketball and that helps. We have discos, like I go to the discos and I dance with all the young kids. So we just form a big circle and they just bop with me and so it's good.

Are there problems . . . like teen pregnancy?

Not as much in our community, no. We're all family in our community as well. We're all related to each other, so I don't . . . I don't see that as a big problem in our community, no.

So is there a marital law because most of the community is related?

You don't go with anybody in the community. You know who you're related to so you don't go with them, even if you're not related you've just got to respect them, maybe through in-laws way.

So if you want a man you've got to leave town?

It's like I was saying only the other day, I said if I want a man I've got to travel 250 k's! If I need to go and have a rage you've got to travel that far!

And what town is around, to have your rage?
Broome or Derby. It's not long that you can stay, just a weekend. It's only for two days but if you find something good, the trip was worth it; if you don't, well too bad.

There's a group of us girls, we'd just get in the car and say we're going to town for a rage. So we'd just book a hotel and just go and party all night. But never ended up finding anyone, partying too much and then end up being alone in the hotel sleeping with each other again. Gee, we could have done this back in our community. We even chartered a plane once!

It's pretty expensive but, you know, it's good if you ... like I say, if you're hanging out for a good time you'd pay the price to go in. Oh, we've got a nightclub, it's mad, that goes on till five in the morning. I'm always closing the doors there. The Nipon Inn in Broome.

Bit of a party animal?
Yep.

What's your poison?
I like bourbon. I'm a bourbon drinker. I love bourbon. I can't drink beers. I can't drink wine. I remember one time when I had wine, we went to an alcohol and drug conference! And I was our promotion officer! They gave me wine and that was poison. I was in the spa at three in the morning. I was terribly drunk from it. I couldn't handle wine.

And did you have to do any lectures the next day?
No, we had to go into workshop groups. I didn't end up making it for the morning session. I was sick. I was so sick!

You could have said, 'Well, last night I experienced ... '
That's right. That's what I had a laugh about the next morning, and they said, 'Oh.' I said, 'Yeah, just think eh? We're here for

an alcohol and drug conference and the representative was drunk! Couldn't get out of bed!'

Oh, you're a ratbag!

Is domestic violence a problem up that way?
Not a major problem. It's a problem when they're drinking. Not so much up home there because it's a dry community. It's never been a problem really.

Domestic violence runs through black and white families, it affects all the family and we need to put a stop to it.

My feeling from you is that I am not worthy to sit in the same room as you, I am envious in a respectful way... it's like you are complete within your core or soul. I've never connected with anyone like this before. Like I know you enough and that you have opened up to me and that we are contemporary women... this feeling is quite overwhelming... is that because you have a strong foundation of culture and connection to your land and customs?
My grandfather, he's one of the strongest tribal elders in the community. He's the boss man for Law as well. He's still alive. He's pretty sick at the moment but... you know, he's one old man who knows like when you have your songline and things like that for Law. I can't really go into it, but he's one old man who knows... like for ceremonies they've got to go and get him. To make sure that they're doing it proper way.

Has he passed on his knowledge?
Through initiation. Yeah, we have corroboree in our community still. It's very strong, our traditional ceremonies where we go and dance. My son was initiated. He's eleven, he went through his stage of Law, and my grandfather's passed on some of his

knowledge to him and to my brothers. It's always passed on through generation through generation.

And what stage is your boy at? Has he got other processes to go through?
He's got a long way to go before he becomes a man.

Do you think that's so important? Like for our people and communities to bring that in again, and keep it strong?
Oh yeah.

Like from where I'm from, me and Cilla, there's nothing like that, you know? And my aunties say, 'Well, you know part of our process to become women is like child-bearing, that's one sort of process of becoming a woman; there are other ceremonies but unfortunately they are lost, gone.' That's why I feel we are lost. We don't know our ceremonies and don't know our rights in our societies of Aboriginal nations, clans, tribes and mobs. The very few old people we got won't pass anything on because the receivers are not worthy.
I think it's important to keep the Law, especially the corroboree's alone, because it's a part of your culture. It shouldn't be lost, you know. It's been there since Dreamtime. God knows how long it's been there, you know. And it's true, for every song and dance that you're keeping, you're keeping your culture alive! And it's true, like you say, that song and dance keeps your spiritual memories of your ancestors alive; it's their songs that you're singing! And it's their story that they're telling through that corroboree. And how they dance and the process that they go through in the corroboree, it's . . . it's very important because it's our Dreamtime, it's our history.

It's a part of us.
It's a part of us, yes.

It makes you the person you are.

And it's a part of our culture that shouldn't be lost. I mean, it's only been lost because, like you say, Aboriginal people have been modernised. They're now living in cities so you can't really practise your . . . your corroboree or your initiation ceremonies because, you know, where you going to go to? A park or something? Unless you've got that land, that spiritual connection to that land, it's still where you dance. We have Law Grounds. That's why land is so important.

Law Grounds in community, where we have our corroborees and that, no white man, no nobody allowed to go there. Women not allowed to go to those Law Grounds. It's really sacred to the people. My mum's the boss woman as well; the community made her the boss woman. So when she goes down, goes into the Law Grounds, we all have to follow her. So we're still very much, in the traditional sense, keeping that culture very much alive.

There's a process as well. When you start off as being . . . like a secretary. You're a secretary, then you go through all these different levels to become the manager. Well, that's what the boys go through, you know. They start off as like a secretary, and then they go through all these different stages in life. It might take them ten years till they get to be the boss, but by going through the process they become better men. They learn that there's different steps to that level, it's very complex. It is rewarding because they have achieved something; they have worked hard and long to become a man and they can wear that title with pride.

Do all the children up there go through that? Or just certain ones?
It's the boys that always go through it. They start about eight years old.

What about the women?
The women are there as a sole provider. They're very important in that process as well. The mothers especially.

So were you there for your little fella?
Oh yeah! It's a very . . . it's a very sad time as well because you know they're leaving their childhood to become little men. Very touching time as well, especially when we are all crying, and all my sisters, they've got to be there for me as well. There's a real bonding thing as well. Not that we're not close, but it's another . . . it's a different kind of bonding. It's a spiritual feeling. Makes you feel good.

I mean, I cried when my son went through ceremomy. My sisters cried for him. My mum cried for him because he's leaving his childhood ways behind. But my brothers were the proudest people, you know, because they've been through it. Now they're men; soon my son will be able to communicate to them on a different level because he has experienced ceremony. They'd been through all those stages and now they're seeing their little sons or nephews go through it.

You've travelled a bit, so can you tell the difference with the men who have gone through Law and the ones who haven't?
Yeah, definitely. I mean, it goes back to the sense of respect. The ones that have been through Law, they've got a different outlook on life; they know where they are at in their lives. I don't want to sound like I know everything, or uninitiated men aren't any good because I'm sure there are men out there who have found other ways to better their lives, but deep down initiation is so important to remote, community, country or city Blackfellas.

I guess us urban or country Blackfellas feel that, but should that make us less an Aborigine? My partner's family are Stradbroke Island mob, Nunnuccal, but he was brought up with his white dad, so he never had culture or customs. But when he goes over there his family members tell him that he is doing his own corroboree with his briefcase and meetings, and because he is a good man and upholds family values they say he goes through his process by achieving great stuff in his work.

I reckon that every time I do my one-woman show Box the Pony: that's my corroboree. That's my Dreaming and that's my story that I will pass on to my daughter. I would love her to perform it at some stage and add her story onto it. I know every time I perform that I become strong as an individual and all the positive feedback I get from other people who I have helped along the way, and even the negative stuff, makes you stronger. I was told in a dream that I needed to dance more, so I added more dancing to the play and people say that's what takes it to the next level and I know that I am working for my ancient spiritual ancestors. I call on the care-taker of this land Pamanyungan, Australia, when I need guidance and direction and I know if I was not a good person then I would not be having such great fortune. So I think that we too can create our own ceremony and be connected to the land we call home and make our spirit strong by simply giving and respecting all things.

There's that spiritual connection and knowing who you are—And where you're coming from—which helps you to make the right decisions. But it's about reconnecting again. Reconnecting to who . . . and from in here [Rosanna touches her chest over her heart]. Get back to your old people. Talk to them about the old stories, keep that alive. Put it into books. Talk about it more. Make that feeling come alive again. I've been through the cities where a lot of Aboriginal people are . . . it's not their fault that they've lost their culture in some ways. A big part of it has been taken away from you mob, and that's . . . and that's sad.

You just got to get those beliefs back, bring them to life and pray to our ancient spiritual ancestors for guidance. We were here long before Christianity, we got our own higher beings.

Do you believe in recording certain cultural or traditional things?
Not really, because there's things in certain cultures that other people shouldn't know about. Like, it's for that mob alone. For

my culture there's things that I shouldn't even talk about, because it belongs to us. Only for Bardi people, you know? It's good to share the value system of tradition and culture, to let people know that it's important, but other than that within your own culture, you should not be documenting things. We have to keep it documented old ways and that's orally and must stay within the men, or stay within the women. Keeping that spirituality alive.

Get back, get back your culture. You know, it's not too late, you know.

I mean, just because you live in the city, there's still stories about this place.

Like when I travelled to Sydney last time, there was a tour guide on the bus and he was talking about the birthing areas of certain women, and talking about where their communities were once, now you've got a big shopping mall or something that's been built on it. And I was so sad, you know. Because the Aboriginal people of this area didn't have . . . no say, really, in how their own community is going to be shaped and developed.

So land rights is quite an important issue really, isn't it?
Yes, it's very important. Like, in our community, we're lucky because we didn't have that impact of white settlement . . . as the Aborigines in the city have. Like I say, they were stripped of their land and culture and, you know, replaced with all these big buildings now that you've got here and they call . . . that's white man's culture. That's not your culture. But with us, we've still got our land. We've still got our culture, and that's so important for identity, for knowing where you are, for ceremonies, so our men can be men—so they have their role in society, not only Blackfellas' world but to have that diginity to walk and hold his head up high in the white man's world . . . we don't have that if we don't have our Law Grounds. That's why we're fighting for land rights. And like white man would say, 'Why . . . why, why

are you fighting for your land?' Well, we're fighting for our land because we don't want you people to come and develop on it! To rip the guts out of mother earth and scar her, all for progress and money, and that's very sad. Tradition areas and Law Grounds and birthing places, we want to keep it as it is. How our ancestors remembered it. And how our kids are going to remember it in the future.

I never, ever thought of it like that, as you have just said it, but now I understand.
Ceremonial place, it's a spiritual place as well for Aboriginal people to come together, to share that spiritual bonding with each other. Especially the men. And the women. When we walk away from the Law Grounds, we don't go back on there, we don't look back on to it until the next time we have our ceremonies. In our community, when you're growing up, people learn to respect that. You don't go there, that's the Law Grounds.

Like one time there's . . . oh it's sad. We had a nurse . . . I don't know if you should really talk about this, but there was a nurse in the community . . . like every white person that come into our community, we always tell them when Law ceremonies on, you learn to respect them and you stay away. You don't go into this area, you don't go into that area. They get updated on what's going on here or there. But one time that nurse she jumped on a horse, went into the Law Grounds, and since then she's never been the same. She's been affected by it. She's retarded, looks retarded now. My uncle found her. She was frothing in the mouth and eyes were bloodshot, and we don't . . . like even as Aboriginal people, we're frightened of the Law Grounds! We know that it's got that spiritual strength and presence there; when them old people say, 'Don't go there', you don't go there! But I don't know, she went there and it affected her. That's why it frightens a lot of people who come into our area. Our Law is so strong.

Some black people don't understand how strong Aboriginal Law is.

I went to another area, like you say, you talk about respect, so in Aboriginal culture you've got different kinds of Aboriginal customs and beliefs because of all the different tribes and clans etc. Aboriginal people everywhere learn to respect their Aboriginality and the other mobs' beliefs. They have their ways, and their stories and their Dreamtime, because you've got the saltwater people, the riverside people and then the desert people. Desert Law is still very strong, right, and so is riverside and so is saltwater.

The Fitzroy Crossing area, they're still very strong in their culture as well. I went out there on a tour, I had my tourism student and my mum as well, so we went to the Gibb River where *Wandjin* . . . you know, the legend of *Pideon,* he was a warrior, an Aboriginal warrior; but it was in the Fitzroy Crossing area where he was hunted down and shot. That's pretty interesting that story. But we went up to those areas and when we got there my mum, we felt this really . . . like, connection to that place.

This is really strong—like we say we're feeling from in here our *ly'rhn* [Rosanna touches her chest over her heart]. I went up to have a look at this Aboriginal art on the rocks, and I'd never seen Aboriginal rock art before. And we went up to the rock, it was like that art was drawing me to the place, I was seeing marks that the ranger had never ever seen in all the years he'd been working around that area.

Then it showed itself for me. I would look up and like every place I looked it was there, it was just drawing me to have a look at certain parts of the rock. Every time I looked way up I'd see little figures, and I asked the ranger, 'Have you ever seen these things before?' And he goes, 'No, I've been the ranger for ten years. I've never seen that.' That 'thing' drew me to a certain part of the rock and made me . . . I went to one area and I stood there and I reckon, 'No, it's not here.' I felt like it was wanting me to look at something and I reckon, no, it's not here. So I went back to another part of the rock and I stood there and I said, 'It's here!' And I looked straight up and there was a massive snake painted on the rock, and he goes, 'I've never seen that before.'

It just showed itself more clearly and that ranger's been going there for years and years, he'd never seen it. Like, I was crying because I had a different connection to that place. It was like it was a birthing ground as well, I was in tears. I didn't want to cry but it was just the feelings—all beautiful. And I told the story to one of the people on a tourist trip I was doing, on my cultural tour, and she was crying.

I know what you mean when you visit places like that, if you have that special awareness to spirituality then you feel it big time. Whitefellas too, you know?
Aboriginal spirituality is very powerful in every which way. It just depends on how you use your sixth sense. How you connect to it. I think it will guide you. Trust it.

Is there a sixth sense?
Aboriginal people have a natural sixth sense, I believe, anyway. You know, we're spiritual people, so that sense comes from deeper than us. And that feeling of . . . it's just natural. I mean, it's like intuition, it's something . . . it's natural to us. We call it our *ly'rhn*, it comes from within here, our heart. It comes from the heart. I mean, you think through your head; some people don't think about things, they feel it. It feels right to do it, instead of you think it's right to do it. But it feels right. It's just a way of guiding yourself as well. Know your *ly'rhn*. When you get into a situation you might think, should I do it? Then your *ly'rhn* says, yeah, do it! It's like a gut feeling of whether it's right or wrong. And then you feel it and you're thinking, yeah, I'm going to do it. You go with it if the feeling's right and you know it's the

right decision that you're making whether or not to do something. We lived with this sense for centuries.

And, by calling it a name, you can accept that there is a sixth sense. When you talk to people and say the words 'gut feeling' or 'instinct', they think that you're on some new age trip, but to give it a word and know that our culture has been acknowledging this sense for centuries is so empowering. I am quite excited that I now have the word for what I live by. We have a sixth sense called 'ly'rhn'! Excellent!!

Do you think the . . . like the non-Indigenous people should . . . do you think they listen to their ly'rhn?
No, I think they think straight from their head. Comes straight from within here [Rosanna touches her head]. They don't 'feel' about what their actions could do to people. Just think about our wildlife, rainforests, rivers and land scarred by mining.

And have you followed your ly'rhn *. . . throughout your life?*
All the time. You learn to develop that connection and to trust your sixth sense. Trust within yourself.

Do you pick up on other people's ly'rhn?
Yeah, all the time!

How did you feel when you came here for this?
I felt good! Because you met me at your front gate. You made me feel real good, you know. Like, I mean, if I didn't feel good about things, you'd probably wait in the house for me to come and I wouldn't feel good about being here, but I felt comfortable. The minute I saw you, and like with Bain . . .

Yeah, he's got a ly'rhn, *eh?*
Yeah, definitely. You can feel it.

What do you think about mining?

I guess if you have traditional claim on your land then your community can benefit from the profits of sale. But they're ripping up our land. People have different points of view on this. When you dig into the land, you're taking out things that Aboriginal people connect to. Like those minerals and things that the trees live off, that the earth makes ... what the earth has made so that we as humans can live here, what makes this earth go around. If I took your heart out, if your heart was removed from your body and someone put another heart in there, it wouldn't be you again. It wouldn't be the same you. You'd have to adapt to that new heart, it's a new replace ... it's something different. I said mining is like ripping out the heart from mother earth. You're taking out all the minerals from the land, to only make bombs, or steel, to only start wars or build more concrete jungles.

They're doing wrong with it, with the goodness that mother earth has provided. These mining sites leave a deep hole like a boil on your body, that takes its time to heal, but it leaves a scar and that scar is numb, you have no feeling there, and that's what mother earth has to deal with. We are just hacking into her; the pain she goes through. Sometimes I think I wouldn't blame her if she said enough is enough, and put an end to this greed-driven race.

The land's never going to be the same again. You could replace it with more sand, grow more trees on it, but it's never going to be the same.

I live off the land and still practise our beliefs ... oh, it's frustrating!

I'm sad how things like ... progress, they call that. And the Aboriginal people got no say in what's happening. I don't know, it's just a big political arena now for everybody. That's why I'm happy to live in my own little community.

Community is so important, even if it's in the country or city. We all need to be involved a little more. Even if that is just to know your neighbourhood.

There's politics involved there in our own communities, but not as major as the outside world and I'm happy to deal with and heal our own problems.

There's always room for compromise in everything, it's whether the other parties want to.

In your community do you reckon you're going to become boss woman?

Oh, well, they'd be sorry then if I became boss woman! Like, they say, 'Why don't you run for council?' I said, 'If I run for council, everybody will be sorry!' What decisions we make as a council, I back them up, you know? And I'm really strong and firm on that. Don't go back on your word! I'm very straightforward.

Would that be something you'd like to do in the future?

If someone voted me in and if my time came, like you say, there's always a right time for doing things. If it's meant to happen, it will happen. And then it will be the right time to make decisions and things like that.

When your time comes what sort of things would you do for the community?

I'd look at any situation with an open mind. Making decisions for all . . . for every part . . . every generation in the community, young, middle-aged and old. Taking interest in the kids, because they're our future. You've got to look at the kids and make changes for them, and make decisions for them, because they're going to be living with this decision for the rest of their lives.

They are our future! They have to not only live for the future but carry on with the values of our past culture. To make sure of that, I tell the young people: sit down and listen to your elders. When the old people go, all the knowledge goes with them. If you don't sit up and say, 'Hey, I want to learn', or 'I want to listen to you', you're going to be too late, because everybody's crying after they go, 'I should have sat down with them' and 'I should have done this, and I should have done that'. My grand-parents, they're living . . . they're living legends. They are carrying so much knowledge, information. I feel so sad that if they go, everything goes with them, and if I don't find the time—that twenty minutes, that half an hour, two days to sit down with them—everything is gone.

And do you do that?
Oh yeah!

Knowledge that they pass on to me, about certain cycles, cer-tain changes in the environment, the seasonal calendar, we know all about the seasons. What's ready for one season isn't ready for the next. Like bush fruits, the flowers . . . we know when there's certain flowers in the season that there are certain things ready in the sea. The oysters are ready, the fish is fat, you know, things like that.

We look at our land for the changes. This year with all the rains, we didn't have much bush tucker. The rain affected the growth. When the wattle trees come up we know when the bush honey is ready. When we feel the *barrgana* isn't coming and the *lulin* time, well, we know that the stingrays are fat.

We've got five seasons in the calendar year for Aboriginal people, when . . . we've got *lulil* . . . season is when the turtles are mating. Mating time, that also means it's a cold time. We have a whole year planned out like that by looking and watching the changes of the land. Like, turtles are fat at certain times of the year with their mating. And that's the time they are richer in goodness and that's when we can go and hunt for them. You got to have good eyes to hunt for turtle. Because the men up home, they cruising along on a motorboat now, you know? They go hunting for turtle at night as well, we still have that.

We called that *Bingard* time. Yeah, when they go out, they go hunting at night because in those little . . . *junguming,* lights in the water. Mate, there's . . . what do they call that? We call it *junguming* in our language, but there's . . . it's a little light, it's little insects in the water.

Phosphorous lights. They give off this luminous light in the water. And they just stick to the turtle, so at night you can see the turtle going anywhere. When the turtles go out of season, you leave them alone and we go hunt for the stingray because they have come into season and they're very rich and they're fat.

Cool time. When that goes out of season, like it's warming up season, warming up time, that's when the bush tucker is starting to come into season. That's when we live off the land and leave the sea alone to rejuvenate. You can feel the environmental changes, and you know what's coming into season.

After the bush tucker, then you've got reefing at high tides. High tides is when everything is ready. It's reefing time. Every three months there's a change in the environment.

So that's a fifteen month calendar. Hot, warm, cool, cold, high tide. We can also judge from the Milky Way. Like, when you're looking at the Milky Way, you look at the emu in the Milky Way, you know that the emus are starting to lay their eggs. Just from the different ways the Milky Way lays, you know certain things as well.

Sometimes the Milky Way lays this way, and something is ready, but when it lays that way you know something else is in season. You learn to read your environment. You know how to read the trees. The feeling of the wind, the changes. Aboriginal diet was so healthy when they could live off the land and the sea or the desert. But when they were put on settlements ruled by white people, they weren't allowed to go and live off the land

and then they just had to take the white man's rations of sugar, flour and tea . . .

. . . and that leads to generations of poor health. The sad thing is that there is a generation, of mainly men, that are dying at a young age because of poor health from those times of poor diet.
And you have to be so in tune with your senses. I guess the closest we'll get to some white people knowing this would be the bush people, the farmers. Because they live by the seasons too.

To feel a different sense in the breeze and wind, that's beautiful. And here they are in the city in twenty-four-storey-high concrete buildings, nine till five in front of a computer, and the only sense that they're using is sight. They turn off because the sound around them is just a tap, tap of a keyboard.

This time of the year the frill-necked lizards, they only come out. They don't come out at the beginning of the year. They only come out toward the end of the year. Rain time. It's raining time. Like clouds, you're looking at clouds as well. They know when rain's going to come, if it's building up for the wet they'll just look at a cloud and say, oh, look *junjarl.* You know, *junjarl,* meaning different build-up, clouds and rain clouds.

And, like, the smell too, different smells . . . you can smell eucalyptus when you stand at certain areas. You can smell certain flowers, you know other things.

It's just common sense really, a simplistic tool that is part of your make-up. We forget that in the city.
Yep.

With our names as well, we have bush names. Like my name is *Yardood.* Bradley is *Emeil* and Jesse is *Nyinimardi.* Those names are from the elders from long time ago, it's passed through generation to generation. So if I ever have a girl in the future I might give her my grandmother's name, which is *Mungung Rowdji,* I might name that girl child *Rowdji* after her. Because that's keeping her name alive. And that's a part of her that hasn't been lost, so the others will learn that from generation to generation. And people identify with you, like I say to the elders if they say, 'Who you?' I'll say, '*Yardood*'. And they'll go, 'Oh, we know you.' I won't say Rosanna, they won't know Rosanna. When I say *Yardood*, oh yeah, I know, *Rowdji*. For granddaughter.

It's sort of like a traditional practice of renaming. I guess that's one tradition that all races have in common. I think it's beautiful. It not only keeps the name alive but the spirit. My daughter is named after two wonderful people who have passed away and I often tell her the stories of these two great women. It's like a connection.

My last name is Angus. Angus, you think, oh yeah, that sounds a bit Scottish. But Angus comes from my grandfather, his name was *Ungudj*. Black name, them whitefellas couldn't spell his name. To be able to put it in a black and white context, as on paper, they put him down as Angus. That's where Angus comes from. It sounds similar to the way you pronounce Angus, but his name was really *Ungudj*.

That old man . . . because Aboriginal people in the early days only had one name. They never had surnames, you only identify them by that name. Like *Digan*, his name was old man *Digan*. Like, one name. Now you've got the *Tigan* [D to a T through translation by whitefellas] family in the communities. So you know that family and their connection and who they come from. Those names haven't been lost, because you got kids with that name. Still carrying on that name now.

My oldest boy is named after one of my uncles who was a great fisherman. See, those great stories of my uncle are my boy's because that's his namesake.

That's beautiful.

But my youngest is the better fisherman out of my boys, so Jessie says, 'I'm the fisherman, hey, Mum?' I told them: not Jessie,

Bradley. And Jessie would say, 'Mum, you should have named me that because I'm the fisherman, not Bradley! I'm the one who gets all the fish!' He does too!

They go five o'clock in the morning. They go with the tides.

Yeah, they go with the tides, my kids. They know everything. They know what time to go hunting, we can look at the water and will tell you straightaway, oh, tide coming in or tide going out.

Makes you homesick for the bush.
You'll have to come home.

I reckon!
You'll have to come to my country and I can tell you all about it. You'll have the connection when you first get there too. We give people names too, you know? So my grandmother might give a bush name for you when you come up there, and make you feel special. It makes them feel special, hey. I'm part of this family now, you know.

Deadly.

And what do you want to do in the future?
I'm actually in the process of setting up our own family business. In tourism. I'm doing these cultural tours at the moment.

So you enjoy that?
I love doing it. I love doing cultural tours because I'm so proud of my culture that I love telling people about it, and making people understand about Aboriginal culture. How they come with pre-conceived ideas about Aboriginal people. I give them a different impression, one that is positive. We're all different in different ways and there are bad people in all cultures. Yet we all have similar values, you know. It's good to tell about

Aboriginal culture. I find through doing cultural tours you can tell them about the land, tell them about bush tucker, bush medicine and the history. How different . . . and why our cultures are the way they are.

I want to set up a business for my family, so we can be self-sufficient. So we're not relying on government for money. We can do something that we enjoy and get paid for it. And make a living out of it.

What's the employment rate like up that way?
Oh, we're all on CDEP [Community Development Employment Program], which is basically Working for the Dole. They're making us work for the dole, and all those other people they can sit down and collect the dole without doing any work.

There's a big discussion about the CDEP in the cities at the moment, but Aboriginal communities, they've been doing that for ages now. What do you think about this?
No, it's not a really good thing because it doesn't give people an incentive to want to move on with their life. Because CDEP is a basic wage. They only get about 130 dollars, by the time you get your rent and all your taxes taken out of it. So 130 dollars a week doesn't give you any incentive to want to work. I don't think it's good unless you get top up, you know? These young people are . . . they can look at the people in the towns and the cities who collect the dole, they get more money than what they collect for working for it. So it doesn't give them any incentive to want to work at all or to move forward or better themselves.

But doesn't it bring them together in the community? Give them a sense of community. The jobs might not be great but at least they are doing something where it's not grog related, or drug related. And a time to socialise maybe. But I guess you could get caught in a rut and not move on from there. I guess it really comes down to the individual—they are given a chance but it's up to them to make the choice.

It is their choice to go out there and see what's on offer, what's in the real world, and then come back in. At least you've been open-minded.

I was kind of lucky, because I tell people I've changed my attitude toward life and everything around me because I went out, had a look at the real world. Come back into my community, I can either make changes, or at least I know the difference to what's out there compared to my community. And I can speak honestly. I worked outside of my community for a long time. I went and studied in the cities, I've travelled a lot . . . but some people don't want to move from the comfort zone. That's their comfort zone, that's the way they've grown up. But then your way of thinking doesn't change either, because that's just the way you've lived your whole life, it makes it hard for them to change their attitude about things because they haven't seen what's out there. What other people are like. How to understand. It opens up your horizons.

You've got options. You've got choices.

You can understand why people do things in certain ways. I understand why people think a certain way. Some people may say this person is ignorant. Yeah, but why is he ignorant? He might come from a background where he had no choice but to just think like that, you know. So you can understand why people feel and do things in a different way to you. But from the community's perspective, if you stay in the community for too long then your ways of thinking don't change. Because that's just the way you've always lived . . .

Sort of stagnant. We need to evolve as a people?

Unless you break the cycle, you cannot change your way of thinking.

Do you believe that's part of your life cycle, to do all the things that you have done? To open up your mind by seeing what is out there and then going back to your community? Is this part of your path that has been laid for you?

I reckon I was special because, from when I was young, Mum used to tell me I had a choice to go to Broome—Broome to do my high school—but Mum said, 'No, I think you special. I think you can make changes.'

The opportunity to explore, I like the change it's brought in me, and being a Scorpio as well. All things, I feel, are challenging and I want to take it all on. I like to be challenged.

Where do you think your mum got her insight from?

Well, Mum . . . seeing the way people live in the commuity . . . some of it not a good thing. They'll never change their ways.

Mum worked in a hospital in Broome and I grew up with my grandmother. When she was working . . . like I was only eight months old or something when I went to my grandparents to bring me up on the community. I grew up with different old people. My mum, she grew up with nuns. There was a Stolen Generation in our own community as well, where the nuns built their missions and put my mum in a dormitory till she was eighteen. My grandparents were living in the community camp . . .

. . . but they weren't allowed to mix?

Yeah, yeah. She had to do things with the nuns. They were allowed to go and see the old people and that, but they were still living with the nuns, not living with their parents or their people.

She was really young. Really, really young.

True.

And how was her relationship with her mum and dad when she came out of the dormitory?

Yeah, made it good, you know. Made it good, like this is the right thing, you know. But my aunty always say that it was good that they were brought up in that environment because they learnt to cook and clean. But not that you didn't in your own culture. It was part of their life, you did that anyway, you know. Aboriginal people were clean people, but, you know, in their own way, in their own way of doing things, you know. Yeah, fair enough, they showed them how to fold bed sheets properly and iron things. But Aboriginal people didn't have that technology, so how could they know?

I've got a different point of view to that. I believe that their culture was taken away from them and it's replaced by the Catholic system. The Catholic way of thinking. There were new laws that were placed, like the sacred law of Jesus Christ—for Aboriginal people they didn't have Jesus Christ, they had their own religion. There was dance and the corroboree. That was theirs, that was their sacred rituals. And church got their own sacred rituals. But there were a couple of good priests. Aboriginal people would have lost their culture altogether, but one priest came back and didn't see the people practising their culture and said, 'What's happening here?' And they were allowed to prac-tise their corroborees again.

. . . ever since then they've been dancing. Carrying on their ceremony ways, ceremonial ways of doing things.

I still feel really angry at what happened to our parents in the dormitories, but maybe . . . this nun, she did the Suicide Workshop with us—when I was doing my warden's training for that two weeks, well, for four days we did Suicide Workshop. And the first thing that nun said, she looked at the class . . . And this old nun, she taught my mum and my aunties when they were little. She looked at the group and she goes, 'I had some of you when I was teaching here in the early days here at the mission. And if I hurt you, I'm sorry.' She went . . . she used to whack them, whack them around like that, with the cane, you know.

She said, 'If I hurt you, I'm sorry, but I didn't know any other way', she said. 'That's the way I was told to do things because it's supposed to make you listen.' She said it like that!

Did you say anything?
No, I was a little shame. But they did get whacked around a lot, you know. They did get hurt. In every which way.

Did your mum ever talk about those times in the dormitories?
They only talked about the good times because they talked about bonding with other groups. Other kids from different areas were taken away from their parents and placed in the mission. Mum used to say that kids used to cry and everything, and they used to bond to my grandmother because Mum had a mum nearby that they could bond to. Although they didn't have blood, they were still bonded by that anyway.

That's something that I've just learnt regarding my grandmother and why we were related to certain people. It wasn't blood, but because they were all taken from a certain area, all those people looked out for one another. I think that's beautiful. That's what I love about being black—the more the merrier.
When I left the community to come down here, I told my sister, 'Make sure you look after my kids.' And she said, 'Yeah, they'll stay with me here.' I rang back and I said, 'Mum, where's my kids?' 'Oh, they're sleeping with me, one sleeps with me and one sleeps with his grandfather.' It's that smell, that security. I used to do that to my grandparents, you can't blame them.

I do that with my daughter. See, I never moved into my own bedroom until I was sixteen. Amanda would always sleep in with me or where I could see her. And when we got settled in life, and she got older, she said, 'Mum, I want my own room.' And I went, 'You can't sleep in your own room! What about me?' She said, 'No, you'll be right.' But every now and then I've got to go and sleep with her, it just satisfies me to know that she's all right.

Yeah, I'm always like that.

I'm like that for my babies, definitely. I mean, Bradley is like a little man now, he's not allowed to sleep with his mother because that's ancient Law. He can't do that, but with Jessie, he'll say, 'I'm tired now, I'm going to sleep.' And I'll turn my head and I'll look around—he's not in his bed. I look, he's there in my bed! And I just go snuggle right up close and I hold him so close to me. His little bum! I just love that feeling, you know, I just love it all over. I love my babies.

Is there anything else that you would like to tell us about?
Yeah, like with that touring job, I've now got the opportunity to travel on the *Coral Princess*. The *Coral Princess* is a cruise boat. I get to travel up the Kimberley coast for ten days. I get to see the good part of that country, see the coast and go to all the waterfalls, and places that I've never been to in my life!

I will be spending ten days on it. I can't wait!

So, it's a bit of a holiday?
It's a big holiday! But the only work I have to do is two lectures. Two half hour lectures—you know me, I talk more than half an hour. I do two half hour lectures, one on my life, and the other one is about Aboriginal people up the Kimberley coast and how they survived, and the wardens, they talk about the culture, their culture.

Are they genuinely interested when you're yarning to them?
They genuinely are. Sometimes some might get someone not interested. When you're talking to a group you just kind of target

for us. And that's how history is kept alive, if we keep practising it.

We have certain corroborees that we can dance for the public as well. And those stories they only dance to keep the spiritual memories alive for our ancestors. Because they've been writing those songs for a long time and dancing those songs for a long time, and those dances and those songs haven't changed. So you're still dancing . . .

Do you dance?
We have a family one, my sister dances. I haven't been able to dance . . . I don't dance with my sisters. Like, for the young kids, like, we get the little ones involved.

It's more like a family gathering?
I dance when we go for the Law ceremonies and that. You got no choice, if you don't dance you don't make your children strong. To connect yourself to the earth, and your son gets strong.

It's beautiful.
That's why you dance on those sacred sites. It keeps making yourself stronger. If anyone gets sick and you go down to the Law Grounds, it makes you feel good, you know. It makes you . . . I don't know, it does something to you, that spiritual energy.

Without those sacred sites we can't dance, if we can't dance then we can't get strong and we don't have that spiritual energy. Without that spiritual energy and strength, we stay sick. Without those sacred sites we are nothing. But now, in modern times, we have to find another way to connect to our culture and customs and Law. We need to find the sacred lands in the cities we are in and hold our ceremonies on a personal or community basis, or in our own backyards. When I perform my play Box the Pony I am making myself stronger—and my daughter and man. That was given to me by a greater power that is my songline or Dreaming.

A lack of culture, customs, law or colour doesn't make you less of a Blackfella in this country in today's society. It is what you hold within your heart and soul. You can grow and achieve in the white man's world, that does not make you less Aboriginal. If you did not grow up with hard times, that does not make you less Aboriginal. If you don't connect to your mother's or grandparents' land, that does not make you less Aboriginal. The only way you are not Aboriginal is if you don't acknowledge it, and that is your business.

But to the rest of Australia, Pamnayungun, you must accept the change in the culture as we are changing with the times; you can't expect us to all run around in nargars (red lap-lap), that is for special time. Society plays such a huge part in anyone's life, yet we have to toe the line, otherwise we are ridiculed.

But to all my brothers and sisters, it's okay to not know, it's okay to live life in the way you choose, it's okay to make choices that you can benefit from. Life is about choices, it's okay to choose. It's okay to go with the times. The opportunity is out there for all of mankind—embrace it. Even if it is just on a community level, that's a step. We have to work forward for the future—education black way and society way—and be great, the way we know we all can be.

Dinner

I was late, late for a very important date! Having a feed with my new tidda girls, nine of us, going off, flash restaurant in Sydney town, rock on!

When I finally get there—there being Edna's Table II, Australia's finest Aboriginal cuisine—the girls are cool, but happy that I have finally arrived to get the show under way, ease their nerves and tell them what the hell is going on here. A brief intro for everybody about why we are here and what the night will hold for all.

First thing was sound and where everyone would be seated . . . Well, I made that up on the spot—making out I put a lot of thought into who would be great sitting next to each other. That turned out really well, actually. The ancestors are working with me here.

The girls were warned that they would be wired for sound. So the first question was, 'What about going to the toilet?'

Our sound guy eased their minds: 'We all sound the same when we go to the toilet.'

I tell him to turn them down because if he doesn't I'll clip him around the binung—I throw that in before the women decide to get up and leave.

I secretly show them how to turn it off as long as they remember to turn it back on, just don't drop the pack in the toilet. They were cool about that. Drinks in hand, mostly soft drinks—damn, how am I going to get them fired up and open to talking? I'm gonna have to work hard at this. There were no big drinkers at the table.

I sat at the head of the table, I was steering this ship; Deb to my left, Cilla to my right, Rosanna was next to Cilla, then next to Rosanna was Sharon and next to Sharon was Frances. Coming back to my right, next to Deb was Tammy and then Kathryn and then our late arrival—so late, in fact, she missed the first course of croc-odile soup—Liza. When she did finally arrive she slipped into her seat, picked up on the conversation and ran with it, rock on! The sista had great energy, which was needed for the night. Things are looking good!

One black chick couldn't make it due to work and that was Rachel Perkins.

Naturally the first topic we discussed was strippers! There's a group of Aboriginal and Islander boys based in Brisbane who call themselves 'Hot Chocolate' so we spoke about that—far too late to arrange anything. Then our French waiter offered to take his clothes off; even the sound man was propositioned, as long as he kept his glasses on, but we dropped that idea too and decided to leave it for next time. Then the waiter started speaking French and we all melted. This dinner could get right off track if I'm not careful!

I had my questions prepared if the conversation didn't go in the right direction, but I knew that wouldn't be needed, all these women were on the ball.

The big discussion was the main course, and guess what? We all became vegetarians! Shame! Good Blackfellas! There was emu and roo but we went for the asparagus, shame!! Our waiter kept hanging around. He told us he could not help but be drawn to the beauty in the room!

Then it was time to get down to some serious stuff.

There was discussion about where the girls came from—their mob. The Murris outnumbered the others but we had Koori, Nunga, Nyoongar and Palawa around the table too. Sort of like the twelve knights around the round table.

There was mixed conversation from everybody as we were ordering our meals. Just little chitchat from the girls as we got to know each other. Everyone took a great interest in Rosanna's country, its beauty.

And fishing, each girl had a story. Tammy once caught two barramundis on her line and had to reel them in. And she did, by herself, and she took them to a friend's place up in Kowinyarmun, that's where she caught the fish, for a big cook-up. Sharon and her swapped stories about locations because they both travel a lot with their work in communities.

Cilla asked Deb about Radiance; Cilla said that she loved it and thought that Deb was great. Who didn't?!

Kathryn and Rosanna spoke about children and that Rosanna missed her boys. But Cilla piped up and said she's having a good break from her children, four girls, and that she doesn't miss them at all! But then she said she was only gamin, but the break is nice.

As I listened to the taped conversation, I thought, no wonder they call women chooks—we were all gabbing on . . . it was great really, we all just hit it off.

We all spoke about our occupations. Frances started and everyone commented on her dancer's calf muscles.

Frances: I love dancing, it's a great way of expression and healing and getting the message to other people.

Sharon was next, filled us in on who she is.

Sharon: I'm really passionate about what I do out in the communities with the young girls that come to participate in the netball clinics.

Rosanna was next and she just compared how small her little community is to this big city and how she loves her work as a tour guide because she loves to meet people, and most importantly how she loves talking about her culture because she is so proud of it.

Cilla was next but she told me to go down the other side of the table, that she was too shy, but we didn't let her get away with that. She told Sharon that all her girls were netballers. Then Cilla got shy and said she didn't have anything else to say, only that she is just a mum. Sharon jumped in and said, 'One of the hardest jobs.' Cilla wouldn't say any more so I piped in, to fill in the gaps, that she was my mate and that I started her on Malibu and coke, but that was a long time ago.

Then Miss Mailman was next and she told us about her new program, 'The Secret Life of Us'.

Then Tammy, who told them she was my cousin, and then on the other side, her mother's paternal side, she was related to Cilla. That Cherbourg connection. And then Tammy went on to talk about all her ambitions.

Then Kathryn's turn and, on hearing Tammy's ambitions, Kathryn said she didn't want a turn and that she wasn't as together as Tammy, but that she was having a great time at the moment living in Sydney; she had only been here for five weeks. She was a little reluctant to talk about her Miss Australia achievement but, of course, I pushed it. But she was more interested to hear from the other women about Aboriginal culture as she felt that was lacking in her life. Kathryn felt that she did not have the same connection to her culture as some of the women around the table. She thanked me for allowing her to be a part of this night and allowing her to meet the other women, but more importantly for involving her in such a great project. Sharon says that she probably was in the same boat as Kathryn as she didn't feel she had grown up with culture either.

The first question that I wanted a group discussion on was 'What is Aboriginal?' and Kathryn and Sharon had led into that perfectly. I told ya these women are deadly.

Sharon: I guess for me, I grew up with a white father because Mum and him split up, but Mum didn't know a lot about the culture side because of the circumstance of her being put into a home and then adopted out to a white family. So she had nothing to pass on to me. I grew up in the city so I didn't grow up in a typical Aboriginal community.

Leah: But that is the question: what is a typical Aboriginal community or family, what is that? I'm guilty of saying this, 'Orh, they're not proper Blackfellas because they didn't grow up in that struggling black family way or on a community.' It's what you feel in your heart and soul that matters.

Kathryn: Is there a 'typical'? Why is there a category? Is it only skin deep? Is it being brought up with the traditional stories? Is it living on a remote community? Is it wearing the colours?

Leah: We have been influenced by the media with the image of the poor down-and-out black person and then we feel less worthy to call ourselves black if we didn't come from struggle street. But that's wrong because every race has its own levels of society in their own communities. And we fall prey to the stereotypical negative image the media and politics portray of the trouble spots in our communities . . .

So what is 'black' today?

Of course, no one wanted to go first, so I chose Frances.

Frances: I really found out that it made more sense to me when I left this country and went overseas and I didn't have any friends or family or that community around me, I was by myself. But, wherever I went, I felt an energy inside me, it didn't matter where I went or what I did . . . I had this sense of belonging and a sense of place and a sense of home because this is what this country Australia does to me. I would watch all those people in New York rushing around and I would sit back and watch and think that they don't have what I have. I felt safe because I knew that

I had a special place to come home to. Our [Bangarra] style of dance is so layered, it's not just a move or a body formation: it means something to a race of people. The stories behind the dance deal with issues relating to that race of people, to give strength to them and to give the outer world an understanding of that race of people. It's ancient, yet modern, and has such meaning. It is being familiar with the feeling of this land—that dirt and heat and that smell of rain, the wind and the cold. We know it . . . but we know it because of all the stories that are this country's history, this country's soul.

Deb: I agree, I agree matey, not that I've done a lot of travelling but when I was overseas it really hit home for me what I actually have back here in Australia. It is a belonging . . .

Leah: Not just an address, but something rooted in culture, no matter how involved or not your knowledge is; it's the blood connection to this land.

Deb: And that I can be myself.

Kathryn: I don't know whether it was the jetlag but I actually wanted to get down and kiss the ground. You lunge onto the earth and kiss it because you are home. You feel an inner calm . . . a complete feeling.

Sharon: You really feel at home when you jump on that plane and you hear the Aussie accent.

Kathryn: The footage they show on the video screens.

Sharon: You just feel pretty proud.

Tammy: I had been to America and had felt those same feelings that you were all talking about, but it was even stronger when my friends, they are African-American, came over and stayed for about a month. See, they made me realise something. We took them to the Murri community in Brisbane and up to Cherbourg and the whole while they were with us they kept saying, 'You don't know how blessed you are. Sure, a lot of culture, so to speak, is taken but at least you have a spiritual home.' See, a lot of the African-Americans are drifting around. They said, 'We were taken to America and all I know is my people were from Africa, but Africa is such a big bloody continent and access to trace family history is not very good, but at least you've got a place you can call home.' They just have a place, a house, that they call home. And it is easy, well, easier for us to find out things about land, culture and family.

Rosanna: I think, 'What is Aboriginal?' It's a sense of identity firstly, there's a lot of different Aboriginal people and where we all come from . . .

Leah: Tonight is an example of that.

Rosanna: But to be Aboriginal is a sense of identity. Identify with who you are in here—your heart—before you go out and say where you come from and where you belong to. It's a connection to country and that could be simply a place you identify with. Even if it's the place where you were born.

Leah: In some cases your parents may not know where your country is, so claim the place you were born—there is nothing wrong with that. Of course, there is black politics regarding land rights but you can just state your connection and that should be okay. You know, when I give talks to the white communities, I tell them to claim the titles we give them. Like 'migloo' in Queensland for white person, claim it. Find out the area in which you live; i.e. if you're white and you live in Murgon, you say you are a migloo and you are from the Wakka Wakka region, and so the white people can be a part of that community. I recently did a talk at a university and the students got so excited when I told them to do this that they all said they would go and find out stuff about the town where they were born or where they call home. It's about feeling that you belong and that there is a connection in the communities. It's what you identify with that puts your heart at ease, whether you're black or white.

Rosanna: You feel from the heart and if you feel you belong there, well, that's you, in your own personal right.

Kathryn: Something that's not tangible . . . it's not being in that location—still living, still doing the same thing. It's a feeling that's spiritual.

Rosanna: It's a feeling within you; it's not because you're fair . . . there's all different colours that Aboriginal people come in and a lot of differences in how they are brought up and thoughts on how you should be judged on how Aboriginal you are. It's in your heart, it's what you identify with . . . you know yourself that you are Aboriginal and that you are beautiful.

Leah: Cilla and I were talking about this in my backyard the other day. It's the fair-skinned ones that try extra hard to be black. You're not black enough or you're not white enough and it is very confusing and frustrating.

Cilla: You get it from both sides. You get called yellow.

Our first course has arrived and I announce that we work from the outside in with the cutlery. It took me a fair few meals at flash dinners I was invited to to learn that, you always wait for someone else to pick up the knife or fork first. I remember my first dinner and I pretended to drop my serviette and then made out I was looking for someone and by the time I turned around someone started eating and away I went. The crocodile soup is great.

Rosanna: A lot of our people grew up in the cities, it's not your fault that you grew up there. Identify with your different areas.

Tammy: You made the perfect point before when you said you have to know who you are before you can grow externally and help other people.

Deb: When I was growing up in Mt Isa, I never had a strong connection to the community and that came from my dad not really wanting us to have that connection. But I guess it was that whole shame thing that came with his generation and for so long I grew up not really understanding the mob from up that way or why they were the way they were. I had white friends and they would come over to play but I was not allowed to have black friends over. Then when I went down to Brisbane and started to meet people like Wesley Enoch and you, Leah, who had a stronger sense of community . . .

Frances: Did you go looking for that?

Deb: I think so, I think when I was studying I really held onto that and really wanted to be with people who had that strong sense of identity. The struggle that was done by the black pioneers in the entertainment industry pathed the way for us young Blackfellas now. And that comes from strength as a community and standing strong together and I love that and realise how important that feeling and understanding is. Because I didn't have it even though I grew up with my black father and my black skin . . . I was shamed out too that for so long I didn't actually want to connect to that part of me. And I was really embarrassed about that. The education system that I went through didn't allow any kind of exploration of culture. I didn't have it with my family and I didn't have it at school, so I didn't have it.

Sharon: Same with me. I went to a very multicultural school so I just blended in with the rest of them. I could have been anything. And my Aboriginality was never an issue for me. It was never spoken about, I was just Sharon Finnan.

Deb: Actually, same here.

Kathryn: At my school there was a feeling of angst against Aborigines when we would talk about certain issues, government grants etc; people were misinformed and I didn't know enough about it myself to stand up. But it was something that someone would say that was misguided and it's amazing how many people latch onto that and all bulldoze forward with this naive view and then not care about the ramifications of that. But I couldn't stand up; I wanted to, but I didn't know enough or have the confidence to either. And then some of my friends would tease me about being Aboriginal and I told them, 'So what if I'm Aboriginal, I'm proud of it.' And, you know, the next day it was dropped and you know what? Sometimes they were envious. It goes to show, sometimes you just have to show those sorts of people that whatever they do to you or say to you it just doesn't have or make any impact and 'it' loses its power. 'It'— could be their narrow-mindedness, racism or naivity.

Rosanna: I remember when I went to school and all they were teaching us was about Captain Cook. And I'm saying, hey this is not right! My family has been practising different lore and we have different views on things through our stories we have carried down from generation and generation. We had no story about sitting around waiting to be discovered by this man Captain Cook. We had our own societies and systems long before. And later in life I became very angry about this, this is why I do tours so I can tell people that that's not the way it is: us Aboriginal people were here first; and also identifying with the culture, which allows them to understand. I'm lucky I come from a very strong cultural background. But it also doesn't mean that I am not affected by the society we now all live in. I guess my knowledge of culture gives me a firm foundation.

There was a lot of agreement around the table. I brought up a story about how the Mutitjulu community get urban black women to go and talk to the young girls about some of the opportunities that are out there in the big bad world. But has anyone told them that they are the luckiest young people in the world? Because their culture is strong and they have their language too, because with them Top End mob they locate you by your language. That's how some of the women, when they first met me, tried to place me: they asked me what my language is. I told them that I didn't know it and I felt sort of degraded and actually questioned my Aboriginality.

But I will never do that again because I am an Aboriginal woman. Maybe a general language that is still strong can be taught in schools. It may not be your area or mob, but it's a part of our culture.

Deb: Like in New Zealand, Maori is actually taught in their schools to all children.

Leah: Like when you see the New Zealand football team all singing the haka and they sing their national anthem in language. Wouldn't it be cool to sing the national anthem in an Aboriginal language? I would love to do that. I should do it.

Rosanna: You should just do it. You up there on centre stage. They can only cut ya mike.

Leah: But I should, shouldn't I?!

Sharon: You should have done it when Cathy Freeman won the four hundred.

Rosanna: How did you fellows feel when she was told that she couldn't run with the flag? Didn't that make you guys angry? That's her identity.

Leah: There are rules in every job and that's her job and it was really up to her whether she did it or not. But if I had been her and the opportunity arose, then I would have taken it. But the biggest achievement was that this whole nation was wishing a black woman all the best and wanting their children to be like her. That's a bigger statement than anything.

Tammy: But even if she hadn't run with it, that doesn't make her less a Murri. Like a black woman . . . despite all that our people have been through, even if she hadn't won the gold medal, the fact that she got to that point . . . our people have produced this.

Kathryn: How did people feel about the bridge walk?

Leah: I was up at five in the morning, up with the first lot across. It was a beautiful crisp morning. We were all rugged up but it felt so good to be up enjoying daybreak on such an occasion. I did my salute to the sun and prayed to the ancestors for a great day.

Deb: It was the most amazing feeling I've ever felt. I was getting off at the North Sydney station and seeing families, people with little kids and different sorts of people who I didn't think would support a day like this. They were coming out in droves and the carriages on the train were jam-packed, it was like you were sardines. It was the most incredible feeling going over that bridge [Sydney Harbour Bridge]. It was such a dignified march, such a respectful march—it was beautiful. You could really feel that people want change.

Sharon: A friend of mine went there and heard a little girl in front of him say to her dad, 'Do you think the Aboriginal people know we are marching here for them today?'

While the serious conversation was happening around the table, and as I listen to the tape and transcribe, I'm straining my ears because the table talk is really faint. I focus on the foreground talking and it's bloody Rosanna and Cilla going to the toilet. I don't know why their mikes were up so high; they weren't holding the conversation around the table, anyway. I heard the squeaking of the toilet door and then Cilla said that it would sound like Niagara Falls. And Cilla couldn't find the clip to unclip it from her jeans. Then I think the sound guy realised and turned them down. Anyway, they were all talking over me.

I was talking about the walk across the bridge, about how I was up the front with them old people that were cruisin' in those little golf carts and, halfway across the bridge, I looked behind and it was amazing—it was this sea of people moving as one. A huge mass of bodies. I went over to a couple of them old people, they were all them Stolen Generations mob and I told them to look behind and a couple of them just couldn't believe it. This one old girl said, 'This is the best sight I've seen in a long, long time. These people cared about what happened to me. I know that there are good Australians out there that do really care. Now I feel better about myself. They care for me.' It brought a tear to my eye.

As the tape progresses Rosanna is not turned down and from the dunny she says, 'I'm actually glad I decided to be involved in this project.' Cilla agrees from the other cubicle (these two are going to kill me for writing that they were in the jilawah/toilet). I think she said it was brilliant. This will make for interesting stuff if we pick up what the others say as well as they're in the jilawah. Darn, shouldn't be saying that they are in the jilawah but I am pissing myself laughing as I write this. I know them girls and they'll probably double me when they read this. Luv you, my sisters!

Back at the table.

Kathryn: It was powerful to all Australians to show that, okay, the government may go in this direction, but the power is with the people.

Deb: This sort of thing rises above politics!

Tammy: And it transcends.

Kathryn: All of us are so happy that so many people participated and that it went for a lot longer than what was planned. I just wanted to know what it was like to be there because I was still in Tasmania.

Leah: Liza, did they do anything in Brisbane?

Liza: Yeah, they did.

Deb starts to laugh.

Deb: I walked there too. I was walking all over the place!

Tammy: They reported that they had about sixty to seventy thousand people, with Miss Compere Mailman. We were supposed to walk to City Hall and the route that they took was symbolic because Blackfellas weren't allowed to go into the city centre over that bridge, the William Jolley Bridge. But when we finally arrived at the Town Hall they told us to keep walking because the forecourt there was jam-packed and they couldn't fit any more people. So they told us to keep walking to the

Botanical Gardens. And here's the police giving us this escort. It was ironic to see the police walking with us. You don't see that a lot in Queensland. It was really great for the State.

Liza: You know, with that people's movement, does it stop there? What else are they going to do? You know, they've all come together for that day but what else is going to be done for reconciliation?

Leah: Good question. Are black issues only ever going to be acknowledged in NAIDOC week? Is it only for Sorry Day and reconciliation days that support is going to be shown?

Deb: The current government is not even doing that. John Howard can't even turn up. He doesn't acknowledge anything.

Kathryn: Is there the controversy if he does say sorry that it will have dire ramifications?

Tammy: I have a few points to make. The first point, I'm not an expert in this, but the problem I see with that argument that if he says sorry on behalf of an institution that was responsible then it can set a legal precedent . . . but the argument from the Premier of Queensland, Premier Beattie, is: yes, the Commonwealth government were partially responsible but all the States were partially responsible and they have apologised and Blackfellas didn't go ballistic with lawsuits. And even if we did it's our legal right to.

And the second point I wanted to make is that I am actually a little disappointed with some of our self-appointed leaders in the way that they have attacked the argument. The argument they have is that John Howard should say sorry on behalf of the Australian people for what happened, on behalf of the government rah, rah, rah . . . So therefore it's easier for the public and the media to cut that argument down because John Howard just puts his hand up and says that he can't say sorry on behalf of all these people because they didn't take the kids etc. Instead our leaders should reframe the argument, say: John Howard, you should apologise on behalf of the institution, as if the government is a company and John Howard is the representative or the CEO of that institution. That way the public have no right to say that he has no right to apologise on behalf of me because I didn't take those kids.

Leah: But do we really want that little man to say sorry to us? I want someone who will mean it. But it's a good point in the fact that he is a part of this government institution and that on behalf of the past government wrongdoings he apologises.

Kathryn: It's too late now for him to have his say, if he says it now it means nothing.

Sharon: We've seen his true colours. It's like he's been pushed into it.

Leah: And as I say at the end of Box the Pony, *'When you see them old people smile, it was a smile of relief that people care and those smiles will release the anger in our young people because when our old people are hurting we feel for them.' But when they go, 'Nah bub, I'm right now', then you go, all right then, I can start to work on healing myself or the individual.*

Kathryn: It's the protective mechanism we have for others. And one more thing on what you just said. Whether you agree or disagree as to say sorry or not, we have to acknowledge the past wrongs but without thinking, what's going to be the outcome if we do say sorry. You don't think, what if we do this. What will the repercussion of our action, or in this case the word 'sorry', be.

Liza: I wouldn't want John Howard to say sorry. I mean, words to me . . . that means nothing. I think action. They took our language away from us. Put language back in schools. Instead of teaching Japanese and German why not teach a traditional language? Australia Day, to us that's Invasion Day. If you mean reconciliation why not change it to maybe a day in NAIDOC week?

Leah: Or a day that we as a nation can agree upon. Where we can start anew. That's what it's all about—starting something new.

Liza: We are into the twenty-first century, times are changing. And we all have to come together as one. And also as Indigenous people we have to unite together and support each other and educate our children to go forward and learn to adapt with the changes!

Some fun stuff now, I called it 'Spin the Camera'. I put a little camera on a 'lazy Susan' (one of those things that you find in Chinese restaurants in the middle of them round tables—you put the food on and spin it and watch the food fly off, nar, gamin, you spin it slowly to allow better access to the food). I had the camera sitting on a box and gaffed down—rough job, but it worked. I thought it would be a great way for the women to have some fun and just talk silly. So 'Spin the Cam', where it stops nobody knows. First was Cilla, she just ducked under the table. Next was Deb, who got all camera shy and couldn't think of anything to say. Liza said hello to her mum and sisters. Kathryn gave a speech in appreciation of being invited into the book and to have dinner with nine other beautiful chic black women. Then it became serious, with a few more speech-type responses from Frances and Sharon. And Rosanna just said that she missed her babies. I thought that was a nice intro to the 'Spin the Camera' game, so when I want some juicy stuff later they won't be afraid.

The next issue was the word 'tolerance' that the government and a few politicians have been saying. Here's what Tammy had to say.

Tammy: I have a real problem with the government and some politicians' use of the word tolerance. I don't want to be tolerated; I want to be loved, respected and valued, so I wish they wouldn't say the word tolerate. And even some of our people, our self-appointed leaders, are asking for tolerance. Don't ask on my behalf! I want to be accepted for who I am, I don't want people to accept me because they have to or because it is politically correct.

Leah: Every single one of us here is different but we are all Aboriginal women and this book will show our individuality.

Kathryn: I liked it when we were having our photo taken and she [the photographer] said, 'I think I've got a nice blend of colour.'

There was a big laugh up from the girls.

Kathryn: I think she was talking about our clothes?

Tammy: And our hair colour.

Leah: What do we think about the international view of Australia?

Liza: My forté is Indigenous tourism. I've been in that for over ten years and the last job I worked at was Tjapukai Culture Park and we had over five hundred international tourists visiting that park a day, and I think with my job now, the first Indigenous women's calendar, that the international market will accept it more than what Australia will domestically. Especially the Germans—they just love our culture, they just can't get enough of it. And especially with the big events that we are having in Australia at this time, and in the near future, the international visitor will experience our culture in some sort of way, and they want that.

Leah: Is there enough support out there in our own communities for our up and coming young people?

Liza: I don't think there is, like, take my company for example, we have been struggling to get our ideas up and running with the first Indigenous calendar. We are promoting our beautiful women, promoting our traditonal lands . . . there is another young male enterprise, 'Hot Chocolate', they were the first Murri male review strippers . . .

Leah: I was gonna bring them down.

A cheer from the girls . . .

Liza: And the brothers are good lookin' too (another cheer from the girls). They went for funding and got nothing. Our financers need to restructure and put money aside for young black entrepreneurs who are trying to make a go of it.

Leah: I know we have other issues like health and issues involving detention centres . . .

Deb: Sorry, but usually when you are looking at the arts it has always been the last to get funding; always has been. When you try and deal with the welfare of our communities in health, housing etc, the arts will always take second place. When there's budget cuts the arts are always first to go and as an artist you always have to validate your position as an artist. We are just as important as anyone else as artists. Frannie, is that right? As dancers and actors and singers . . . it's really frustrating when the arts has always had a backfoot when it comes to funding, and not to belittle anything else in our communities, cause, God knows, some of our communities are in bad states, but with arts it's frustrating not to have that support.

Leah: You've made a good point. But I guess the next step is for us to get out of the government handout mentality and go out there and push for success on our terms. That's what we are trying to do with our company and it's bloody hard. But it makes it all worthwhile when you do the hard work on your own . . . and then to succeed, it is so rewarding. If you get a grant that's great, but they are so few and far between.

Then we got talking about another photographer, who is a lovely lady from England, Penny Tweedie, who came out here and was captivated by the culture and she spent some time with one of the mob from up in the Territory way and they made her part of their family. But she has great shots which big companies could buy to help sell their products, but they won't touch them.

Liza: Why is that?

Leah: I don't know, but I did speak to a director of commercials and he said that the companies might not think that it is politically correct. But then I thought, if you had an Aboriginal writer for those ads then they would be done proper way and everything would be okay, wouldn't you think? But I don't know.

Liza: Is it their naivity?

Leah: They say that the white community isn't ready for it. Well, when are they going to be? If someone doesn't offer it, how the bloody hell will we ever know? Anyway, who are they to say anything regarding anything to do with our culture? As long as we say it's all right, then it's all right.

You lookin' sad there sister, you don't like your emu?

Rosanna: It's too raw. This fulla still gallopin' . . . When you was talking about international tourists . . . I came here to Sydney for an international tourist conference and they said that ninety per cent of the visitors are looking for Aboriginal culture, to experience or just to be exposed to it. So I applied for funding through ATSIC and they said that the business isn't viable. Yet we do our own research, we had questionnaires, and every single person who filled them out said how great this was and that they would go and spread the word . . .

Kathryn: I hope it doesn't not happen just because it isn't marketable.

Rosanna: It happens in some places where the tourism is properly set up because these people want to meet an Aboriginal person, the interaction.

Kathryn: It would be fine for Australia to say that there is a call for this because we want to show this to the rest of the world. Because we are proud of our culture and we are not trying to just make a dollar out of this.

Tammy: And there needs to be some serious legal protection of our culture. Our children were taken from us, we were taken from our land, language elements from our culture were taken and at present there is no copyright for our art, our medicinal remedies and wisdom. Like, a lot of Americans are taking on empowerment, but they are deriving a lot of that wisdom from Indigenous teachings. None of that is being protected. Why aren't our people given opportunities to receive royalties from pharmaceutical companies, because a large percentage of the plant-based pharmaceutical scripts are derived from Indigenous wisdom from throughout the world. I've had discussions with non-Indigenous people about this and they say that this idea is in contravention of their culture and I said, 'No, you are not even asking the people; you are not empowering them to make the decision themselves, whether they want the money or not. Who are you to decide to take that knowledge, exploit it and don't even offer anything back?'

Rosanna: Money has no value when it comes to culture. You value your culture, you value your family, you value your land. Money is just a totem.

Tammy: But at least give the people an opportunity to say no, thank you, or yes, thank you.

Leah: Or give it back to communities so that they can become self-sufficient in getting things that the communities need.

Liza: Like Nathan Blacklock, deadly footballer, goes back to his community of Saint George. They had no pool there so Nathan is trying to raise funds to give back to the community and because of his position and profile in the public eye he has created an awareness of the needs of the kids out that way. It's just great to see the brother doing that; there should be more of that happening, creating awareness for our communities. Because the way things are going with our political situation in this country ATSIC will be abolished in another five years, and we have to start being economically independent of government handouts, creating our own business and creating employment for us and making money. If anyone is to make money out of our culture, shouldn't it be us? And we need to make sure that the international tourists are aware that there are stores that are ripping off the Indigenous artist and a logo for authenticity needs to be made known to the international tourist. I know of backpackers from overseas painting didjes and boomerangs... anyway, getting off the track here, don't get me started on that, but yeah, Nathan Blacklock has done the right thing and set a great example and I support him a hundred per cent.

Tammy: There needs to be a lot more support for our brothers from the communities like that, there's too much two-face... jealousy.

Cilla: True! I got run down for coming to this, for being involved in this project.

Liza: Why is that?

Cilla: Jealousy! They're just bored.

Leah: Isn't it up to the individual in how far they want to succeed? And why do they have to pull others down? That's why I chose someone like Cilla to be a part of this project, because she is a community mother and we should support each other, whether you are at the pinnacle of some profession or (the hardest job of all) a mother.

Cilla: But that happens a lot with Blackfellas, they gotta tear each other down. Why not support?

Leah: So what do we do?

Liza: We keep on succeeding and continue to enhance the lifestyle of the Indigenous communities of Australia.

Deb: But that 'pulling down' comes from a deep psychology. It comes from a deep place.

Leah: That's true too. But we are moving forward in that area.

Cilla: Yeah, out at Cherbourg, for the Olympics, the torch came through and there was a lot of people involved in that and that whole event lifted everyone's spirits... it's hard to describe but there was this feeling over the whole place there was something special happening for the people.

Sharon: It's also great the future generations are now having great role models out there in sport and academics and us here around this table showing that we have achieved, and all we can do is spread our message and they take it on board and gain from it, or they don't.

Kathryn: But we're okay with whatever they say. And we're not going to listen to their negatives.

Leah: You take it on board, it may hurt but you trudge on. Maybe it's the Super Abo Syndrome, you always bring and take ya mob with ya. Even if it's just your family, that's usually pretty bloody big anyway. But if the determination could be handed out in tablet form, I know I'd be passing it out. And then we could all move up and onward.

Tammy: Something else we need to address in our way of educating our people. Of course everyone achieves when they are enjoying what they are doing, but it is also important to give other options in careers, like why not stockbrokers or an international investor? Then you go ahead. A lot of TAFE courses are, like, park rangers, but there are still no jobs. Like, for example, they still bring workers from Cairns to work on the houses in the community; the community is still not self-sufficient in offering training courses to the locals and there is still no work. What we have to do is be strategic in what's going to happen in the future, tomorrow. Not let disaster take hold and then go, 'Oh, they said that could happen, what do we do now.'

Leah: I think you are all looking a little dry, you want some drinks.

There was orders taken and then Sharon congratulated Deb on her efforts in Radiance.

Everyone went off into private talks and congratulating each other on the individual achievements around the table. It was an opportunity for myself to have a break and think about my questions and plan for the rest of the evening.

My sound guy did a great job in mixing the conversation: it is interesting to listen to them all talking at once. The girls were just nattering away. It's great they were all eager to know about each other.

Leah: What do we think about our black brothers?

There was a pleasurable growl from the table.

Sharon: Have we all black men?
    Leah: I think there's a bit of a mixture.
    Rosanna: I don't mind either one. Not with any as we speak.
    Liza: I stick to my own kind, keep the culture strong and growing strong with my little black babies.
    Sharon: Mine is a TI boy from up Cairns way.
    Deb: Mine is white but I have chased the black boy many a time.
    Frances: Well, my boy is Spanish.

That got a howl from the table.

Cilla: Mine's a Murri fella from home.
    Liza: I'm single at the moment, just came out of a seven year relationship and no children.
    Leah: Tammy, what about you?
    Tammy: Maybe!
    Leah: How do you keep the spice in a relationship?
    Liza: Hot sex!
    Kathryn: Real feeling.
    Tammy: Spirituality.
    Deb: Madness and laughter.
    Cilla: Communication.
    Rosanna: Affection, loving affection.
    Sharon: Honesty and integrity.
    Cilla: Contraception!!

Big black chick cheer on that one. Hhhhhheeeeeyyyyyy!!!!!!

Frances: Respect.

There was another fun game of 'Spin the Cam' and this time the question was 'Who would you invite for dinner?' There were names like Macy Gray, Nelson Mandela, Mum, a couple of footballers (AFL) and someone wanted to lick Anthony Mundine for dessert. You get the general gist of how the dinner went. Dessert was great (no, it wasn't Anthony Mundine).

    And we yarned for another two hours over coffee . . . it was a great night for connecting and knowing that I have found nine new friends that share a passion, a drive for success, to bring something special forward and upward for our people. But we also bonded on a black level as well . . . it was very earthy and sincere . . . yeah! And with the last word of conversation from Miss Frances Rings: 'Respect', I'd like to leave it there!

Special Thanks to the following people for without their help, expertise and support this book could not have been possible.

Bernard Shirley and Stephen Mahoney formerly of QANTAS for their support and vision for the project in the early stages, and the wonderful Emily Choo who followed in their positions and has been a revelation. I would also like to thank the organisation QANTAS for being the major sponsors of the book, which allowed the chicks to fly from all over Australia for portrait sittings and interviews for the book. Without QANTAS this would have been a very different book.

Robert Hannaford for his magnificent portraits and the fact he waved all and any fees for the paintings so we could interview the chicks and have the paintings in the book.

Scott Rankin and his company BIG HART for their ongoing support and expertise.

Liz Croll from Cercus Design for all her hard work and excellence with presentations, pitches and artwork over the years with the *Black Chicks Talking* project.

Jennice and Raymond Kersh for their love and support and the run of their restaurant Ednas Table II over several *Black Chicks Talking* dinners. And all the other ways they've helped me in my career and my company Bungabura Productions.

There have been numerous photographers used in the *BCT* book. Brenton McGeachie who photographed the portraits for the book, Lisa Tomasetti who photographed the *BCT* Dinners, and Jo-Anne Driessens who was the stills photographer on the *BCT* documentary shoot and whose images are seen throughout the book. Thank you all for your fantastic work.

Stephen Page, artistic director of Bangarra Dance Theatre for the use of his dance studios for the portrait sittings and also to Accessible Arts for their support with a number of the portrait sittings and the use of their space.

Giselle Bingham for transcribing all the initial *BCT* stories and for her wonderful and insightful feedback.

To Bain Stewart for all his devotion, support, drive and professionalism in carrying Bungabura Productions across the success line again.

Last, but not least, my agent Harry M Miller who crunched the QANTAS sponsorship deal and his staff, in particular James Thane and Michael Cassell from the agency.

Thank you,
Leah Purcell

their art on the caves. It's named after an explorer who found it. Of course they're not going to name it after the local mob or something of some significance to them. They just don't get it, eh?

No.
But what I was getting at was the fact that this artwork just sends all my senses ablaze with emotion, they are unreal.

So this has become like a permanent job now?
I got offered to do the tours because that's the kind of person I am, I'm motivated. I'm interested in telling people about my culture. I was recommended by somebody, they introduced me when I came down last year for the tourism conference. I got introduced to the owner of the boat, the *Coral Princess*, then he offered me that job.

It's working towards reconciliation. Like, they see an Aboriginal person as part of the tour. We are working in with the geographic mob. The expeditions mob, they talk of how they landed here and things like that. We can talk on behalf of the Blackfellas, saying, 'No, you wrong, we were here long before you landed. We just hid, we didn't run away.' When they talk about the 1700s, I say, 'We've been here longer than the 1700s, because where could we have gone? We never went . . . we never went anywhere. We never left, we're still here!' That's what I say. Where did we come from? And our culture, I talk about how you've been here only dated 1788. Well, Aboriginal people didn't have anything to bloody . . . to record their history or know how many years they been here?

In the sense of days, it wasn't relevant.
Doesn't mean nothing. We're talking about Dreaming. But the way to keep our history dated is through the songlines. Through the songs, through the art! That was the way of keeping history

pictures there, because I wanted to show you something from my country because I can see you come from a very strong cultural background. I wanted to show something to make you believe.' He's saying that to her in her sleep, 'To make you believe that this culture is still alive in my country too.' And, anyway . . . and when Mum told me that story I was just sitting there crying. I went back and I developed the films straightaway when I got back to Derby the next day. I went to the chemist, got the film developed, but, you know, that photo didn't come out?

True?!
He said to Mum in that dream that night, he said, 'That photo your daughter went and took, I'm not going to let it come out because I wanted you to see with your own eyes, and to feel that.' He said, 'That photo is only white man way of holding on to memories. Your memories should be in here [pointing to her head] forever', and he say like that to my mum. And Mum never told me that part when she was telling me about her dream, but when I tell her that photo never come out, she reckon, 'I knew that. I knew that photo wouldn't come out.' I took three or four shots of it at different angles, and nothing came out.

The film was just black. Black, it was black. For those four photos it was just black on the negatives, it was black black black! But every photo before and after it came out. Amazing, hey? Like, incredible. I felt so, so . . . words can't describe it.

And he said, 'For that feeling that you seen in that rock, you've got to keep it in here forever, in your *ly'rhn*,' he said. 'You don't need a photo to remember it.' He said, 'Your feeling, that's the main thing.'

I'm glad I've got a good memory, from way back, I'm glad I've got that. It's all them old memories and the feelings that they trigger. Feelings, that's right. We're going up to a certain part of the coast where there's the Bradshaw Art done by Aboriginal people; it's

Rosanna on one of her cultural tours

those people and they get into it. They get into it, they come and then they ask you questions later and so you tell them: this is the truth about this and that. I put them straight and it changes their attitude. It changes their perspective on Aboriginal people. And that's the best part for me about doing a tour, seeing someone's attitude change.

That's, like, an achievement for me. That's why I love doing it. Because it's challenging. To challenge someone . . . to challenge someone's way of thinking. You're challenging. You're not going to change it. But to be able to at least get them to see a different point of view, that's an achievement.

These tours can be part of the reconciliation process because they're interested to know about our culture, well, then, they're interested in maybe changing their way of thinking, their views on Aboriginal people. Not the way the media portrays them. But our way.

Aboriginal people dream about certain things. Like Indian [Native American] people, Aboriginal people can astro travel. Mum seen this warrior coming up to her and that warrior said to her, 'I know you. And I seen you today, you and your daughter walking through' . . . we were walking through this rock gorge, and on the other side of that rock it's got a big canyon. This big, big black limestone rock on both sides, and a river between them. We were walking along there, I was mucking around with my camera, Mum said, 'Come on!' And I said, 'Why?' And I ran up to her. And one of the other girls, Vivienne, this young girl, found a stone head, a stone spear head!

Wow!

In the river bed. Now, thousands of people walk through there every day. Tourists, every day! They never seen it. But Vivienne wanted to pick it up, and Mum said, 'Don't pick it up! Don't touch it, you just leave it where you found it.' And I took a photo . . . like, I took a photo of it with my camera. We just looked at if for a while, not touching, just looking, then we covered it up and then we went on our way. We didn't worry about it after that. And that night that great spirit from our area came to Mum in her sleep and said, 'I'm glad you told that girl not to touch that, because I wanted to show you something from my country.'

It's that connection people have from different cultures. And he said, 'I wanted to show you something from my country, that thing was there for a long time, in my days', and his days would have been in the 1700s. He said, 'I wanted to show from my days', and he said, 'Your daughter, when she went up to that rock' . . . I was telling you, I cried, for that rock art. When I went up to that rock, he reckon, 'I make her feel that way.' That's *ly'rhn*, he changed my *ly'rhn*. He said, 'I'm showing her all those